Don't Block the Blessings

G·K Hall &Cº

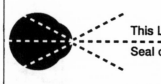

This Large Print Book carries the
Seal of Approval of N.A.V.H.

Don't Block the Blessings

REVELATIONS OF A LIFETIME

Patti LaBelle

with Laura B. Randolph

G.K. Hall & Co.
Thorndike, Maine

Published in 1997 by arrangement with G. P. Putnam's Sons.

G.K. Hall Large Print Core Collection.

The text of this Large Print edition is unabridged.
Other aspects of the book may vary from the original edition.

Set in 16 pt. Plantin by Al Chase.

Printed in the United States on permanent paper.

Library of Congress Cataloging in Publication Data

LaBelle, Patti.
   Don't block the blessings : revelations of a lifetime / Patti
LaBelle with Laura B. Randolph.
    p. cm.
   ISBN 0-7838-8069-3 (lg. print : hc)
   1. LaBelle, Patti. 2. Soul musicians — United States —
Biography. 3. Large type books. I. Randolph, Laura B. II. Title.
  [ML420.L17A3 1997]
  782.421644′092—dc21
  [B]   96-52283
                                                 MN

This book is for Zuri. I pray that knowing your past will help you be comfortable in the present and never, never be afraid of the future.

To my loved ones who are no longer with me: Chubby, Daddy, Vivian, Barbara, Claudette and especially Jackie for bringing me out.

Acknowledgments

From the Authors

This book would not have been possible without the help and support of dozens of people who were generous with their time and knowledge and who cared deeply about making sure this story was told.

A very special note of gratitude and appreciation is owed to George Peters and Rudy Calvo. George, thank you for your long memory and deep dedication to doing whatever it took to uncover long-forgotten facts and long-lost friends. Rudy, thank you for your encyclopedic knowledge of all things LaBelle. You know what your passion, support and Herculean effort have meant to this project — and so do we.

To Stayce Holte and Hattie Mae Sibley, thank you for unlocking the mysteries and the memories with such openness, selflessness and tenderness.

Thank you, Al Lowman, for your vision, early encouragement and commitment to making it all happen.

To the Riverhead family — Mary South, Susan Petersen and Marilyn Ducksworth — thank you for your expertise, faith and support in all stages of this book.

Thank you, John H. Johnson — without your unconditional support, Laura Randolph's participation in this book would not have been possible.

To Cindy Birdsong, Luther Vandross and

Arsenio Hall — thanks for the memories.

And thanks to: Bernard and Mary Montague, for sharing their extensive archives and helping fill in the blanks.

Richard Parsons, Richard White, Richette Haywood, Barbara Best and Karen Lee, who helped in so many ways that only they know.

Allen Arrow and Gail Ross, for taking care of business.

Rachel Cobb, for always being there.

Numerous people helped with research and remembrance. Among them we particularly thank Zuri Edwards, Billy Holte, Dodd Stocker-Edwards, Stanley Stocker-Edwards, Joshia Mae James, Thomas Hogan, Joan Groce, Verdelle Robinson, Hazel Souder, Percy "Butchie" Rogers, Anna Edwards, Percy Edwards, Mary Palmer, Michael Joshua, Fahja J. Page, Pizell Robinson, Nellie Smith, Norma Harris Gordon, Christopher Williams, Naomi Thompson, Josephine Peters, Marlene Benton, Gertrude Benton, Llona Lockman Gullette, Zara Bradley, Sally Beatty, the Reverend James Butler, Tommy Mitchell, Yvonne Hogen, Jean Brown, Johnnie Dawson, Diann Reid, Rafiq Sabri, Sundray Tucker, Ira Tucker, Richard Glenn, James Jones, Jim "Mudcat" Grant, Georgia Lloyd, Charles Walker, Bobby Martin, Morris Bailey, Harold Briskin, Eileen Brown, James "Budd" Ellison, Jayne Edwards Stovall, Kenny Gamble, Ellin Lavar, Sami McKinney, Vicki Wickham, Ken Reynolds, Mike Ecker, Edward Leak, Robert

Pruter, Suzanne Flandreau, Peter Grendysa, David Nathan, Julie Shore, Andre Milteer, Marilyn Batchelor, Dyana Williams, Allen Toussaint, Linda Distefano, Alan Fox, Kevin Tong, Mike Tarsia, Gered Mankowitz, Sam Fine, Shelly Bromfield and Diane Beifeld.

From Patti LaBelle

I never knew I had a book in me. Surprise! Thank you, Laura Randolph, for making our sessions so easy. It's too bad we don't own stock in Kleenex. We'd be rich!

To Zuri, Billy, Stayce, Dodd and Stanley, thank you for filling my life with so much joy and making me prouder than you could ever know.

To my brother Thomas, thanks for turning me on to Ella, Sarah, Nina, Dakota, Gloria and James Moody. I know Chubby is proud of you — and so am I.

To my siblings Monica, Henry and Joshiala, thanks for loving our father and me through good times and bad.

To Aunt Hattie Mae and Aunt Joshia Mae, thank you for mothering me. You both picked up right where Chubby left off.

To Norma Harris Gordon, thanks for your love and loyalty — and for never, ever telling me no.

To Hunchy: I love you for helping me believe I could. You made it easy for me to share things and never made me feel embarrassed or uneasy about anything Laura and I felt was important to the book. Thank you. I finally know that by writing this book I have gotten rid of all the dust and dirt, and now I can shine.

From Laura Randolph

To Patti LaBelle, thank you for opening your home and your heart to me. But most of all for always making me feel that even though this was your life story, it was our book.

A very special thank you to Armstead Edwards for his belief in me. I will never forget it.

To my mother, Anna Randolph, for her unconditional love, faith and support. And for telling me, from the time I was a little girl, "There's no such thing as can't," and somehow making me believe it.

To my father, Horace Randolph, whose love is always with me and whose spirit I feel watching over me.

To my sister, Susan Randolph Leonard, who is always there right when I need her.

To Christopher Benson, whose spirit, wisdom and guidance are behind everything that has appeared with my byline.

Somewhere in the music you discovered the way past pain. You have experienced it — the calm, the cure, the heights. Now you want to throw out a lifeline on a string of sound, show others how to grasp it, navigate beyond obstacles, and steer toward the light. For even in utter darkness, you know they can feel the music. And somewhere in the music is harmony, body, and soul.

— Liz Brown-Lavoie
Berklee College of Music

Chapter One

This day had been planned for weeks. We were shooting the video for my single "If You Asked Me To." Everything was in place. We were all set to go, and everyone was waiting for me. The camera started rolling, the music began to play — it was time for me to perform. As I moved to my mark, I could feel all eyes following me. I knew what they were thinking. It was written all over their faces: Could I do it? Would I be able to hold it together?

The night before, my husband had asked me if I wanted to cancel this shoot. I told him no. I had to do this. It didn't seem, at the time, that I'd *ever* feel better and I had to find a way to push past the pain. My husband had come in case I needed him. So had my youngest son. But when the shoot began, it was just me — standing all alone in the spotlight dressed in black. It was the first time I would shoot a video solo, without anyone else in the scene, and I had never felt so alone in my life. That was as it should have been because I was alone in my pain and there was no one else to blame for what I was feeling but me.

This was my sister's birthday. July 12, 1989. Had she lived to see it, she would have been forty-four. But she didn't make it. As everyone in this room knew, I had buried her just the day before. They knew *that*. But they didn't know the worst part. Most people don't. Most people have no idea why it has become so important to me to reach out to so many others. Yes, the causes I support — Big Sisters of America, Save the Children, the United Negro College Fund, the American Cancer Society, and the National Minority AIDS Council — are doing important work. Yes, my contribution to these and other groups has earned me civic awards, which I treasure and hold dear — three NAACP Image Awards, a medal from the Congressional Black Caucus, even a cancer research laboratory dedicated in my honor. But what drives me to say "yes" to all these organizations is more, much more, than the joy of helping others. That's only part of it. The other part is something few people know about me, something that haunted me for years. I say "yes" every chance I get now because once, when it really, really counted, I said "no."

It was such a little thing that my sister had asked of me. I've done much bigger things for perfect strangers. And anyway, how long would it have taken me to do it — fifteen, twenty minutes, tops? But I said "no." I refused. There wasn't a good reason. Not really. It wasn't as if I was busy or had something pressing to do that couldn't wait. I just didn't *want* to do it. I had been going back and forth to the hospital for days and I finally had a quiet moment at home to relax. That's when the phone rang. It was my sister. She wanted me to do her a favor. The chemotherapy treatments had made her so sick she didn't want to touch any of that hospital food.

"Please, Patsy," she said. "I'm hungry — hungry for one of your egg sandwiches. Your egg sandwich is the only thing I want. It's the only thing I have a taste for. Will you make it for me?"

"Now?" I asked. "Do you have to have it this minute? I don't feel like it right now. I'm tired. I'll make it later."

After that phone call, my sister got worse. Much worse. And later never came. She was on a respirator and in and out of consciousness. Days after that call, she died. The thought kept tormenting me — that I had refused to do the one thing she asked of me, the one thing that could have given my sister some small amount of pleasure as she was about to leave this world.

That's all I could think about as I gave the director the signal I was ready to begin. Maybe I was being punished. Maybe I deserved to be. Maybe it was poetic justice that I would have to sing *this* song, *these* words, *this* day:

If you asked me to, I just might change my mind . . .

I couldn't hold back the tears. The more I sang, the more I thought — about what I had done, what I *hadn't* done, what I would never be able to do again. The more I thought, the harder I cried. Those tears you see on that video? There's nothing phony about them. They're real. The pain you couldn't possibly see was *very* real — almost unbearable. It got so bad that, before the video could be released, most of the tears ended up on the cutting room floor. That whole shoot was agonizing, but I made it through. More than anybody, my sister would have wanted me to. I know that sounds like a cliché; but it's true. More than anybody, she wanted me to soar. In my heart I knew that. In my head, I tried to convince myself that she had forgiven me. But still, every day for the next five years, I was tortured — by grief, by guilt, and most of all by fear.

That probably sounds unbelievable, especially the fear part. Most people who have seen me perform don't think I could be afraid of anything. Not Patti LaBelle — that brazen, outrageous diva who will do and say just about anything onstage. If you've ever been to one of my shows, you know they're part concert, part revival, part confession, part church. Sometimes, okay a lot of times, I even get to preaching. I know people come to my shows to listen to me sing, but in between songs, I make sure they listen to me talk. About faith — in God and in themselves. About hope — for today and tomorrow. About love — in good times and bad. And while I believe every word I say, Lord knows I do, here's the unadorned, barefaced, not-so-pretty truth: I didn't always practice what I preach.

The truth is, I wasn't always the woman you see today, the woman who tries to keep her feet on the ground and her priorities straight. That's only half the story — the cover. This book is the other half — the *un*cover. The half that tells the whole story. The half that took me most of a lifetime to face. The half I kept hidden from my

16

fans as well as myself. Until now.

For years, people begged me to write my story. But I wasn't ready. I know me. I knew that if I ever did a book, I would do it like I do my shows. I would just give it up. All of it. Just the way I do on the stage — I would lay it all out on the page. And I just wasn't ready to do that. Not then.

But I'm ready now. Not just to talk about *my* life, but to talk about how precious life can be. If, that is, you know how to live it. If you don't block the blessings. I know this now the only way you *can* know it: by being on intimate terms with death. All my life, it's been in my face, taking what was mine; what I needed the most and loved the best. I lived in constant dread of death until finally, thankfully, I let go of that fear. And ever since then life has taken me on a magic-carpet ride, a ride that started the night I once thought I would never live to see.

May 23, 1994. It was a night I'll never forget — the eve of my fiftieth birthday. I had always been convinced I'd die before I was forty-four and even when I made it to my forty-fifth birth-day, I thought I had as much chance of living to see fifty as I had of living to see one hundred and fifty. I wasn't being paranoid. Not at all. My belief was based on family history. On facts and figures, dates and data. On nature's arithmetic, not mine.

You see, not one of my three sisters lived to see her forty-fourth birthday. Not Vivian, not Barbara, not Jackie. Neither did my best friend,

17

Claudette. I watched all four of them die; every single one of them eaten alive by cancer in the prime of her life. I saw the worst happen to the best. One day they were young and beautiful and planning their futures. The next, it seemed, they were weak and weary and planning their funerals. In between, I stood by helplessly as diabetes and Alzheimer's claimed my mother and father before their time.

That's why, for so long, no matter how hard I tried, I couldn't shake my fear of dying. I thought about it day and night. When it would come. How it would take me. All I would leave behind. How can I explain how real death was to me? It was everywhere, not just taking my family, but even my fans — so many of them — whom I've watched perish from this scourge called AIDS. My life had become a slow dance with death.

God. How do you live with so much heartache? I had no clue. To cope, I threw myself into my work. I toured the country like a mad woman. I gave concerts everywhere — in big cities and small towns, in huge outdoor stadiums and small indoor clubs. Touring kept me moving. And, as long as I kept moving, I could run away from everything — from my guilt and my grief, from my feelings and my fears and, most of all, from that bottomless pit of pain in my heart. I wrapped my very soul in my song. I had to. For comfort, for consolation, for camouflage.

Within no time, I became a master at hiding my fear. It wasn't too hard. All it usually took

18

was a smile and a song. But as hard as I tried, I could never hide it from myself. You push it down but it's always there. The hurt, the hate, the horror.

For the longest time, I refused to even hope that I would be the lucky one, the only one of my mother's four daughters to beat the family curse. Hope hurt too much — I learned that each time I put someone else I loved in the ground.

When I got too crazy, my husband tried to reason with me. Other than a slight heart murmur, I was healthy as a horse. Hadn't all my doctors told me so? In my head, I knew he was right. But where it counted — in my gut — I couldn't shake the feeling that death was just toying with me.

Of course, the crazy thing was I had so much to live for. Most people who have spent as much time as I have thinking about death feel as if they have nothing in life. As my husband always reminded me, I had plenty. Everything anyone could want and more. A wonderful marriage. Three beautiful sons. Money. Fame. A fantasy career that filled my life with so much joy. I had seen every dream I'd ever had come true. I had toured the world, sold out Broadway, starred in my own prime-time television special and series. I had sung everywhere that was anywhere — from the Olympia Theater in Paris to New York's Carnegie Hall.

It was wonderful beyond description. All of it. But, it never seemed to help. At least not for long.

If there was one thing I knew, it was how fast it all could be taken away. Everything could be planned, but nothing was ever promised.

I suppose every time we lose someone we love we all ask questions. Questions that might help us — even in some small way — to face death. Theirs and ours. I asked God all the time. Every single day for five straight years. Why had He spared me and none of my sisters? Was there something I was supposed to do? If so, what? What was the purpose of my life? If there was some larger reason for me to be here, then why was I suffering so much trying to figure it all out?

The answers to my life-and-death questions didn't come in a way that I recognized then. And so I started the countdown. Since my youngest sister's death, I had felt as though I were living on borrowed time. I knew what I had to do and I had no time to waste. Because I know what it's like to lose someone before you've had a chance to say your good-byes, I started saying mine. At every show I gave, I bid my fans — many of them friends — farewell. Not in so many words, but in my own special way. I did it by leaving what I hoped would be a lasting gift, a legacy of love to all those who had given so much love to me. That's when I started the talking between the singing. I didn't hold anything back, either. Nothing. I talked about everything my mistakes had cost me. I thought by holding a mirror up to each and every one of them, then maybe, just maybe, I could save somebody else from making the same ones. I was preparing myself by purging myself.

So imagine my surprise when I actually made it to fifty. I'll never forget it — the night before my fiftieth birthday was one of the most vivid, most amazing, experiences of my life. I remember everything about it. Lighting the candles in the bedroom of my L.A. condo to fill the room with a golden glow. Lying awake, watching the clock, staring out at the Hollywood Hills stretched out like a blanket below my window. I felt this incredible calm and peace. At last. It was complete, it was total, it was absolute. I felt as if I had finally been released. After all those years of begging God for answers, I realized that He had been answering me all the time. In every song I sang. In every person I touched. In every spirit I lifted. At last, the messenger was getting the message: I hadn't been preparing to die at all — I was learning to live.

Sipping a glass of wine and staring out the window at a thousand lights dancing across the Hollywood Hills, I imagined all those people in all those houses, living their lives, thinking about tomorrow and the day after and next year as if they would live forever. I imagined how all those people out there were taking life for granted, as we all tend to do. I thought about how I had learned to take nothing — not one single blessed thing — for granted. How I wanted to live every moment as if there would not be another.

And that night, for the first time in years, I felt free. Free to live again. Free to believe again. Free to dream again. As I drifted off to sleep, I knew I really had only just awakened. I couldn't wait to greet a new day, a new year, a new life. And, most of all, to share the revelations of a lifetime. That's why I finally wrote this book. It's all here. All of my experiences — the good, the bad, the ugly — and the lessons they have taught me.

This book is about me. Who I am. Who I've been. All that I hope to be. My soul, my sorrow, my secrets. The deepest ones. The darkest ones. The ones I wasn't even sure I was ready to admit to myself.

So here it is. This is what you've been asking for. A front-row seat to the show, a backstage pass to my world. The life and times of Miss Patti Boom Boom. But it is not an autobiography, not a traditional one, anyway. It is a confession — of all the things I've done and all the things I wish I hadn't done. It is a song — a bittersweet hymn dedicated to my FAMILY, my FANS, my friends. This is not a life story as much as it is a lesson in life: how to endure it, how to accept it, how to embrace it.

This book is not a journal but a journey. From where I've been to where I belong. From where I was to where I am. From Hell to here. And this is not a chronology as much as an apology: to myself, to my sons, to my sisters: three beautiful women who lived too short and died too young; three adoring sisters who loved me the best while I treated them the worst; three generous souls who gave me the most while I gave them the least.

Hey Sister, Soul Sister, Soul Sister, Soul Sister.

This is not about dates, times, and places. It's about experience, about acceptance. It's about sinking below, rising above, giving up and going on. This is not a diary. It is a declaration of faith, shaped by everything that has happened to me up to now, shaping everything that happens from now on. Because of the life I've lived, I know there is only one way I can live the life I have left — as a spiritual odyssey driven by an unbreakable promise, a solemn oath, a sacred vow to my mother, to my father, to my sisters, Vivian and Barbara and Jackie, and my best friend, Claudette; to shine their light, to carry their torch, to illuminate their spirit in every song I sing and in every place I go. And, most of all, to meet them all again. Somewhere over the rainbow.

Chapter Two

I was a homely little child. Just as funny-looking as I could be. When I heard Maya Angelou say how ugly she felt as a little girl, I wanted to call her right up and say, "Girlfriend, you too?" Maya said she was certain that a cruel fairy stepmother had turned her into a too-big Negro girl, with nappy black hair, broad feet, and a space between her teeth so big it would hold a number-two pencil. Well, Maya didn't have a thing on me. Only I didn't have nappy black hair; mine was red. And it wasn't my feet that were broad, it was my nose. Of course, a big nose was a thousand times worse than big feet. At least you can hide big feet in some big shoes. But there was absolutely nothing you could do to hide a nose like mine. It was always there, front and center, right between the eyes.

If there was any question in my mind about just how homely I really was, one look at my three sisters was all the proof I needed. I was an ugly duckling living with three beautiful swans. Whether it was true or not, that's how I saw myself. And it wasn't just looks either. Where they were graceful, I was gawky. Where they were smooth, I was shy.

And I *was* shy, too — really shy. I know that amazes people; just blows their minds completely. People see me onstage now and think, Wow! What a wild, crazy, totally uninhibited woman —

Hah! That person you see onstage, that's not me. Not the real me, anyway. That person you see onstage, the singing, strutting, throw-the-mike-down-get-the-audience-up performer with the guts, the gowns, and the glitter, that's my stage image, a gig wig I've put on over more than thirty years in show business. The fantasy me I've wanted to be. I'm a Gemini and, true to my sign, I've lived most of my life as two completely different people — one I made up to share with the world, in the spotlight, the other I kept to myself, in solitude. Until now.

As a child, I was horribly insecure. I saw myself as an ugly little black girl without much going for her. I honestly believed that people wouldn't like me. "How could they?" I thought. "I'm the homeliest person in the world." So, instead of getting my feelings hurt, I did the only smart thing. As much as I could, I stayed to myself. I stayed in my house. Away from other kids.

One of my earliest memories is standing in the kitchen shaking my head furiously as my mother and my adopted aunt, Naomi, tried to get me to go outside and play.

"You've got to get out from under my apron, girl," my mother would scold me.

"You need to make some friends your own age," Naomi would chime in. "You need to play with the other kids."

Play with the other kids? Were they serious? The reason I spent so much time with them is because I had no friends. I couldn't seem to fit in with other kids. I didn't like people. No, that's not really true. I was afraid of them. I felt like such an oddball, like a stranger in a strange land. My shyness was so intense that even the thought of speaking in front of other people — actually talking out loud — sent me into a panic attack. I just wanted to be invisible. I would do just about anything to keep from drawing attention to myself. When I was in elementary school, for instance, I did something that scarred me for a long, long time. I lost control of myself in front of all my classmates. That's right. In the middle of the entire fifth-grade class of McKean Elementary School, I peed all over myself. It wasn't like I hadn't been potty trained for years, okay? And I heard nature calling loud and clear. The problem was, in order to answer the call, I had to raise my hand and ask permission to go to the bathroom. *I had to speak out in front of a classroom full of people.* Not only did I have to speak up, but I had to tell everybody that I had to pee. I tried everything to hold it, to squeeze it back, to keep that slow trickle from becoming a gushing stream, but I just couldn't bring myself to raise my hand.

More than forty years later, I had the chance to think about that humiliating day at McKean Elementary. It was at a sold-out jazz concert in Virginia. I sang so hard, I peed on myself again. In front of thousands of people. But this time I didn't run home crying. This time I stood center stage laughing and joking. I told the audience the truth: I didn't have time to put on my Depends.

But, at least they could go home and tell all their friends that Patti sang so hard she peed on herself. I gave them a choice: I could stop the concert and go backstage and change or I could just keep on singing. They said, "Sing, Patti, sing," and that's just what I did. Little did they know that inside the big star laughing it all off in the spotlight was the painful memory of a little girl desperately trying to hide from it all.

Things weren't a whole lot better outside the classroom. Kids can be cruel, especially when they know you're afraid. I got my butt kicked a few times by the class bully. She would wait for me at the corner and beat me up halfway home. It took a trip up to school by my older sister, Vivian, to put an end to that.

My early school life might have been far from perfect, but there were so many good times at home — much of what a child could hope for. While I felt lost and lonely outside with strangers, I felt safe and secure inside with my family. My parents made sure my sisters and I had everything we needed, and they tried their best to give us everything we wanted.

From the time I was a little girl, my father bathed me in affection. He was always picking me up and hugging me and, even when I deserved it, he rarely spanked me. Even then, the thing I remember most about those whippings is not how much they hurt, but all the apologizing he did afterwards. My father couldn't stand to see me cry. He felt so guilty, he would go out and buy me my favorite treat — a bottle of ginger ale. "Daddy's sorry, Sugar," he would always say, as he wiped away my tears. I was his "Sugar" — that's what he always called me — and he was my sun and my moon.

Since my mother didn't know how to braid, it was my father who did our hair. Not the weekly washings, but the daily brushing and braiding. Every morning before school, he fixed my pigtails. My sister Barbara hated the way he braided. When her turn came, she would cry and scream and carry on. She said my father's plaits made her look like Buckwheat. To me, they were beautiful. To me, they were the only things about me that were beautiful.

When he finished fixing our hair, my father would fix our breakfast — grits, eggs, pancakes, bacon — anything we wanted, he made for us. We had the coolest father on the block. Everybody said so. Everybody who knew him said the same thing: He was so smooth, he could sell ice cubes to an Eskimo.

And he could sing — Lord, could my father sing. He had a voice like Nat King Cole, so lush and rich it would make the little hairs on your neck stand straight up. On weekends, he sang around town at different bars and clubs and he always packed the house. He could get everybody on the dance floor with this song he wrote called "Strike a Match, Light a Light, It's Dark and I Can't See."

He wrote songs for me, too, and, on Sunday

afternoons, we'd sit in the living room and he'd try to teach me, my sisters, and some neighborhood kids how to sing three-part harmony. With my daddy and my music, I could handle the crowd. With my daddy and my music, I could handle anything. Our early rehearsals were pretty pitiful, but Daddy never gave up on us. He'd haul out his tape recorder and play the "The Lord's Prayer" over and over until we got our parts right. We had so much fun back then.

But for me, the real fun started when everyone else left us alone. That's when my dad and I would sit on the front steps and sing our special songs — the ones he had written just for me. We were a team, my father and I, like Fred and Ginger, George and Gracie. He made me feel like a star. "Daddy," I told him one night, "one day I'm going to sing rings around you." He looked down at me and smiled. "Yes you are, Sugar. Yes you are." Daddy never played favorites with us kids, but I was convinced deep down that he surely must love me the best. He was my hero, my idol, and I loved him blindly.

My mother spoiled me rotten, too. She wasn't a hugger or a kisser like Daddy but, in her own way, she let my sisters and me know she was always there for us. She was strong and smart, and she gave me my strength. It's true that, for much of my life, I've been a pushover, but my mother, you couldn't mess with her. She believed women should stand up for themselves. Because of her, when I really needed to, I could too.

Everybody called my mother Chubby, even us kids. To this day, I'm not sure if it was me or one of my sisters who gave her the nickname, but it fit her perfectly and so it stuck. She may have been on the plump side, but Chubby dressed like a fashion model. Beautiful clothes filled her life and her closet. And I definitely inherited her genes. That's the only way I can explain why I'm a clothes horse with such a high-heel shoe fetish it would put Imelda Marcos to shame. (At last count, I had three thousand pairs of pumps.)

If clothes were Chubby's passion, baseball was her obsession. I can't remember her ever reading me a bedtime story, but I can't forget all the baseball stories she told me. She was crazy about the Brooklyn Dodgers, and there was nothing she didn't know about them. She could reel off their players, their stats, their records, everything. I didn't keep up with the Dodgers the way Chubby did, but they were special to me too. I guess they should have been. I was born just one year before they changed the color of the major leagues forever by bringing Jackie Robinson out onto the diamond. Years later, when I dated a professional baseball player, he and Chubby would spend hours sitting on the living-room sofa talking about the ins and outs of the game.

Then there was Naomi. Naomi Thompson was Chubby's best friend, and I can't remember the time she didn't live with us. She was like a second mother to me and loved me like I was her own. When I was knee high to a piano bench, she used to bathe me in the kitchen sink. "Girl," she'd say, shaking her head, "you got the rustiest behind I've ever seen." I can't tell you how many hours of my earliest childhood were spent in her arms, in her lap, in her bedroom behind the kitchen.

Our kitchen. When I was a little girl, there was no place on earth I loved more. If I try to trace back the roots of my passion for cooking, it probably started right there. Almost any time of day, you could smell the sweet aroma of some mouthwatering meal Chubby and Naomi were cooking up. And when I say cooking, I mean these sisters could burn. They did some serious, down-home, southern country cooking: fried chicken and fried corn, barbecue pork smothered in barbecue sauce, hot ribs and hot rolls, greens, grits and gravy. Everything was seasoned just right. It could make a grown man cry.

It wasn't just Chubby and Naomi cooking up a storm, either. My father knew his way around a kitchen, too. Daddy could cook his butt off. His eggs and grits made you happy to be alive, and the things he did with pepper and hot sauce made you think you had died and gone to heaven. It was pure magic. He made this barbecue that was so good people talked about it all over Philly. In the summer, he would buy a whole pig, dig a hole in the middle of the backyard, and roast it to golden-brown perfection. That pig was so good, people would buy the skin off its back. When it was up on the barbecue crackling and turning, just the smell of that thing was enough to make

you start speaking in tongues. Never smelled anything like it before or since. It would make you
hurt yourself. And one time I did.

It happened one August afternoon. I must have
been about nine or ten when my father was frying
some fatback for fried corn and I couldn't wait
to taste it. I just couldn't help it, so I decided to
help myself. I stuck a fork in the pan and, as I
was trying to fish out a nice fat piece, I turned
the whole thing over on me. When that hot grease
hit me, all I could think was: "I'm dying, I'm
dying." And if I wasn't, it hurt so bad I sure
wanted to. My skin peeled away like the top layer
of an onion. You think my lungs are good now,
you should have heard me scream then. Thank
God, my clothes protected me from most of the
spilled grease, but the hot fat burned my neck so
badly I had to be rushed to the hospital. To this
day, I carry the scars. My neck is discolored in
several places.

You'd think that being burned by a pot of hot
fatback would be enough to keep me out of the
kitchen, but it wasn't — partly because I just
loved the kitchen so much, but mostly because I
hated the outside world even more. To get me to
go outside, Chubby and Naomi would offer to
pay me. Fifty cents apiece was the going rate.
Some days the bribes worked, but most days they
didn't. My mother got to the point where she just
couldn't stand me sticking up under her anymore.
"You don't have to go outside, but you're getting
out of this kitchen," she would say. That's when

I would head for my hideout. Next to the underside of my mother's apron, the shed in our backyard was my favorite place. Sometimes I pretended it was my own kitchen. A bucket was my "sink" and a Sterno can was my "stove." I would spend hours cooking everything I had seen Daddy, Chubby, and Naomi prepare: collard greens, spareribs, potato salad — you name it, I fixed it. Whenever Chubby cooked roast pork, I would smuggle some out to the shed and make my own barbecue sauce for it. It was as hot as a firecracker but, honey, it was some kind of good. Even Chubby and Naomi — the high priestesses of cooking — had to admit that.

Because I shared a room with my sisters Barbara and Jackie, the shed was my refuge, my retreat. It was the place where I could be all alone with my fantasies. When it wasn't my make-believe kitchen, the shed became a playhouse for my playmates. Pets, not people. Because I had no friends, animals were a big part of my childhood. They were the only playmates I had or wanted. Skippy was my cat and Bambi was my dog. Who knows what kind they were? A bunch of different kinds, I'm sure. But they were my babies and I loved them to death. Poor babies. I used to dress them up in wigs and hats and scarves and pretend they were people. I even put makeup on their little faces — lipstick, powder, false eyelashes, the works. I guess they couldn't take all that love and attention. Skippy ended up disappearing into a sewer and Bambi ran in front of a car. My sisters swore they committed suicide just to get away from me.

Lightning bugs and butterflies were like pets to me, too. I was always fascinated by things that flew. I loved catching fireflies on hot summer nights and watching butterflies glide through the early morning light.

To a shy, homely little girl, fantasies can be everything. Your salvation. Your lifeline. To tell you the truth, I have no idea what I would have done or what I would have become without my fantasies. Fantasies about cooking magic food. Fantasies about dogs and cats in wigs and hats. Fantasies about butterflies and fireflies taking off into the sky.

Chapter Three

I was born in Philadelphia on May 24, 1944. My parents named me Patricia Louise, but everybody called me Patsy. Until I was fifteen, I lived in Elmwood — a close-knit, mostly black, working-class community out near the airport. Our house was on the corner of South Eighty-fourth Street, at the end of a long line of brick row houses all similar in shape and size. It had four bedrooms, three floors, and front steps that looked out on a park. What I remember most about Elmwood is there were no strangers there. Everyone had a link to everyone else. People were connected. Neighbors watched out for neighbors.

We weren't rich or poor. My father, Henry Holte, Jr., worked at Baldwin Locomotive, a nearby train factory, and my mother, Bertha, served food at St. Agnes Hospital before she quit to stay home with us kids. There were five of us. My brother, Thomas, and my older sister, Vivian, were born long before I was even thought about. Thomas, or Junior as we call him, is older than me by fourteen years; Vivian was older by a dozen. I never met their father, Thomas Hogan, Sr. He and my mother separated when Vivian was just a baby, and he died in 1972. I was my mother's fourth child, two years after my sister, Barbara, and a year before my sister, Jackie.

Our family was squeezed into four small bedrooms on the top floor: one room for my parents, one room for Vivian, one room for Vivian's son, Butchie, and one room for Barbara, Jackie and me.

As a little girl, I thought our house was the most exciting place on earth. It was *the* hangout — *the* gathering place for everybody in the neighborhood. The front door was never locked, and there was always a steady flow of friends and neighbors dropping by. Weekday or weekend, our living room was always jumping, always packed with people laughing and talking and boasting and bragging. The best part was, I could watch all the action from a safe distance: the top of the stairs.

On weekends, Daddy and Chubby would throw card parties, and it was always a full house. To this day, folks in Elmwood still talk about those parties. That's how live they were. People would come from miles around just to have their face in the place. The living room was the center of the action. Furniture was pushed against the walls and card tables were set up side by side in the middle of the floor. Between games of tonk and pitty pat, Chubby and Naomi sold homemade dinners — fried chicken and potato salad went for around a dollar a plate. If you wanted greens, they were extra. You had to get your order in early, though. I don't care how much money you had in your pocket, come nightfall, there wasn't a chicken bone left to be had.

Unlike the fried chicken and potato salad, the

liquor and the card games were never in short supply. You could play for two dollars a game. Or, if you wanted some real action, you could go to the basement. The basement was for high rollers, serious gamblers only. In the basement, the game was poker, not pitty pat, and it was meant for the people with real money and real nerve. On those nights when folks were really in their cups and I was sure I could sneak through the living room unnoticed, I would stand at the top of the basement stairs and peer down into the darkness. I couldn't see much, just shadows and shapes and silhouettes of people sitting at card tables or gathered around the bar. But I could hear everything — the poker chips tossed into the pot, the cards slamming down on the tables; the cheering by excited winners, the cursing by sore losers. Ray Charles or Billy Eckstine was usually playing on the box. I was drawn to the magic and the mystery of it all. Little did I know that I would grow to hate basements because of the nasty, smutty, unspeakable thing that would happen to me in my own. But, that's something I'll tell you about later. In those early days, there was nothing but wide-eyed wonder.

Summer was the most wonderful time of all for me. When school let out, Chubby usually took us down South to Florida to visit her mother and father. My grandparents, David and Ellen Robinson, had a farm in Green Cove Springs, a beautiful little city on the St. Martin River about twenty-seven miles south of Jacksonville on Highway 17. To me, it looked pretty enough to go on a postcard.

I don't remember much about my grandfather, just that he was really quiet and gentle and we called him Uncle Dave — don't ask me why. His wife, my Grandmother Ellen, was anything but quiet. She was a character, honey. Short, petite, and black as the night, Grandmother Ellen was as fiery as a wildcat. She cursed as much as she spit and she spit chewing tobacco all the time. She loved to sit on the front porch and spit the juice across the yard. Lord help you if you crossed her path when she was about to let loose with a jawful. You and your clothes would be wearing some tobacco juice. Nothing stopped Grandmother Ellen. She would just keep right on chewing and spitting, spitting and chewing.

I can see the farm now. For a city kid, it was a wonderland — the gardens planted with corn, cane, peas, and greens, the wide-open fields, the squawking chickens. I loved that place. I would run around outside all day, laughing and playing, then come inside and fill myself on Grandmother Ellen's homemade biscuits. Even dinner was an adventure, although it wasn't one of my favorites. That's because, before dinnertime there was chicken-killing time. Before I started going to the farm, the only thing I knew about chickens was what I had seen at Henry Colt's, the poultry market down on Ninth and Washington Avenue in the heart of the Italian Market. Every Saturday morning, Chubby and I would head over to

Henry's so she could do her shopping for the week. Chubby refused to buy her chickens anywhere else. She said Henry Colt had the freshest chickens in Philly. He also had the freshest chicken plucker in town. Pudgy little Ernest Evans used to entertain customers with songs and impersonations before he did his work in the back. With all his singing and joking, I never had time to think about what was happening to the chickens. I sure never had to watch. But on the farm, I saw everything. Grandmother Ellen would pick a nice plump bird, grab it by the neck, and swing it around and around until its neck just snapped. A few hours later, that chicken would be in the center of the table, cleaned, cut, feathered, and fried. For the longest time, I couldn't bring myself to eat it, knowing as I did how it had gotten to the table. After all, the animals were my playmates. But after going to bed with an empty stomach a few times, my hunger pangs won out over my friendship with the chickens.

Even with all the fun times, there was one thing about the farm that I just could not stand. Or I should say there was one thing I just couldn't sit still for. The bathroom facilities. Since indoor plumbing was a city luxury, Grandmother Ellen told us we had to take our little big city behinds to the outhouse. The first time I saw it, I nearly fainted. I thought it was so disgusting, I vowed to hold everything inside until I got back home to Philadelphia. Obviously, I couldn't hold out for long. Half a day was usually the longest I could go before I had to go. The smell and flies were bad enough, but they weren't what bothered me the most. Don't ask me why, but I was convinced that the minute I sat down, a snake was going to shoot up and bite my butt. Nobody ever had to worry about waiting too long in line behind me.

At bath time, Grandmother Ellen would heat kettles of water on the stove, then pour them into a huge iron tub that sat in the middle of the kitchen. If somebody sat down and tried to dream up the worst thing you could possibly do to a shy little girl who wanted nothing more than her privacy, I know what they would come up with. A stripped-down, buck-naked bath in an iron tub in the middle of a kitchen in front of every-damned-body.

As much as I hated the baths and the "bathroom" at the farm, that's how much I loved waiting for the watermelon truck. I never even let it get stopped good before I was climbing up into the back searching for treasure. Once I found the perfect watermelon, I would roll it off the truck and break it wide open. I never waited for it to be cut. I was in way too big a hurry. I always went right to the middle. That's the sweetest part, you know, the center, the core, the heart. And I ate until I couldn't eat any more. Caught up in the sweetness of the moment, in those precious, innocent times in Florida, I never realized that there would come a time when I would have to break through my own shell and dig deep inside

40

myself to find what was at my center, my core, my heart. Sooner or later, it's something we all need to do on our journey through life. And it's worth the trip, too, because once you get there, to that source, that purest part of you, you realize that you have everything you ever will need to make it. I should know. It was the part of me that would get me through the terrible times ahead.

Chapter Four

Iadored my father. People said I looked a lot like him, but I never thought so. He was fine. Lord, was my father fine! He had coffee-and-cream-colored skin, Indian-like features, and thick, dark hair that he wore combed back. The first time my mother brought him home, Grandmother Ellen teased her for days about her "pretty, wavy-haired man." And my father put the *C* in *clean,* too. Day or night, he would be dressed to kill, or, if not kill, at least seriously hurt somebody. Dirt didn't touch him, at least not for long. He took three showers a day — every day. There's no doubt in my mind he's the reason I've always been such a neat freak.

As good as he looked on the outside, that's how good I always thought he was on the inside. As far back as I can remember, he worked night and day so that he could afford to give Chubby, my sisters, and me whatever we wanted.

As I would learn years later, he had always been a good provider. He had to be. By the time he was fifteen, my daddy had lost both of his parents. His mother, my Grandmother Tempie, died of leukemia and his father, Henry Holte, Sr., was walking to work one morning when he just collapsed right there in the middle of the street. The doctors said he died of a massive stroke, but people who know more than doctors know about these things tell a different story. My Aunt Hattie

Mae says my grandfather died from something much more painful. You see, Granddaddy Henry loved my Grandmother Tempie more than life itself. When she got so sick that he could no longer take care of her and their five young kids — William, Daddy, Hattie Mae, Joshia Mae and Addison — they had to make a very hard and painful decision to move her in with her parents. The day they came to get her, my grandfather said his good-byes and watched from the window as they started to drive her away from him. He couldn't take it. He ran outside and screamed for them to stop the car. He jumped into the back-seat, gathered my grandmother in his arms, and confessed his everlasting love for her. He told her he couldn't, he wouldn't, live without her.

"Temp," he said, "if I never see you again, if the Lord takes you, I won't live long behind you."

True love makes promises that can never be broken. Grandmother Tempie died in July 1938, and eight months later my grandfather was gone. The doctors said my grandfather died of a massive stroke. But people who knew them both tell a different story. Granddaddy Henry died of a broken heart.

Losing both your mother and father in less than a year is hard enough. But, for my father, it was even worse. He never got to tell my grandfather good-bye, at least not the way he would have wanted to. He never got to lay him to rest; never got to give him a proper burial. To this day, no one really knows what happened to Granddaddy's body. It remains a mystery. The only thing we know for sure is that when my father sent the undertaker to the hospital to bring him home, he wasn't there. The hospital officials had "disposed" of the body, though no one could ever find out how.

Sometimes, when I hear stories about Granddaddy Henry and Grandmother Tempie, I feel like crying. When I hear those stories, I realize just how much I have felt their absence in my life. Even so, there's one thing in this world I know for sure and for certain. My grandparents live on in me. All of our ancestors live on in each of us. I honestly believe that. A piece of them is always with us, inside us. People who knew Grandmother Tempie tell me that I sound just like her, that if they close their eyes when I'm singing, they could swear it's her voice they hear. She had the sweetest voice, my Aunt Hattie Mae told me. She was the church organist and people would come from miles around just to hear her play and sing. Hattie Mae says the way she could hold a note and just let it float through the air would give you the chills. They called her "Mockingbird."

With Henry and Tempie gone, all their children were sent to live with their grandparents. All of them, that is, except my father. Henry was the second-oldest child and, years earlier, when times got hard, he took it on himself to go out and earn the money needed to support his two brothers and two sisters. The only place he could find work was in the Civilian Conservation Corps, the program that gave jobs to millions of young men during the Great Depression. He was only fifteen and so to get in, he lied about his age, pushing it up three years. Within months he was working in Jacksonville, Florida, planting trees and building roads. But, before he left his home in Georgia, he made a promise to his sister Hattie Mae. He wouldn't marry until she did. Until she found someone to take care of her, he would continue to take care of all of them. And that's just what he did. For years, Daddy sent his check home to his grandparents to care for his sisters and brothers. It's hard to imagine, but $25 a month supported the whole clan. When Hattie Mae wed in 1940, my father bought her wedding gown and her ring. Afterwards, he told her it was the first time in his life he had felt free — free to go out and pursue a life of his own.

Not long after Hattie Mae married, my father met my mother. It is my Aunt Hattie Mae who tells the story, the story about a whirlwind, fairy-tale, made-for-the-movies courtship that started in a heartbeat in Jacksonville in 1940. One moonlit December night, Henry walked into a party and saw Bertha sitting alone at a table. She was twenty-five at the time, three years older than Henry, and the moment he saw her he got a rush, an electric jolt that ran straight up his spine. Bertha was a real looker, all right. She was on the short side — about five three or so — and she had this smooth-as-silk skin the color of gingerbread mixed with honey. But it was more than her looks that cast a spell over Henry. Bertha was cool. She had style. She had attitude. For Henry, it was like looking at the female version of himself. To buy himself some time and some composure, Henry went to the bar and ordered a drink. For half an hour, he just watched Bertha from across the room. When he finished working on his drink and working up his nerve, he smoothed back his hair, straightened his tie, and eased over to her table.

"What's your name?" he asked her. Okay, so it wasn't exactly original, but at least it broke the ice.

"Bertha," she said and smiled that megawatt smile of hers.

"Bertha," he said, "you're the woman I'm going to marry. I'm going to make you my wife."

Just like that, it happened. Henry probably didn't even know what made him do it, what made him go right up to this woman he had never seen before and decide to marry her. He didn't know anything about her past. He didn't know that, by fourteen, she was expecting a baby and, by sixteen, she was the mother of two. He didn't even know her last name. But none of that would have made a difference. Henry didn't need to analyze the attraction or question it because the only thing that mattered to him at that magical moment was what he saw in Bertha. He saw his fantasy, his future, his forever. And Bertha Lee Robinson of Green Cove Springs, Florida, saw something, too. She was caught up in that whirlwind, that cool breeze that blew her way from the bar across the room. She was swept up in the cyclone of Henry Holte's charms. Five months later, on May 12, 1941, they were married.

During those early times, you never have seen two people more in love. My parents shared an unbreakable bond that connected them, and I believe in my heart that each loved the other until the day they died. But not every fairy-tale beginning has a happy ending. Many years later, the magic spell was broken and my parents wound up tearing at each other constantly. To tell you the truth, some of their fights were so ugly, so brutal, they haunt me to this day. If there is one thing I learned from those experiences, it is that you can love someone with all your heart but still not be able to stay together. As Chubby once told me, to save yourself, sometimes you just have to walk away.

Chapter Five

Everything started out just fine with Daddy and Chubby. Not long after they got married, Chubby found work cleaning houses in Atlantic City, and for a short while she lived there alone while my father looked for work. When friends in Philadelphia, Oliver and Florine Lockman, helped my father get a job with Baldwin Locomotive, Chubby left Atlantic City and joined him. Their first "home" was a bedroom at a friend's house where they stayed for several months. When they bought the house in Elmwood, the whole family was finally under the same roof. But Junior missed Florida so much that, after only one summer, he returned to the farm to live with Uncle Dave and Grandmother Ellen.

Like Junior, I loved the farm. But unlike him, I spent the happiest moments of my childhood in that house on South Eighty-fourth Street, either curled up in my daddy's lap or hanging on his arm. That's why when things changed between him and Chubby it tore me up inside. Emotionally, I couldn't handle it, and I sure couldn't understand it. To tell you the truth, it opened a wound in my heart that has never completely healed.

I was around ten years old when my world began to fall apart. That was when the arguments between Chubby and Daddy started to get really bad. Suddenly, everything in our house was different. I didn't know what was going on at the time, just that something in our family was terribly wrong. Now, I have some idea.

The arguments started over my father's gambling. The weekend card parties in our house always seemed like such a kick. Whether you won or lost didn't seem to matter. Everyone came just to eat, drink, and party. The betting was just part of the fun. At least that's what I had always thought. I didn't know there was a dark side, a side where winning and losing were taken seriously, a side where people play for keeps, a side that was anything but fun.

My father had always been a good provider. But there came a time when his gambling got the better of him, when his side wagers got out of control and the poker games in the basement could no longer satisfy him. He started playing in the street. Cards. Craps. Whatever he could lay a wager on. When his bets got bigger, so did his losses. And when he lost everything, that's when he came home. And when he came home, that's when all hell broke loose.

The fights always started out the same way. My father wanted Chubby to give him money — money he had given her for bills, for groceries, for us. When she refused — and Chubby always refused — my father got mad, and when my father got mad he got rattlesnake mean. He would scream at Chubby at the top of his lungs. "Give me the money, bitch. Don't make me ask you again."

Chubby's answer was always the same. "I'm not giving you a damn dollar, Henry, so take your gambling ass out of here and get out of my face."

It got worse, a lot worse. Sometimes my parents' arguments got so loud I could hear them all the way upstairs, even when I closed my bedroom door to shut out the screaming and shouting. It didn't do much good. I could still hear my father banging his head against the living room wall. I could still hear what he said every time he did it. "Woman, you're going to make me hurt you." And he made good on this threat. He stopped banging on the wall and started banging on Chubby. That's the part I hated the most, when the shouting crossed the line into fighting. Still, Chubby never backed down, no matter how ugly things got. She was the type of woman who always stood her ground, always fought back. That was Chubby. She took no mess. Believe me, you did not want to get into an argument with Chubby. Not unless you wanted to be cursed up one side of the house and down the other. Like Grandmother Ellen, Chubby could be as mean and foulmouthed as any man. She would call my father every nasty name you've ever heard and some you haven't: "Loser." "Lowlife." "Lowdown lying motherfucker." Excuse the profanity but, for a long time, that's the language I heard. What can I say? With every passing day their fights got more vulgar, more vicious, more violent. And when Daddy would hit her, she would hit him right back. They fought and they made love; they made love and they fought. To them, I think sometimes it was the same thing.

The arguments weren't always violent. There were some lighter moments, even if they were few and far between. Like the night my father was on his way out for the umpteenth time and Chubby decided she had had enough. She got dressed in her Sunday best, then waited for just the right moment. My father was headed out the door when she made her announcement. "Henry, I'm going out tonight. You'll have to take care of the girls." The whole time he was screaming and protesting, Chubby was quietly getting her hat and coat. They both hit the front steps at the same time. When they got to the street, my father turned left and Chubby went right. Unlike my father, she never once looked back, Chubby never blinked. When he saw she meant business, my father turned around and came right back home, but we didn't see Chubby again until late that night. The next morning, when our neighbor Josephine Peters asked Chubby where she had gone, my mother told her the truth: "I caught the trolley and took the loop." She had ridden around in circles all night, down to City Hall and back again. They had a good laugh over that one.

Most of the time, though, there was nothing funny about my parents' fights. For a while, I thought I could make them stop. What can I say? I was a kid. Kids don't know any better. I figured if I could just get them to see how much their fights upset my sisters and me, they would never raise their voices, or their hands, at each other again. And so I would stand between them and beg them to stop: "Please, Daddy. Please, Chubby. Don't yell at each other anymore." But they couldn't hear me. As loud as they were screaming, I wonder if they could even hear each other. They were just too caught up in their rage. No matter how hard I cried or how long I pleaded, they just kept right on fussing and cussing at the top of their lungs. Like I wasn't even there. That's what I remember most, how helpless I felt. I just couldn't understand how people who were supposed to be in love could do that to each other. That was the beginning of the end for them. And in a different way, for me too.

You see, those fights almost drove me crazy. They did something terrible to me. How can I explain it? They shook me hard and deep, way down to my very center, my core. I became a nervous wreck. Every time my father and Chubby fought, which was almost every day, it would start all over again. The shaking. The vomiting. The hysteria. I couldn't control it. I would start trembling all over, like a leaf caught in a hurricane. When the shaking stopped, I would break out in hives. My whole body — my arms, my legs, my back — everything except my face would be covered by huge red welts. To calm me, Naomi would put me in a warm tub and bathe me in boric acid. But soon, not even the baths could soothe me. That's when Chubby took me to see a doctor. Every Monday for five straight years, Chubby and I would go to his office on Spruce Street where I was given pills and shots. Even after all these years, when something really scares or upsets me, I break out in hives. It's like I'm a little girl again. Watching. Listening. Trembling.

By the time I turned twelve, there never seemed to be peace in the house anymore. My father was a gambler and a lover and he loved women at least as much as he loved wagering, probably more. He had a restless, roving soul and, though he loved us all, an Ozzie and Harriet family life wasn't for him.

As the tension between him and Chubby grew, he spent more and more nights away from home in the company of other women. Chubby may have loved my father blindly, but even she couldn't ignore the evidence staring her in the face. The truth cut a hole in her heart — especially the times my father came home at six or seven in the morning and asked my mother to make him breakfast. Once upon a time, he had made breakfast for her; once upon a time, he had served it to her in bed. "You should have asked whoever you were with last night to fix your sorry ass breakfast," Chubby would say to him. She called him on all his bullshit.

When she found a credit card bill showing Daddy had bought one of his girlfriends a fur coat, Chubby really went off on him. Then she went out looking for "her." I don't know what happened to the other woman. All I know is that Chubby came back with a fur coat.

For a while after that, things calmed down. At least they weren't fighting all the time, and when they did it wasn't like World War III. That is, until one night — the night my father went berserk. If I close my eyes, I can still see the standoff, I can still hear the screaming. I can still feel the shock. It was the night my mother had gone out looking for my father and found something she couldn't handle. Her worst nightmare. An apartment. His apartment. "Their" apartment. A love nest right there in Philly, right under her very nose. This time my father couldn't talk his way out. Chubby had seen it for herself, in black and white, right there on the apartment door: "Mr. and Mrs. Henry Holte." As if whichever one of his lady friends staying at his bachelor pad at the moment was really his wife.

Chubby waited in our kitchen for my father to come home. And this time it would be a fight to the bitter end. They went at each other like two wildcats. Chubby called him everything but a child of God. Suddenly, Daddy snapped. He screamed: "I'm warning you, bitch. Leave me alone." Chubby kept right on screaming and, in a blur of anger, my father slammed his fist into the refrigerator. There was a sickening crunch. Chubby and I both saw it at the same time: the handprint he left in the door. Then he turned on Chubby. He had this crazed look in his eyes. I was frozen; she was not. Seeing what he had done to the refrigerator door, Chubby was not about to wait to find out what he was going to do to her. For her, what came next was an act of desperation and defiance. It was an act of self-defense. In a flash, I saw the knife in her hand. It was clear she meant to use it. She held it out in front of her. "Come near me," she said, "and I'll cut your throat."

They just stood there, motionless, staring each other down. My mother, my father, and the knife between them. It was only a moment but it felt like forever. The knife wasn't pointed at me, but I felt like it was my life that was on the line. In most fights, there is a winner and a loser. In this one there would only be losers. In most fights, you naturally root for one side or the other. But how does a child choose between her mother and father? You can't. It's impossible. At that moment, everything I loved was balanced at the point of a knife.

Thank God my father came to his senses. He looked into Chubby's eyes. He looked at the knife in her hand. He turned and walked away.

I learned something that night, something that would carry me through so many days and nights to come. From my mother I learned where to draw the line. That it is never too late to start over; that you can always say good-bye. That "I love you" doesn't mean "I'll be a fool for you." From my father I learned another valuable lesson. I learned that, in life, as in poker, there are rules. You have to play the hand you're dealt.

You can't bluff your way through forever. And, most important, you should never — not ever — gamble with something you can't afford to lose.

Chapter Six

When my father moved out, I thought that was as bad as it could get. I was wrong. For me, it got worse. Much worse. It's hard for me to describe my feelings. I was a twelve-year-old daddy's girl who had lost her daddy, and a lot of herself in the process. He had been my life raft and my anchor, and once upon a time our house had been my safe harbor. I watched in horror as the storms rolled in and destroyed it all. Even though I knew Daddy and Chubby couldn't live together anymore, nothing had ever hurt me as much in my life as the day Daddy moved out.

For a while, the only relief came on "Daddy Days." Chubby may have kicked him out of our house, but she didn't kick him out of our lives. As ugly as their separation was, to my parents' credit, they worked it out so my father could see us as often as possible. And he would come by a lot — two, sometimes even three times a week. Sometimes he just wanted to see his girls and sometimes he came to bring Chubby money. I couldn't wait for those visits. It wasn't the same as it used to be. It would never be the same again. But, at least for a short time, we were a family again. Well, sort of. There was one big difference. In addition to the money, sometimes my father brought the flavor of the month. His latest girl-friend. Honey, during those visits, it was a whole different movie. At least my mother could play the role. She became good at acting. Like she didn't care. Like it didn't hurt her. Like seeing her husband bring his girlfriend over to their house, around their children, like it was no big thing. Looking back, I don't know how Chubby did it. But, no matter how many times Daddy showed up with some pretty young thing on his arm, she kept her cool. She would walk around laughing and talking and making chitchat with Daddy's friend as if she couldn't care less. Like it didn't even faze her. It was an Academy Award–winning performance. Daddy wasn't quite so good at it, I'm afraid. When Chubby started dating, my father couldn't handle it. One day he came by and saw the brand-new car one of Chubby's boyfriends had given her. It was parked right in front of the house. Daddy went off. He grabbed a brick and, slowly, methodically, smashed out every single window. First the front, then the back, then the sides. One by one until there wasn't a single pane of glass left. When he finished, he calmly put the brick down on the sidewalk, brushed the pieces of glass from his pants and walked away. After seeing what he did to that car in front of the house, Lord only knows what my father would have done if he had seen what was happening to me in the back of the basement.

What was happening in the basement was a foul and nasty nightmare. That's the only way I can describe it. Not knowing what to do with my pain, I got a little weird. I don't know any other way to explain some of the things I found myself doing. Don't ask me why, but, for some strange reason, I was drawn to the basement. Not when there were parties and people. But when it was still and silent. When I thought nobody else was around. There was something down there I couldn't resist. Something I couldn't stay away from. It was the smell of the damp cement floor. I *loved* that smell. It called me. It pulled me to it. It drove me a little mad. For whatever reason, I began to crave it. I would sneak down the stairs, get down on my hands and knees, close my eyes, and breathe in as deeply as I could. It turned me on so much that soon just smelling the floor wasn't enough. I wanted more. I needed more. So I began to lick it, to see if it tasted as good as it smelled. And it did. I know how weird this sounds. I never understood it and to this day I can't explain it. All I know is that I did it. And I kept going back, again and again, to indulge my secret obsession. As much as I craved this little thrill, I knew something about it wasn't right. So I was careful, very careful, to make sure nobody knew about my secret trips downstairs. Or so I thought. Never in my wildest dreams did I think this crazy compulsion would lead to such suffering.

I've been so ashamed of the things that happened to me down there that, for almost forty years I have kept them inside. Other than my husband, I have never told a living soul about them. Not until now. Even now, after all this time, it hurts so much to tell the story — a story that plays out in my head over and over again like a bad dream I can't shake:

It's cool and dark and quiet. I am kneeling on the floor breathing it all in — the intoxicating smell of the wet cement. I am lost in the moment. I bend my head closer to the floor and stick out my tongue. Just as I am about to press it against the cool concrete I feel something I've never felt before down here: something behind me. It is a hand, a large hand, reaching under my skirt. I tense up. I am shocked and embarrassed — shocked to realize that someone else is down here and embarrassed that whoever it is has discovered my secret. Maybe they've been watching me all along. Maybe they've been laughing at me. Maybe they're going to tell. Oh, God, I hope they don't tell.

"Don't be scared, Patsy." It is a man's voice coming from the darkness behind me. "I'm not going to hurt you."

I recognize the voice instantly. It belongs to one of my mother's boyfriends.

"What are you doing down here?" I say, even though I feel that I'm the one with the explaining to do.

No answer. Now I'm really scared.

"What are you doing down here?" I repeat, trying to keep the fear out of my voice.

More silence. The hand begins to move. It reaches into my underpants and stops between my legs. I freeze. I have never been touched there before. I know it is wrong but I don't know what to do, how to stop

60

it. Now I am terrified, but I'm also confused. I want to scream for Chubby to come and help me but I can't. I'm too afraid — afraid about what is going to happen to me, but just as afraid about upsetting Chubby. If she finds out, she'll be furious; she'll probably pull a knife on him, just like she did on Daddy. Then she'll have to kill him. And it will be all my fault. I never should have been down here in the first place. What if Chubby asks me about it? How would I explain it? What will I say? Oh, God. I'll have to tell her about the floor! How will I be able to make anyone understand something I can't even figure out myself? I can hear my heart pounding in my ears. I know I'm in trouble. Deep trouble. I know that I need to get out of here. But I can't. I try, but I can't. He won't let me. Then, suddenly, it happens. He pushes his finger inside me. There's a piercing pain. I am lying there, a million miles away but there, crying silently, waiting for him to finish what he is doing to me down there. I blank out.

Did he rape me? To this day, I honestly don't know. I know that wasn't the only time he got me alone and took advantage of me. But, how many other times and in how many other ways he violated me, I just can't remember. Whenever I try to call up the memory, my mind just shuts down, goes completely blank. I can only remember that first part of the nightmare. It doesn't take a shrink to figure out the reason. It's like Maya Angelou says: "I haven't so much forgot as I can't bring myself to remember." Maybe one day I'll be able to, who knows? Maybe one

61

day, I will no longer need to.

Just as I can't bring myself to remember everything now, I couldn't bring myself to tell anyone back then. Not Chubby, not my father, not a single one of my sisters. I felt too dirty, too guilty, too ashamed. I have always wondered if he did the same nasty things to Barbara and Jackie. But I never asked them. Now I will never know. But there are things that I *do* know now that I didn't know then. I know that sexual abuse doesn't just happen once or twice or even several times. The horror of it continues long after the act is finished and the physical pain is over. Like a slow torture, a fever blister that will neither erupt nor heal. I also know now that there is no pain so deep, no secret so dark, that you can't share it with the ones you love. After all, love is understanding, love is forgiveness, love is protection. I only wish I could have understood these things a long time ago. Before it was too late.

Chapter Seven

Some kids run away from home to get away from it all. I had nowhere to run. So I took flight in a song. Music was my escape hatch. It gave me something to hold on to when I thought I had lost my father. It gave me something to believe in when I thought I had lost my faith. It gave me something to strive for when I thought I had lost my way. Singing was sort of running away — from my secrets, from my sorrow, from myself. How can I explain it to you? Music was like a drug to me. It transformed me. It transported me. It saved my life.

For as long as I can remember, music filled our house. It was always there at the card parties. It was always there in my father's serenades. And my older sister, Vivian, made sure it was always there when she got home from work. Vivian loved herself some blues. For her, B.B. really was king. In the evening, before she even took off her coat, the first thing she did was turn on the record player. I can see her now sitting on the living room sofa, legs crossed, head thrown back, body swaying to the rhythm and the blues. Johnny Ace and Bobby Blue Bland and B.B. King with his number-one hit "3 O'Clock Blues." Oh yeah, and much later, "Sweet Sixteen." That was Vivian's song. She'd light up a Pall Mall, close her eyes, and sing that song over and over. I remember thinking how beautiful and sophisticated she looked sitting there singing and smoking, smoking and singing. Her voice may not have won her a Grammy, or even a recording contract, for that matter, but she had something that attracted a fan club from miles around. Drop-dead-go-to-hell-don't-speak-to-me-because-you-know-you-don't-know-me looks. All the neighborhood boys had a crush on Vivian. Why not? She was stunning. At five feet six, she was shaped like an hourglass. And she didn't so much walk as stroll. She moved with the grace and power of a lioness, and when she spoke, she purred with this slow, sexy, southern drawl. She dressed to kill. Just like Daddy. Just like Chubby. I swear Vivian had some serious drag.

Everybody in Elmwood talked about the way she dressed. And walked. And talked. And looked. She was the Countess of Cool. All the guys were jealous of Vivian's boyfriends, especially this guy named Zimmerman. In addition to Vivian, he had something else they all wanted: a 1954 Oldsmobile convertible. With Miss Thing beside him, Zimmerman would drive up with the top down, the radio blasting, and Vivian's hair blowing in the wind. They would stop traffic. The moment they rounded the corner, everything went into slow motion as all eyes turned their way. I wanted so much to be like Vivian. I idolized her. She was everything I longed to be and wasn't.

Maybe I'd never look like her, maybe I'd never have a handsome boyfriend who drove a convertible, maybe I'd never really be that cool and popular, but I could damn sure pretend. After all, I was the master of magic and make-believe. I mimicked every move she made. And in my head, I was the star. Everybody loved me, just like Vivian. Using a pencil as my Pall Mall and a rolled up newspaper as my mike, I gave my first concert at the age of nine or ten. It was me, my mirror, and my imagination. I played to a standing-room-only crowd and, honey, I killed them. That was the beginning, the start of my no-holds-barred concert performances. All thanks to Vivian, I learned how to play the role.

It wasn't until I started junior high school, though, that I plunged deep into music for the sake of my soul. One night, when I was upstairs playing alone in my room, I heard voices. They were lush and beautiful, and they were coming from downstairs. I understood these voices. My heart recognized their suffering. It was just as Tony Morrison says: "a knowing so deep." I was drawn to these voices, pulled to their source. My body seemed to float down the stairs on their melody. With each step I took, their power, their passion, their pain grew stronger. They were talking to me. About me. We were connecting. When I got to the end of the staircase I found my brother, Junior, sitting there in the living room listening to the voices.

"Who's that?" I asked him.

Junior introduced us. Gloria Lynne. Dakota Staton. Dinah Washington. Sarah Vaughan. He pointed to the stack of albums near the record player; a few of his favorites he had brought up from Florida on one of his regular visits. From that moment on, I was hooked — on their music, on their voices, on jazz. I heard my history. Music created by black folks. Music I felt deep in my bones. When Dinah sang "I Believe," I did. When Sarah sang "Body and Soul," she touched mine. I heard something sacred in their music. I had made new friends. Thanks to Dinah and Sarah and Gloria, my world began to shift. My bedroom became my nightclub, my concert stage, my sanctuary. When I got home from school, I would grab a broom or a bottle or a brush — anything I could pretend was a mike — and stand in front of the bedroom mirror singing my heart out. I didn't care who heard me, either. I found myself wanting to be heard. I wasn't homely little Patricia Louise with the big nose and the nappy hair and the broken family and the dirty little secret. I was beautiful. I was powerful. I was popular. I was Billie Holiday hypnotizing an audience. I was Nina Simone mesmerizing a crowd. I was Cinderella — Cinderella with a band and a beat and a tick and a tock that would never strike midnight again.

Even though Vivian had become my model of poise and perfection, Junior was the one who turned me on to the magic and the miracle of music. From then on, whenever I sang, I didn't feel sad about my father leaving or guilty about my mother's boyfriend. Nothing bad or ugly could touch me. I wasn't tortured by nerves or fear. It was there, singing in my mirror, that I came to understand the power of music. A healing power. A bonding power. A power that rises up from deep down inside. A power I would finally learn to share with other people — real people.

It happened one summer when Chubby took Barbara, Jackie, and me down to Georgia to visit my Aunt Hattie Mae. One of the neighborhood kids came by with a new record. I don't remember what the song was or who was singing it, but I do remember what it did to me. The moment I heard it, something happened to me. It was like I went into a trance, like I was back in my bedroom, just me and my fantasy fans. I started dancing. Aunt Hattie Mae says the way I was moving to the music was so hypnotic, so mesmerizing, that no one could take their eyes off me. At first I was just swaying to the rhythm but then I got completely lost in it. Moving my hips to the beat, moving my lips to the words. I don't remember the exact moment I realized that I wasn't at home. That I wasn't singing in the mirror. That I was out on Aunt Hattie Mae's front porch. That the audience wasn't inside my head. Everybody was right there, in real life, clapping and cheering and shouting. Somewhere in the distance I could hear people chanting: "Go, Patsy!" "Go, Patsy!" "Go, Patsy!" Everyone was watching me but, you know what? I didn't care. I couldn't stop. I didn't want to. The only thing that mattered was the music and the moment. I was there, the center of attention and I liked it.

It was a moment of discovery. It was the first time I really felt the energy of the music moving through me to the crowd and from the crowd back to me. It was like an amazing cycle — a life-giving, love-getting, spirit-lifting cycle. Like deep breathing. Pumping it in. Pumping it out. When I inhaled, I drew love from everyone there. When I exhaled, I just blew them all away.

Chapter Eight

After what happened to me on Aunt Hattie Mae's porch, I was different. That fall, at Tilden Junior High School, I started coming out of my shell. I was still quiet and shy, but I wasn't running away from people anymore. I had learned that there was something about me they liked — something inside me. By the time I started ninth grade, I no longer had to rely only on make-believe fans or fireflies for company and companionship. I had finally made some real-life human friends: Brenda Austin, Sally Butler, Claudette Henderson, Gloria Robinson, Llona Lockman, Marlene and Gertrude Benton. We all lived in Elmwood and we were pretty inseparable. After school, we'd hang out at my house or at the park across the street. But Tuesdays were different. On Tuesday nights, all the neighborhood kids would meet at the local skating rink. That was the night local deejay, Georgie Woods, "the guy with the goods," spun records and, believe me, when Georgie Woods spun records you couldn't sit down. I sure couldn't. From the moment I laced up my skates, I was hell on wheels. Literally. I would practically fly around the rink singing and swinging and skating to the music. It was a party. It was a performance. When I was out there on the hardwood, I felt so graceful — so free and alive. Like a firefly. Like a butterfly. I lived for those Tuesday nights at the rink.

Chubby and Naomi couldn't believe it. I was starting to believe in myself. They didn't have to pay me to go outside anymore.

It was during this coming-out period when I made a major move — a move to the head of the crowd, a move that would change my life forever. It happened in church, our family church. Beulah Baptist was practically right across the street from our house, just behind the park where the kids hung out. Almost everyone in Elmwood worshiped there. Naomi and Chubby had been members forever, and my sisters and I were all baptized there.

Chubby believed in going to church, but she never forced me to attend. It wasn't until a youth choir was organized at Beulah that I really became interested. Of course, you had to go to church in order to sing in the choir. So I started going all the time. But I wasn't attending church for the sermons. I went to sing my praises. And for me, that was a high religious experience. It was holy. It was spiritual. It was gospel.

This choir was a big deal for the kids in Elmwood. Almost fifty of us joined, even my sister Barbara who couldn't carry a tune in a bucket, and this tall, really quiet nerdy kid named Armstead Edwards who had a monster crush on her. We were called The Young Adults Choir and on the second Sunday of every month we sang. We sang for the congregation. We sang for our families. We sang for God. Mrs. Harriett Chapman, the church organist, was our director, and every Tuesday evening she held practice in the chapel. At that time, the choir was the only thing that could have kept me away from the skating rink. Mrs. Chapman was a wonderful teacher. The kind you never forget. She ran rehearsals with kindness, patience, and love. From the first day of rehearsal, I knew I belonged in the choir. I loved gospel music, all right. But it was Mrs. Chapman's gentle encouragement and support that really made me feel at ease. She made me feel safe and secure. She made me feel at home.

It was because Mrs. Chapman made me so comfortable that I found myself doing something I never would have thought about doing before. One evening, we were rehearsing a new hymn for Sunday morning service. It was called "God Specializes," and it touched me in a special way. Each time we sang it, it moved me deep down inside. When Mrs. Chapman said it needed a solo, for a reason I can't fully explain even now, I raised my hand.

"I think I can do it, Mrs. Chapman," I said.

She was stunned. As much as she tried to hide it, I could see the shock in her face. I could feel it in the brief moment it took her to respond. In all the time I had been coming to rehearsal, I had never said much more than "hello" and "goodbye." But Mrs. Chapman was cool. She just smiled and motioned for me to come forward. "If you think you can, Patsy, I think you can," was all she said.

I was so nervous I began to tremble. What had

I done? What would I do? How could I change my mind? Before I could work it all out in my head, Mrs. Chapman struck the opening chords and I just followed. I followed her lead. I followed my heart. The fear melted away. I closed my eyes and began to sing:

Have you any rivers that you think are uncrossable? . . . God specializes in things that seem impossible and he can do what no other power, Holy Ghost power, can do.

I was stirred by the music and moved by the spirit. Once I closed my eyes, it felt like a dream. It was as if I really wasn't out there in front of the Young Adults Choir at all. I was back in front of my bedroom mirror, singing into my broomstick. I was Dinah and Sarah and Nina all rolled into one. Halfway through the song, I was no longer just singing. I was chanting, I was incanting, I was crying, I was testifying, laying back on the notes until the song was no longer a song, but a sanctified call to God and I was no longer a teenage girl singing in a church choir but a messenger of the Lord singing on the front steps of Heaven. When the song was over, no one said a word. The room was so quiet, you could hear an angel landing on a cloud. Mrs. Chapman was staring at me as if she were seeing me — really seeing me — for the first time. Some people in the choir were actually crying. Mrs. Chapman's daughter, Zara. My sister Barbara. What had happened? What would happen next? Finally, the answer came.

"Patsy," Mrs. Chapman said softly, "from now on you will be our soloist."

For almost three years, I was. I only left the choir in the early sixties when professional commitments kept me from attending Sunday services. Years later, I would think about that special day when something rose up in me and I rose to the occasion. That's certainly what I was thinking about in March 1991 when I did my PBS television special, "Going Home to Gospel." We taped the show at Chicago's historic Quinn Chapel, a church founded by black folks in the nineteenth century in the city that had boosted black gospel music in the 1930s. There I was with some of the biggest names in contemporary gospel. People like Edwin Hawkins, The Barrett Sisters and The Mighty Clouds of Joy. There I was thinking about that one moment in time — a defining moment in my personal history. I thought about how all the wonderful things that had happened in my career started that day in church with a shy little girl singing to the Lord; with a kind and supportive lady who said, "If you think you can, I think you can."

That's why, later that same year when the Beulah Baptist Church honored Mrs. Chapman for her fifty-one years of service, I had to come back home. I had to break another commitment to be there, but I needed to return to the church where it all began for me to pay tribute to the lady who encouraged me to step up. I needed to be a part of it. I needed Mrs. Chapman to know how much her faith in me would always mean. That night, in November 1991, for the first time in three decades, I sang with the choir. I joined them to perform for Mrs. Chapman, to sing her favorite hymn: "Jesus Keep Me Near the Cross." That was the last time I sang with the choir and it was the last time I saw Mrs. Chapman. We didn't know it at the time, but she had lung cancer. Eight months later, she died. But, in an important way, she lives on. We've all had that special teacher or neighbor or coach who believed in us enough to make us start to believe in ourselves. Mrs. Chapman must have known that when you reach someone the way she reached me, when you touch someone so deeply, when you inspire someone to reach into themselves, to reach their potential, they can't help but pass on that inspiration to so many others. That's what I have tried to do with my life and my music. And because of that, Mrs. Harriett Chapman — and anybody else who has ever taken the time to touch a child's soul — is immortal.

Chapter Nine

With Barbara and I singing in the choir, Sundays became very special days in our house. The place was alive with energy. It was electric. Like backstage on opening night. With six women and one bathroom, it was always a race for face time in the mirror. None of us — not one single one of us — was about to leave the house until we were Sunday-morning fine. Our outfits had to be out of sight. Our hair had to be happening: dyed, fried, and laid to the side. Especially mine. If everybody was going to be looking at me, I had to be perfect. I always made sure I was the first one ready. While I waited for Chubby, Naomi, and my sisters, I would just stand there in the doorway of our house looking out across the park at the front door of Beulah Baptist Church. Door to door. From my house to God's house. I felt connected, inspired, blessed. Watching the streams of people making their way inside the church, it would hit me like a lightning bolt. *They were coming to hear me sing.* Word had spread throughout Southwest Philly that, at Beulah, there was this teenage girl who was "touched" — touched by the Holy Spirit. Soon, whenever the Young Adults Choir sang, the place was packed to the rafters. Every pew from front to back. It was standing room only. All those people. They were coming to hear me sing. "Yes, Lord," I would hear the sisters shout, as I sailed into my solo. "Sing your song, Sister Patsy. Move a little higher, a little closer to Jesus." And I did. I kept moving, higher and higher, and I was bringing them with me. They wanted to come. After all, they were coming to hear me sing. Just like they did Grandmother Tempie. The Mockingbird.

Even people from other churches started coming. It didn't matter what you were the rest of the month: Presbyterian, Catholic, or Holy Roller. Come Second Sunday, you were Baptist and you were sitting in Beulah. Lots of our neighbors were among the converted. Like the family of my dear friend George Peters, who were devoted members of Elmwood Methodist, but who would come to Beulah to hear me sing. After service, it seemed like the whole church came by our house. All the regulars were there. George, his mother and aunt; Miss Maudie from down the way; Ida Jones, who owned the neighborhood beauty shop and had to be there to get the 4-1-1 on everything and everybody; and, of course, there was Chubby's ace buddy, Queen Esther Black, who sometimes brought her sons, Bernie, Junior, Robby, and Gus. Uncle Pizell, Aunt Verdelle, my cousins Hazel, Marvin, and Veronica were there, too. So was my best friend, Claudette Henderson. While the grown-ups were cooking and gossiping, the young people were playing music and cards. But not me. I was always cleaning. Dusting the tables. Sweeping the floor. Emptying the ashtrays. I had to stay busy, active, moving. It was the only way

I could come down from my high, the only way I could release all that pent-up energy I still had inside me after singing. Besides, as long as I was cleaning, I could be *around* the crowd without really being in it. George found the only way to draw me in. Begging me to sing. He always wanted to hear the same song: Carla Thomas's big hit, "Gee Whiz." Like half the boys in Elmwood, George was secretly in love with Claudette, and the whole time I was singing, he never took his eyes off her. Once was never enough. I could barely get the last note out before he was begging me to sing it again. Soon, everybody in the house was egging me on. My very first encores. My very first fans. My very special friends. I felt a total sense of belonging, which I cherished. I held my breath for fear I might lose it. Taking my bows on world-famous stages, I often flash back to those days in Chubby's living room when my friends and neighbors cheered me on. That's when I began to associate applause with acceptance and cheers with love. Gee whiz.

I was a late bloomer and it was at John Bartram High School that I started to come into my own. In the late fifties and early sixties, the Philadelphia public schools were full of talented kids who would go on to fame and fortune. Earl "The Pearl" Monroe, who was at Bartram with me, would become a sports icon for his silky-smooth moves on the basketball court. Kenny Gamble, who was at West Philly High, would become a music legend for his silky-smooth sounds in the recording studio. (Never in my wildest dreams did I imagine Kenny would wind up being a multiple Grammy Award–winning producer. Not little Kenny Gamble who used to sneak beers for me to drink with him in the alley behind my house. It was Kenny, along with Leon Huff, who would shape the Sound of Philadelphia, producing artists like Jerry Butler, The Intruders, Harold Melvin and The Blue Notes, The O'Jays, Teddy Pendergrass — and one day me.) Back then, none of us had a clue what the future might hold, least of all me. For a teenage girl, the future is Saturday night. And there were plenty of other things to think about at the moment. Pretty clothes. Cute boys. Cool cars. Because of my singing, I had become popular. And my newfound popularity gave me confidence. With my girlfriends by my side, I found myself doing things I never could have done on my own. Like going to parties and staying out all night. One time we pushed it too far. It was the night Marlene, Gertrude, Barbara, and I hitchhiked to a party over in West Philly. When we missed the last bus back to Elmwood, I knew we were in trouble. I just didn't know how deep. We all found out the next morning when we finally got home and our mothers were waiting for us. Chubby was hysterical and somebody had called the police and reported us missing, kidnapped, vanished without a trace. We had to go down to the station and explain ourselves to the officers which, let me tell you, was a whole lot easier than explaining it to Chubby. I halfway wanted them to lock us up to protect us. I knew what was waiting for Barbara and me when we got home. Given the circumstances, we got off easy. Chubby grounded us for two months. Fortunately, being on punishment only stopped me from hanging out with my girlfriends on weekends. Monday through Friday, I had to go to school where I got to pursue the single most important interest of teenage girls: chasing boys. Literally. For a while, my girlfriends and I were into stalking Oliver Chamberlain. His older brother was basketball star Wilt Chamberlain, but that's not why everybody wanted to get next to him. Oliver's attraction was much more personal. His ride. A long, shiny, pretty black Oldsmobile that Wilt had given his parents and which they let Oliver drive. The minute school let out, Claudette and I lined up to catch a ride. But Oliver threw us a curve. Apparently, we weren't among the chosen few, so he and his friends started ducking us. We'd zig, they'd zag. We'd go left, they'd go right. Finally, Claudette and I just gave up. A few minutes later, they passed us waiting at the bus stop, but we were much too cool to let them notice us noticing them. By the time they drove by, we were profiling — smoothing our hair, leaning on the bus stop, striking a pose, giving good face. We were Vogueing long before Madonna ever heard the word. Teenage girls are nothing without their image.

Of course, I was probably more image conscious than anybody I knew. Like my sisters, Claudette didn't have to think twice about her looks. She was beautiful. Not only was I not in her league, I felt I had to overcome so much just to get up to "average." That's where Vivian, the Countess of Cool, came in. She had the baddest drag in town. So bad I thought her clothes could even make me look good. So I took my life in my hands. I broke into Vivian's trunk, the one where she kept her prettiest pieces locked away from her younger sisters. You have never in your life seen such fabulous clothes. Cashmere sweaters. Butter-soft leather bags and belts. Melt-on-your-skin Italian silk shirts. I just couldn't help myself. I would pick the lock and take my pick. I'd always make sure to sneak them back in the trunk before she got home from work. I thought Vivian would never know the difference. What I didn't know was how to fold them as perfectly as she did. Eventually, I got busted. Vivian beat my butt all through the house. But you know what? Those clothes were so beautiful they were worth every bruise. They were the reason I made the Best Dressed list at Bartram High. At the time, it felt like snagging the Grammy, the Oscar, the Emmy, the Tony, and the Nobel Prize all wrapped up together. Even then, I was a "drag queen."

I loved makeup almost as much as I loved clothes. With all those paints and potions, I could change my face. I thought it needed changing. Everywhere I looked — beauty pageants, fashion magazines, TV shows — I saw the face of beauty and it wasn't mine. You have to remember, this was before The Movement. Before The Revolution. Before black — dark skin, full lips, wide noses — before any of that was considered beautiful. It was before the words "dark and lovely" traveled in the same circles. It was way before we crowned even one, let alone five, black women as Miss America. So I set out to paint a new picture of myself — one that might at least minimize the glaring differences between me and all the models on the magazine covers. I piled it on. Heavy, dark, and thick. My makeup was like an American Express card to me — I never left home without it. Every morning before school, I would go down to the kitchen, turn on the stove, and melt the tip of my eyebrow pencil over the open flame. It only took a second or two to get it soft enough to draw a thick, heavy line. Maybe I was trying a little too hard. Between the blue shadow above my eyes and the black liner beneath them, I must have looked like a cross between Tammy Faye Bakker and a raccoon. What I didn't realize is that there are deeper things than physical beauty that make you attractive to people. Long-lasting things. Things that aren't painted on your face or buttoned up your back. Things like warmth, kindness, generosity, compassion. Things like the way you laugh, the way you love, the way you live your life. Those things — not the eyeliner and the cashmere sweaters — were the things that were winning me friends. And eventually boyfriends.

At Bartram High, I had two. James Jones was the first. All the girls were crazy about him. For one thing, he was a senior. For another, he was drop-dead fine. Somehow, we connected, although it wasn't one of those everyday-is-the-Fourth-of-July kind of love affairs. At sixteen, love is so much simpler. Eating lunch together in the school cafeteria, walking to class hand-in-hand, sitting close in Chubby's living room listening to love songs on the record player. It was warm, wonderful, sweet, and short. When James graduated, our romance ended. Just like that.

A few months later, I started dating Richard Glenn, a popular junior who everybody called "Bird." Where James was a looker, Bird was a dancer. We used to do the cha-cha and the bop at all the neighborhood parties. I loved dancing almost as much as singing, especially with Bird. Once we learned each other's moves, we got to be real showstoppers. At one end-of-school party, somebody put on "The Twist," and the next thing I knew Bird had grabbed me and we were out on the floor working out. We were twisting and turning and curling and curving so hard that, halfway into the record, a circle had formed around us and the whole room was cheering us on. I had this big smile on my face, but no one really knew why. It wasn't because Bird and I were in the spotlight, although I had come to love the attention I was getting. I was smiling because I was thinking about Henry Colt's Chicken Market, down on Ninth and Washington Avenue and how pudgy little Ernest Evans used to joke and sing and do impressions for Chubby and me before he'd go in the back and pluck our chickens. I thought about how Henry Colt had put him in touch with Parkway Records and how Dick Clark's wife had renamed Ernest Evans because she thought he was a cute version of Fats Domino. ("Fats" became "Chubby" and "Domino" became "Checker.") I thought about how Ernest Evans had become an overnight sensation with a number-one hit that Bird and I, and every teenager in America, was dancing to now. And I thought about how dreams are played to music and how music brings dreams to life. That's why I just kept smiling and dancing and dreaming.

It wasn't long after that party when I began to think about making my own dreams come true. If Ernest Evans could become Chubby Checker and if Chubby Checker could become a big star, I was convinced that little Patsy Holte could make it, too. After all, even when the only thing I saw looking back at me in the mirror was a homely little black girl, the voice I heard reverberating back to me when I sang in church was the voice of a beautiful angel. Everyone said so. Especially Chubby. "Patsy," she always said, "you got the sweetest voice on this earth." I began thinking about actually *making* the music I was listening to. I began to reach beyond the Young Adults Choir.

It was in the living room of my friend Gertrude's house where I joined my first singing group. Gertrude had to baby-sit her two nieces, and a bunch of us were keeping her company. It was the usual crowd: Marlene Benton, Sally Butler, Brenda James, my sister Barbara, and me. While Gertrude was looking after her nieces, the five of us were just sitting around doo-wopping. Someone put on one of the greatest R&B ballads of all time — The Five Satins' "In the Still of the Night." We started singing over the record, and we thought we were it. To this day, I can't be sure exactly what we were hearing. With The Five Satins as backup, who wouldn't sound great? Right then and there, we decided to form our own group. We named ourselves after our neighborhood — The Elmtones. The Elmtones from Elmwood. A guy in the neighborhood, Tommy Mitchell, had a piano on his porch, and soon we began going to his house to rehearse. We were awful, but you couldn't tell us we weren't the baddest, hippest quintet in town. Many days after school, we would stand around under the trees in the park across the street from my house singing as if we were giving a concert at Carnegie Hall.

After a few months of these performances in the park, we heard about a local talent show that would be held at the Carmen Skating Rink in North Philly. "The Battle of the Groups." We decided to go for it. That was the easy part. The hard part was getting ready for it. We practiced for weeks. But we still weren't quite ready. The

84

problem was that we didn't realize just how not ready for prime time we really were until show-time, when Big Neck Pete and his group finished their routine, and our number was up and we went down. In flames. It looked like everybody from Elmwood had showed up. Even with Tommy accompanying us on the piano, we stunk up the place. Big time. From the moment we opened our mouths, we sounded like a train wreck. Screeching and clashing. Where were The Five Satins when we really needed them? Barbara was the worst. She was hitting wrong notes all up and down the scale. I don't know about the audience, but I just couldn't take it. In fact, I lost it. Right there. In the rink. In front of hundreds of people. Singing was the one thing in my life that made me special; the one thing that transformed me from shy, awkward Patsy to cool, popular Patti. From an ugly duckling to a swan. And now it seemed as if Barbara was destroying even that. When I heard the crowd start to boo, something inside me snapped.

"You stupid, no-talent, no-singing bitch," I screamed at the top of my lungs.

Marlene, Sally, and Brenda just stood there in stunned silence as I kept ranting and raving in a fit of blind rage. They had never seen this side of me before. Neither had I. It seemed to come out of nowhere. This was the night I met "Priscilla," the name I have since given to the mean, selfish diva-bitch who lives inside me. But that was only the beginning. Barbara could always give as good as she got. She wasn't about to just stand there and take all that abuse from her younger sister. Barbara started screaming and cursing right back. We performed at the Carmen Skating Rink, all right. But not the way any of us had planned. Not the way the crowd expected. I was screaming at Barbara, she was screaming at me, and the audience was screaming at both of us to disappear. And that's just what I did. With one last blast at Barbara, I turned on my heels and left all four of them standing there in front of the audience. All I wanted to do was find Chubby. I knew she would be waiting for me. I knew she would understand. I knew she would get me out of there. She was waiting for me, all right. But, as I started to run toward her, the look on her face stopped me dead in my tracks. I had never seen that look before. Not even the night she pulled the knife on Daddy. It was more than anger, more than outrage. It was disgust. It was disappointment. It was disgrace.

"I'm ashamed of you," she said in a low, even voice. "And if I ever hear you speak that way to your sister in front of people again, I will personally beat your ass black and blue."

Barbara heard it from Chubby as well, though it wasn't nearly as bad for her. After all, it was my fault. I had started the whole thing.

Hindsight is always 20/20. Looking back, I realize that I never would have treated a friend the way I treated Barbara that night. But she was my sister, and I knew no matter what I did or said to her, she'd always be my sister; she would always forgive me. It had never occurred to me how deeply I had hurt and humiliated her and embarrassed Chubby in the process. All I cared about was me, my feelings, my ego.

Needless to say, that was the first and last performance of The Elmtones from Elmwood. Unfortunately, that was not the last time I treated Barbara like she was some gum on the bottom of my shoe. It wasn't the last time I would have to think about the lesson I was supposed to learn that night, but didn't. Had I understood it then, I could have saved myself so much heartache, so many years of guilt and grief. I have come to realize that there really is a high price to fame. But public approval shouldn't come at someone else's expense. You can't lift yourself up by putting other people down. And you will never impress everyone by stepping on anyone. In fact, there really is no need to try to impress people at all. Those who really care about you don't have to be impressed. Those who don't care about you never can be. Everybody loves a star, but that doesn't mean they love you. What they love is the image of you, the makeup you wear in public, the glitz, the glitter, the gig-wig. At the end of the day, after your last bow, after the curtain goes down and the lights go up, after you've wiped off the makeup and you just sit there staring in the mirror at the real you, you know what matters most. It is the unconditional love of family and true friends. A love that doesn't start with a hit or end with a flop. A love I didn't appreciate until it was too late.

Chapter Ten

There was so much for me to learn in my years at John Bartram High School. Somehow, I kept missing the point. Chubby tried to tell me. So did Junior, every time he came up from Florida to visit. Over and over again they would give me the lecture about what was really important in life. *It was important for me to study hard. It was important for me to improve my grades. It was important for me to get a good education.* They just didn't understand. None of that was important to me. History, geometry, and biology wouldn't help me make it in the music business. As it turned out, I was the one who really didn't understand. I was so young and naive, I just didn't get it. There was so much for me to learn in my years at John Bartram High School. But it wasn't just in the classroom. I had a lot to learn about the way things worked, about how the system was set up against black kids.

In the early sixties, like so many other urban high schools, Bartram High reflected the racial attitudes of the times. Although black kids made up a big chunk of the student population, the teaching staff was lily-white. Worse, it was assumed black students weren't smart enough to keep up with the white kids. It wasn't until I was an adult that I learned that we had been "tracked" — that is, we were grouped and placed into sections, supposedly based on our aptitude and potential. The top sections were for the brightest kids who were being groomed for college and a better life. The lower sections were for all the other students who were expected to get low-wage jobs, not high-paying careers. You could count the number of black students in the top section on one hand and still have fingers left over. I only knew one — Armstead Edwards, that bookworm from the Young Adults Choir who was in love with my sister Barbara. In fairness, I have to admit that, even if more black students had been moved into the top sections, I wouldn't have been one of them. I was an average-to-below-average student, at best.

I can't count the times I have wished I had listened to Chubby's and Junior's lectures back then. If I had it to do over again, I wouldn't have dropped out of high school, especially just one semester shy of graduation. As an adult, not having that diploma did a number on my head many times. Frankly, it often made me feel insecure, sometimes downright inferior. As a teenager, though, I couldn't see that far down the road. All I cared about was the moment. And, at that moment in my life, all I wanted to do was sing. Music was all around me. It was inside me. Somehow I knew I would make my living on a song. "I don't need A's and B's because I'm going to make all of my money singing," I often told Junior.

Bartram had limited opportunities for black students in the classroom, but I seized my opportunity down the hall, in the auditorium. In my senior year, Eileen Moran, my favorite teacher, organized a talent show to be produced, directed, and performed by the students. But even though I had been aching for another chance to see what I could do in front of an audience, I was still gun-shy, torn about putting myself out there on the line again. Half of me wanted to audition, but half of me wasn't sure I could handle it. Singing in church for the Lord was one thing, but singing in school for all your friends, well, that was a whole different movie. There would be no choir to back me up. No Mrs. Chapman to urge me on. No sisters in the church to get happy with the spirit. What if I got booed again, the way we had gotten booed at the Carmen Skating Rink? I just couldn't take that. And there would be no back-up singers to blame. I'd never be able to show my face in school again.

In the end, my desire to sing won out over my fear of rejection. But once I got to tryouts, I couldn't stop thinking about the Carmen Skating Rink. When my name was called, I walked out onstage and then just froze. Everybody was staring at me. Miss Moran. The panel of student judges. All the kids in the auditorium. Everybody was waiting for me to do something. Dance, sing, joke, juggle, anything but just stand there. Finally, Miss Moran broke the silence. She told me to relax, to take my time, to begin whenever I was ready. I nodded, took a deep breath, and managed to force the words.

"I'd like to sing."

Sing? Miss Moran told me years later that she got a sick feeling in the pit of her stomach. She had only seen the quiet Patsy in her classroom, the one who wouldn't even raise her hand to ask a question, not the one outside raising hell with all her friends. How on earth, she wondered, would I ever raise my voice in front of hundreds of people? She soon found out. So did the student judges who voted me into the show immediately, breaking their policy not to reveal finalists until the following day. So did the student audience six weeks later when they unanimously chose me as the first-place winner. *"This is it,"* I thought, as everyone in the auditorium rose to their feet and gave me a cheering, thunderous, five-minute ovation. *"This is the feeling I want for the rest of my life. Nothing in the world will ever feel better than this."* My heart raced to the beat of hundreds of hands pounding together. We were one — two halves of the same whole. Me and the audience. I kept replaying in my head "You'll Never Walk Alone," the song that had won the audition. The song that had won the talent show. The song that had won over the crowd. The song that could have become my personal anthem forevermore.

After the talent show, I had no idea how fast things would start happening for me. I had no way of knowing that, a few years later, on February 26, 1965, I would stand on that same stage and perform once again by special request of Miss Moran. Only I wouldn't stand alone. I would stand center stage as lead singer of a famous quartet. And I wouldn't sing a Broadway show tune. I would sing a Top 20 R&B hit — *our* hit.

I won something else at the Bartram High talent show, something even bigger than first place — another chance to showcase my talent. My business teacher, Harold "Heshy" Briskin, was a very popular man around school. It wasn't just that he was a good teacher, although everybody agreed he was one of the best. But he was also popular with all the girls because he was so good-looking. I mean, the man was fine. Fall-down-on-the-floor-and-weep gorgeous. I had a serious crush on Mr. Briskin. All the girls did. That's why, a few days after the talent show, when he pulled me aside in the hallway between classes, I thought I would just die. And, when I heard what he had to say, I felt like I had been resurrected. He had been there, at the talent show. He had listened to me sing. My voice had moved him, touched him, rocked him. He thought I could sing professionally. I had the right stuff. He said all I needed was the right break, the right people to hear me at the right place. And he could arrange all three. Mr. Briskin had a friend in the record business who was looking to sign new talent. If I was interested in auditioning for him, he would set it all up. If I was interested? Was he kidding? That's all I *was* interested in. Once I got Chubby's permission, Mr. Briskin would bring his friend to a local club, the Venus Lounge on South Broad Street, where he would arrange with the owner to let me sing. The rest would be up to me. I was only fifteen years old. I had only just decided what I wanted to be when I grew up. And here I was about to get it. My big break. Like Chubby Checker on Dick Clark.

"I'll be there," I told Mr. Briskin. "And I'll make you proud." That afternoon, when I told Chubby about Mr. Briskin's offer, she was beside herself with joy. She was so-o-o excited. That's the way she always was when it came to my music and me — never a pushy stage mother, but always supportive. Always encouraging. Always there for me. Over the next few days, I spent more time worrying about what I was going to wear than what I was going to sing. I agonized over my appearance. I had to look the part if I was going to make the right impression. Finally, I decided on a white spaghetti-strap dress with a wide, knee-length skirt. It was fitted tight in the waist and I hoped it would make me look older, hipper, sophisticated. Like Vivian.

Monday night. My big chance, my big break, the moment of reckoning. It all came much faster than I ever expected. I don't remember much about getting ready, or getting to the club, or getting to the stage. I don't even remember what I sang. I do remember the feeling in the room that night. There was a heaviness in the air. Cigarette smoke hung in the room like a blanket of fog. The smell of booze was strong and stifling. But, more than anything else, the place was heavy with expectation. This was not Beulah Baptist. This was not Bartram High. This wasn't even the

Carmen Skating Rink. This was the Coliseum. The Lions' Den. And I was fresh, raw meat.

Even with Chubby and Mr. Briskin there for support, the pressure got to me. I cracked. I could barely get the words to the song out, let alone sing it with any passion. That Monday night at the Venus Lounge, I didn't sing whatever song it was that I chose: I *butchered* it. The transformation that always happened whenever I sang, that metamorphosis never came. If there was any magic at all in that place that night, it was seeing my golden opportunity disappear. Vanish into thin air. *Poof.* Just like that, it was gone. So was my professional career. Over before it even began. The audience didn't exactly boo me off the stage. That would have been better than what they did. Nothing. I got the silent treatment. As if I had never even been there.

All I wanted to do was go somewhere and crawl under a rock. But I couldn't. I felt too bad for Mr. Briskin. Here he had believed in me so much that he had put his own reputation on the line, and how did I repay him? By making a fool of both of us. I didn't know how I was going to do it, but as I walked off the stage, I knew I had to fix it. I knew I couldn't leave it like that. I pulled myself together, walked over to Mr. Briskin and begged him to talk the owner into letting me sing one more song. I don't know how I thought I would get a second chance. Maybe there was a little magic in the place after all. Mr. Briskin pulled a rabbit out of the hat: the owner's answer was I could sing one more song.

This time I didn't blow my chance. This time, I blew the doors off the place. By the time I had sung the last bar of "Come Back to Sorrento," the audience was on its feet cheering the little black girl in the little white dress. Mr. Briskin's friend didn't sign me, but I didn't care. At that moment, the crowd's standing ovation was better than any record deal. It told me what I needed to hear. I had redeemed myself and Mr. Briskin. I had justified his faith in me. I had renewed my faith in myself. That was what really mattered that night in the Venus Lounge. What if I had given up after the first song? I would never have known that I could do it. I wonder if I would ever have tried again.

Chapter Eleven

There had been a lot of changes in our family by 1961. Jackie got pregnant and, three months before her sixteenth birthday, she gave birth to her son, Billy. Chubby adored Billy and spoiled him rotten. In fact, it was my mother who really raised him. Jackie's pregnancy had to feel like déjà vu all over again to her. Just a dozen years earlier, Chubby had gone through the same thing with Vivian. Like Jackie, Vivian got pregnant in high school and was only sixteen when she had her only son, Percy, or Butchie as everybody calls him. Of course, Chubby knew firsthand what it was like to be a teenage mother — a single teenage mother at that. By the time she was sixteen, she was raising not one child, but two. Every mother knows her child and, in her heart, I think Chubby knew Jackie wasn't ready for motherhood. Here she was bringing a new life into the world before she even knew about life herself. I wasn't there for Jackie the way Chubby was. Truth be told, I wasn't there for her at all. I was too busy with my own life, my own dreams, my own plans. Jackie must have felt it from the very beginning. When she was too scared to tell Chubby she was pregnant, she didn't confide in me. Jackie turned to Miss Moran, our favorite teacher, the same teacher who had organized the talent show. I'm not proud of it, but my attitude at the time was that Billy was Jackie's baby, Jackie's burden, Jackie's responsibility.

Chubby and Vivian were having problems, too. After Vivian and Butchie's father broke up, Vivian fell hard for a married man. His name was Charles, but Vivian called him "Old Faithful" because, no matter how bad things would get for her — and they would get insufferable — he stuck by her every agonizing step of the way. But none of us could know that when they started seeing each other, especially Chubby. At the time, all she knew was that Charles had a wife and Vivian was his "chick on the side." They fought about it day and night. Chubby screaming at Vivian: "Can't you see you're wasting your life in a dead-end relationship?" Vivian screaming back at Chubby: "Can't you see Charles is my life and I want this relationship?" Neither would give in. I don't think either of them could. And the stalemate finally drove Vivian out of the house. After months of arguing, Vivian, the sister I idolized and adored, found an apartment and she and Butchie moved out.

By the time Vivian and Butchie left, Chubby had broken up with the boyfriend who had abused me and the day he left our house for the last time I knew God had answered my prayers. Soon, the rest of us would leave Elmwood as well, but, unlike Vivian, we didn't move by choice. In the late fifties, The City of Philadelphia got the bright idea to target Elmwood for a massive "re-development project." It was a big deal. The largest in the country at the time. A hundred-million-dollar urban-renewal scheme. I don't know what our community's "redevelopment" meant to Philadelphia. I do know what it meant to the families who lived there. It meant losing our homes, being torn from our roots. As the old-timers used to say: "Urban renewal means Negro removal."

When you cut through all the legal mumbo jumbo, the deal boiled down to this: You could sell your home to the city for whatever price they were offering, or you could stay put and run the risk of having your home condemned and taken from you. I'm sad to say that's exactly what happened to many families who tried to hold on to their homes and stood by helplessly when the bulldozers rolled in. By the mid sixties, nearly half of my childhood community was uprooted.

Chubby didn't put up a fight for our house. As much as she loved it, I think she was ready to let it go. It was filled with so much of her past, so much of my father, so much to remind her of a life and a love affair that had ceased to exist outside her memories. With the money she got from the city, Chubby went out and found us another four-bedroom house at 5819 Washington Avenue. It was only about fifteen minutes outside of Elmwood but, on moving day, you would have thought I was leaving for Siberia. I was so depressed, even my blues had blues. For most of my life, I've hated change. Letting go of the old and familiar scared me to death. I was terrified I wouldn't be able to adjust to the new and un-known. That I wouldn't be able to cut it. My fear of change caused me a lot of anguish and heart-ache until I learned to accept some simple facts of life: change is the only constant — the trick is to learn to see it as just another opportunity to grow, a chance to transform yourself from the person you are into the person you want to be. When you fear it, you fight it. And when you fight it, you block the blessing.

Our move out of Elmwood was a perfect ex-ample of this simple truth. It turned out to be the right thing at the right time. In fact, looking back, I believe it was fate. Had we not been forced to move, I would never have met the man who be-came my first manager, the man who gave me my first break as a professional in the music busi-ness.

After my experience at the Venus Lounge, I was fixated on performing. With Chubby's con-stant encouragement, I knew I was meant for bigger and better things. I just needed to find out where. At the time, "girl groups" were all the rage — the cutting edge of sixties soul, rock, and pop. It was the Golden Age of female vocal groups. As songwriter Gerry Goffin has said, "In the sixties, God was a young black girl who could sing." And, back in Philly, we all worshiped these idols.

With the radio pumping out songs by The Shirelles, The Chantels, The Chiffons, and Lord-knows-how-many-other hot new girl groups, I was desperate to be part of it all. So desperate, in fact, that I wiped out all memory of The Elmtones and set out to form a group. I hooked up with three high-school classmates — Yvonne Hogen, Jean Brown, and Johnnie Dawson. We all lived within a few blocks of one another. For the next several months, with visions of *American Bandstand* dancing in our heads, we spent every free moment at one another's houses tightening up our harmony and choreographing dance steps. In those days, you couldn't just stand behind a mike and sing. You had to be able to *move,* baby. As we worked on our routines, we would give shows in my living room. Our "band" was on the radio — the AM band — tuned to the hottest black stations. Sometimes we used the record player, an old clunker that my brother had left on one of his visits from Florida. Chubby and Naomi were our audience. I would give the signal — three finger snaps to set the tempo — and we would start our routine after the fourth beat. We would spin and slide and sing and glide until we were ready to collapse from exhaustion. In our minds, The Shirelles and The Chantels didn't have a thing on us.

It wasn't long before we decided to take our show on the road. We started performing around town at sock hops, school dances, and neighborhood parties. We sang everywhere we could — the front steps, the back porch, the bus stop — for anyone who would listen. Our entire professional wardrobe consisted of one outfit — white blouses, gold skirts, black pumps — which we found at some discount store. We wore those outfits to death. Chubby used to joke that those clothes could stand up and do our routines all by themselves. Luckily, Yvonne's mother took pity on us and made us some new drag. Knee-length gold satin sleeveless dresses that made us feel like little divas. In the tiny universe of our community, I was already beginning to feel like a star.

After our performances, I would come home and sit at the kitchen table with Chubby and dream. One day I would be an internationally famous singing star with millions of dollars and millions of fans. Chubby didn't just understand my dreams. She shared them. More than anyone else, she knew what music meant to me. She believed in me before I believed in myself. "Girl," she used to say, "your voice could make a blind man see." I know that's why she gave me her blessing when, just one semester before my high-school graduation, I told her I wanted to do the unthinkable. I wanted to quit school to sing pro-fessionally. As much as Chubby wanted me to get my high-school diploma, she knew I had to do what I couldn't help doing. That's why she didn't just get behind me as I set out to chase my dream. She wound up leading the way.

One afternoon we were rehearsing at Jean's house. We weren't supposed to be there that day. We had planned to hold practice at my house but, for some unexplainable reason, we changed at the last minute. We were deep into it when Mr. Walt Overbee, a friend of Jean's mom, dropped by. Unexpectedly. He wasn't supposed to be there, either. (But, then again, maybe he was.) He and Mrs. Brown were sitting in the living room shooting the breeze, but he kept tuning out their conversation and tuning in to the music floating up from the basement. Finally, he asked Jean's mother the name of that hot new record she was playing. When she stopped laughing, she told him the "record" he was listening to was her daughter and three of her friends. Mr. Overbee didn't believe her. After he went downstairs and saw for himself, he handed Jean a piece of paper on which he'd scribbled the name and phone number of one of his neighbors.

"Who's he?" we all wanted to know.

Mr. Overbee's neighbor, Bernard Montague, was a former print shop manager who had quit his job to promote variety shows and R&B revues. He lived right around the corner on Ellsworth Street, and he had a reputation as an ace artist manager — a man with strong connections in the local club circuit who could break new acts.

"He's looking for a girl group," Mr. Overbee told us. "And with your voices, he can take you places."

Well, that was all we needed to hear. Before Mr. Overbee could get up the stairs good, we had Mr. Montague on the line. I'm not sure which one of us did the talking, but whoever it was must have been pretty convincing because Mr. Montague agreed to audition us the very next day. We couldn't believe it. We were shocked. Rehearsal was over for the day. After we stopped screaming and hugging and dancing around Jean's basement, I ran all the way home to tell Chubby about our "lucky break." She was excited and she insisted on going with us to the audition, as much for support as to make sure everything was on the up-and-up. I felt like a little kid on Christmas Eve. I didn't sleep so much as an hour that night. That's probably why the next day seems like a dream. Racing through classes, riding the bus home from school with the other girls, the pep talk from Chubby, standing at Mr. Montague's door. We were all nervous, but we were too determined to let anything stop us. Mr. Montague's wife, Mary, answered the door and led us through a large foyer into the living room. There he was — the man with the keys to our future — sitting on the sofa, smoking a cigarette. He wasted no time with preliminaries.

"So you girls think you can sing?" he said. "Show me what you got."

He told us to sing a cappella. He wanted to hear *us*. Just us. Our voices. Our harmony. Our sound. Mr. Montague was so blunt, we froze. But Jean's sister, Diann, who tagged along to watch, jumped up and belted out the Gladys Knight hit, "With Every Beat of My Heart." I don't know if Mr. Montague knew Diann was just showing off, but he looked at her as if he thought she was auditioning. "Next," he said. That meant us. Now, we weren't just nervous. We were terrified. I looked over at Chubby, and she gave me a wink and a nod. No words were necessary. I got the message. It was going to be all right. She wouldn't have brought me here if she didn't believe I could handle it. She would never set me up for failure.

We decided to do two songs that we had been practicing forever, two songs that showed off our moves and our close-knit harmony. I can't swear to it, but I'm pretty sure we did "I Met Him on a Sunday" by The Shirelles and "He's Gone" by The Chantels. When we finished, Chubby was smiling. But there was just one problem. Mr. Montague wasn't. He didn't say a word. He showed no emotion. No reaction. He just sat there smoking his cigarette. It seemed to take forever. In the back of my mind, I kept hearing him say the words I feared: "You girls don't have what it takes." All I wanted to do was get out of there before he had the chance to say them. And anyway, what was taking him so long? Why was he putting us through this? Finally, he finished his cigarette and crushed it into the ashtray. He looked straight at me. I held my breath.

"You kids have potential, but you need a lot of work," he said. "If you follow my rules, rehearse long and hard with my people, I'll put you on my show."

You know the phrase "walking on Cloud Nine"? Well, I was dancing the cha-cha on it. My heart was pounding out the beat. The rest of me stayed perfectly still. Chubby didn't say a word. She just looked over at me and smiled. A smile that said it all. A smile that said: *You did all right, girl. Your world is about to change.* That was all the confirmation I needed. I wasn't dreaming. This was real. In fact, it was a dream come true.

When we left the Montagues, Johnnie, Yvonne, Jean, and Diann rushed home to tell their parents the news. That left just Chubby and me. We walked home arm in arm. Neither of us said what we were thinking. Neither of us had to. Chubby's smile had said everything. Johnnie, Yvonne, Jean, and I were going to be professional singers with our very own manager!

Lying in bed that night, all I could think about was how lucky we were. After all, we weren't even supposed to be at Jean's house the day we met Mr. Overbee who wasn't supposed to be there, either. I fell asleep thinking: "What a lucky co-incidence." Now, I know that what happened that day wasn't a coincidence at all. I believe it was something much more meaningful, much more mystical, much more magical. I had to live almost fifty years before I learned that there are events in life that are so extraordinary and so unlikely, that they can't be chalked up to chance alone. Like when you think about a friend you haven't talked to in twenty years and — bam! — out of the blue, she phones you. Or when you're struggling to find the solution to a problem and — bam! — you pick up the paper or click on the TV and there it is — the answer. I've heard all kinds of stories like these. I've had the experiences myself. There are some stories I could tell you that sound too incredible to be real. Like the one

106

about this man — and I know him personally — whose date stood him up on his twenty-first birthday. Distraught, he decided to visit a neighbor, a woman he had been secretly in love with for years. He knew she was usually at home, but on this night she wasn't home alone. Her date was there with her. Her sister was rarely at home, but on this night, she was. And though she always had a date, on this night she didn't. The man had never paid much attention to the sister and she didn't think much of him, either. But on this night they both paid attention. They connected. They've been happily married for more than twenty-five years.

Whenever events like these occur, I see them now as Divine Guidance. A cosmic reminder of a Higher Power. Evidence that God is always watching us, steering us, sending us messages. I have heard that scientists and scholars have all kinds of terms for these events. Synchronicity. Fortuity. Happenstance. I don't have some fancy name for it. Sixty-dollar words aren't my style. But, I *do* have an explanation. "Coincidences" are the everyday miracles of our lives. Everyday blessings. "Coincidences" are just God's way of staying invisible.

Chapter Twelve

Mr. Montague started managing us around 1961, and he didn't waste any time getting us in shape to appear in his R&B revues. At the audition, he had said we needed a lot of work, but what he didn't say was just how hard he planned to push us. Seven days a week we rehearsed in his basement. On school days, it wasn't unusual for us to practice three, sometimes four, hours a day. On weekends, we practiced all day. Our opportunity was coming soon, Mr. Montague promised, and he was going to make sure we were ready when it did.

Opportunity knocked much sooner than any of us could have imagined. After only a few months of rehearsals, Mr. Montague managed to get us booked to perform at the Orchid Ballroom. This wasn't record hops and roller rinks. This was a serious gig. Back then, the Orchid Ballroom was one of the "in" places to go in Philadelphia. Like the Peppermint Lounge in New York, it was where all the beautiful people went to see and be seen. When our big night came, I was a nervous wreck. We all were. Mr. Montague had delivered on the first part of his promise — getting us the opportunity. But we wouldn't know until we walked out on that stage whether he had delivered on part two — getting us ready. When the curtain opened, we got our answer. All four of us went on automatic pilot. After all those hours of practice, we had our act together. Down cold. The shakes, the shimmies, the steps. And, oh yes, the sound. We blossomed that night at the Orchid Ballroom, and the crowd went wild. We were so good, in fact, the owner booked us that night for several return engagements. It felt like a Hollywood movie. *A Star Is Born*. Four stars, really. And it all happened so fast. There was only one thing missing. A four-star name. As the Orchid Ballroom manager told Mr. Montague when he rebooked us, "Here's Patsy, Jean, Yvonne, and Johnnie" just wasn't going to cut it anymore. We had less than a week to come up with our new identity. We started playing the name game, struggling to find something that fit, something that hit. One of us, don't ask me who, suggested we call ourselves The Orchids. Not bad. It sort of fit. We had gotten our first big break at the Orchid Ballroom. But it didn't hit. The Orchids just didn't have that pop, that sizzle, that snap that we wanted. But we couldn't let it go. We kept playing around with the name — it was "Orchid This" and "Orchid That" — until somebody struck a chord.

"How about The Ordettes?"

It was perfect.

We had the name, we had the numbers, and we had the manager. With Mr. Montague pacing us, pushing us, promoting us, The Ordettes started getting bookings all over town. At night, we played the club circuit in Philly and, in the mornings, we somehow managed to drag ourselves to class. We spent a lot of weekends in New Jersey where we had become the favorites at the Old Soldiers' Home in Atlantic City. What a difference a year makes. On my last trip to the seaside resort, I wasn't a singer; I was a cleaning lady. For a hot minute. Some summers, when money got tight, Chubby would work as a domestic for wealthy white folks on vacation. Jackie, Barbara, and I would tag along to hang out on the boardwalk, eat some good seafood, and try to catch a glimpse of all the big-name entertainers. On one trip, to earn some extra money, I answered a want ad for a housekeeper. Big mistake. The gig was ghastly: washing clothes, washing windows, polishing silver, scrubbing floors and, in between, cooking and caring for this arrogant, rude, rich white woman's blind mother. That was my first and last job outside of show business. That woman hadn't been out of her house a good hour before Priscilla came out. I put down my mop, picked up my bag, and left her "To Do" list on the table and her blind mother rocking in her chair. I know now that, even if that woman didn't treat me right, the way I handled the situation was wrong. Chubby taught me better than that. One sure way to triumph over people who dog you is not to sink to their level, but to bring them up to yours. Kill them with kindness. That day, I gained new respect for my mother and everybody else who has ever earned a living as a domestic.

Not that earning a living as a singer in the early

days was glamorous. The Old Soldiers' Home in Atlantic City is a long way from the Metropolitan Opera House in New York City. But that didn't matter to Chubby. All she wanted was to hear me sing. Even if the place was a dive and she had to drive hours to get there. I was used to seeing her sitting in the audience before the show. I was used to seeing the whole audience before the show. I had a thing about getting dressed early. At least an hour before showtime. It gave me time to size up the audience before we took the stage. You'd be surprised how much you can tell about a crowd when you're peeking through the curtains. One time I was the one who got surprised. Chubby was in the front row as usual. The shock was her date. It was Daddy. The two of them were sitting there laughing and talking as if they were a normal couple. As if they were still together. *As if they were in love.* Seeing them together like that opened all the old wounds. It brought back all the buried hopes, however irrational, that one day my parents might reconcile and we'd be a family again. I couldn't hold back the tears. Shaking and sobbing, I ran back into the dressing room where Jean held me in her arms until I felt I could go on. It was the first night my father ever saw me sing professionally and my performance was bittersweet. It truly was a labor of love. During the ride home, all I could think about were the nights in Elmwood when my Daddy and I would sit on the front steps and sing our special songs. I thought about the night I promised him that one day I would sing rings around him. I thought about how now, it was my singing that had brought my parents together again — even if it was for only one night.

Many nights, when I'm riding home from my concerts, I think about what, for me, is the *real* magic of my music. The power it has to bring together all kinds of people. People who have nothing in common except the music and the way it makes them feel. Gays, straights, conservatives, liberals, Jews, Gentiles, blacks, whites, young, old. When they come to hear me sing, they check their differences at the door. When they come to hear me sing, they are a family. Just like Chubby and Daddy. Even if it is for only one night.

Chapter Thirteen

Despite our early success, the original Ordettes would soon fall apart. I was ready to eat, drink, and sleep music. This was the life I had chosen for myself. But, one by one, Johnnie, Yvonne, and Jean were making different choices.

Johnnie was the first to quit the group when her father decided the only music he wanted her to sing was gospel. Because he was managing a number of groups at the time, Mr. Montague was able to replace Johnnie pretty quickly. He moved Sandra Tucker from The Tonettes, making her the latest Ordette. Sandra could really blow. Still can. Music is in her blood. Her father is Ira Tucker, lead singer of the legendary gospel quartet, The Dixie Hummingbirds, the group that backed Paul Simon on his million-selling single "Loves Me Like a Rock." While we were still breaking Sandra into the group, Yvonne and Jean each fell in love. Soon after, they both left The Ordettes to get married. (Yvonne married Mr. Montague's son, Eugene.) I was sorry to see all the other original Ordettes go. We had so much history together . . . forming the group, working out our routines in front of Chubby and Naomi, the excitement of those early performances. But I understood their reasons for leaving just as they understood mine for pushing on. I wished them well.

That left Sandra and me, alone together. Mr. Montague assured us that it wouldn't take long to find replacements, and we took his word for it. In the meantime, we continued to sing in his revue, but with one big difference: whenever we had a show, we sang separately, as soloists. Even with the changes in personnel, the routine was pretty much the same. We'd hop in the back of Mr. Montague's station wagon and drive two, sometimes three, hours to play even the smallest booking — the Tippin Inn in New Jersey, the Steel Pier in Atlantic City, Sparrows Beach in Maryland. You name it, we played it. If there was a room, a crowd, and a place to plug in a mike, we were there, doing our thing. The show always went the same way. The dancers would open. "Ladies and gentlemen, put your hands together for King Chico: King of the Arabian Fire Dancers." Then Sandra, then me. When Mr. Montague started managing his nephew, Gil, the two of us would do a duet, usually "Starry Night." I always closed the show alone.

As a soloist, I was getting steady work and a good response in the Montague revue. But I wasn't really happy in the spotlight alone. I wanted more. I wanted four. I wanted to get back out in front of a group. At that time, nothing excited me as much as going through the routines we had worked out as The Ordettes. Four girls in tune with one another. Powered by the same force. Stepping to the same beat. Glowing in the same spotlight. But, finding two new members

114

was taking longer than Mr. Montague had promised. It's not like he wasn't trying. For weeks, Mr. Montague held auditions without signing anyone. He said finding the right girls was more than just finding the right voices. Sure, it was about harmony. But, in a group that would be spending as much time together as we would, harmony is much more than just hitting the right notes. It's a total mix. It's personality. It's chemistry. It's symmetry. It's easy to recognize, but hard to define. It's something you just feel. And, so far, he hadn't gotten that feeling. Until the day Mr. Montague hooked us up with Nona Hendryx and Sarah Dash, two other teenagers from Trenton, New Jersey. He had heard them performing in the Del Capris, another girl group on the local circuit, and convinced them to sign with him. He put them in The Tonettes for a while but when that quartet lost another singer, Mr. Montague blended the remaining Tonettes with the remaining Ordettes. Sarah and Nona; Sandra and me. Mr. Montague was right. It was perfect harmony. The way we sounded together. The way we moved together. The way we fit together. It was seamless. Smooth. Sugar-sweet. Together we put The Ordettes back in business.

Once we started getting bookings as a quartet again, Mr. Montague backed us up with the hottest band around to complete the package. In the early sixties, The Bill Massey Band was perfect for our show — a mixture of R&B, ballads, and standards. They were tight, they were versatile.

They also were in demand. Our performances were usually no problem, but rehearsals were another matter. When the band's schedule got crazy-busy, Morris "Mo" Bailey was brought in to run our practices. Mo was my heart. Still is. A talented, creative powerhouse, he played saxophone as a teenager with jazz greats like Albert "Tootie" Heath and McCoy Tyner. He would become famous doing arrangements for great vocalists like Nina Simone and Curtis Mayfield. When it came to our rehearsals, Mo had strict instructions from Mr. Montague: work us from sun up to sun down, until we could hardly stand up. And he did. He worked us like we were gearing up for the Olympics. By the time rehearsals ended, Mo said Montague's basement "smelled like a locker room after a playoff game." But we didn't mind all the work. We were playing to win. And we had a great coach. Not only did Mo help us polish our sound, he also improved our steps. He knew stage moves almost as well as he knew musical scores. It was Mo, in fact, who is credited with creating the seventies dance craze "the bump." It hurt me to my heart when I learned Mo was stricken with muscular dystrophy, a disease that has cost him the use of his legs.

With Mo's workouts, Mr. Montague's bookings, and our silky-smooth sound, there was only one obstacle: school. Between the daily rehearsals and the nightly shows, who had time to go to class, let alone keep up with classwork? That's when Chubby and I had our talk. I know it was hard for her. It was hard for me, too. I had come so close to graduating — just one semester away. But I also was close to the musical success I dreamed about. Too close to let it slip away. Chubby understood that. When she gave me her blessing, I dropped out of high school — a decision that would trouble me for years. It bothered me so much that when I was in my thirties, I went back to Bartram High to finish what I started; to get the one thing that fame and fortune couldn't give me: my high school diploma. Almost twenty years later, studying for those midterms and finals wasn't easy. But I did it. Now I can say proudly that I am a graduate of John Bartram High School.

Nona and Sarah quit school, too, but unlike me they both studied on the road, and it wasn't long before they earned their diplomas through a correspondence course. Sandra wanted to leave school, too, but her parents told her if she was going to quit anything, it would be the group. Just when we thought we had it all together, here we were again, looking for another Ordette. This time we found her in a breeze. With a little luck and a little word of mouth, a songbird flew our way. Cynthia Birdsong wasn't from Philly. Cindy grew up in Camden, New Jersey, and got the word Mr. Montague was looking to sign a girl singer from her hometown friend Alexander Wild, who Mr. Montague also managed.

One afternoon, she turned up on Mr. Montague's doorstep. When she introduced herself, I thought: "Girlfriend, with a name like *Birdsong* you better be able to sing." Cindy handled the pressure like a pro. She remembers all of us watching as she stood in Mr. Montague's living room singing, "It Could Happen to You." When she finished, it definitely happened for her. She more than lived up to her name. She was awesome. And her face was as beautiful as her voice. Of all the girls who had auditioned, I hadn't seen anyone who even came close to her look or her artistry. When she hit the last note, Mr. Montague's face said it all: Cindy was in. We were a quartet. We four were now one.

Chapter Fourteen

In the early days, the four of us really were like sisters. Closer, if you can imagine it. You know that expression: "It is but chance that makes sisters but hearts that make friends?" Well, that was Nona, Cindy, Sarah, and me. Best buddies. Sisters of the spirit. Soul mates. It was partly because we shared the same dream, but mostly because we understood one another. With them, I felt completely at ease. We shared things we couldn't tell another living soul.

Nona told me about her days growing up poor in Trenton where her friend, George Clinton, used to cut her hair. Of course, this was long before George discovered his real calling as "Dr. Funkenstein," head of the musicians who became famous as The P-Funk All-Stars. Nona was one of seven children, and she called herself a "stone ghettoite." Like my father, Nona's father at one time had worked for the railroad. While Daddy was a big-time gambler, Nona said her father was a big-time drinker. Sarah's family was even bigger than Nona's. One of thirteen children, Sarah, too, had grown up poor in Trenton's inner city. Her father, a minister, didn't approve of her singing anything but gospel music. He used to tell her she was singing for the devil. Cindy grew up in the projects of Camden and, like the rest of us, she started singing in church. Though you could never tell it by looking at her, Cindy was five years older than the rest of us. She used to make me swear on my life I would never tell anyone her real age. I kept her secret, but I teased her about it constantly. I always called her "Mom."

We were inseparable back then. Whenever you saw one, you saw four. After spending all day rehearsing in Mr. Montague's basement, we would walk over to my house where Chubby would cook us dinner. My mother loved Sarah, Nona, and Cindy like they were her own. Many a night, when they were too beat to go home, Chubby passed out blankets and the four of us slept on the living-room floor.

In my whole life, I had never felt so close to anyone. Not to Vivian, not to Barbara, not to Jackie. For a while, Sarah, Nona, and Cindy became my sisters, the people I shared everything with, and my sisters became just people who shared my last name. There was a time when people would show me early photos of The Blue-belles and I'd get this sick, hollow feeling in the pit of my stomach. It reminded me of what is lost forever. And how they had hurt me. And how I had hurt them. When we first broke up, those old pictures used to make me recall things that are best left forgotten. Just looking at them would make me remember how the dream became a nightmare. But that's a story I'll save for later. When we started out, we believed we would stay together until the end of time. The four of us — one for all and all for one — together forever.

That unshakable bond became the glue that held us together in the lean years when we were doing wall-to-wall one-nighters for ten bucks a show. As word spread that we were good, really good, we started getting gigs all over the place. By early 1962, we were performing nonstop. Truck stops. Juke joints. Honky-tonks. In the early sixties, the biggest black names in show business played the "chitlin' circuit" — a network of top black clubs and theaters that included the Apollo in New York, the Howard in Washington, D.C., the Royal in Baltimore, the Uptown in Philadelphia, and the Regal in Chicago. In the early days, the only way we could get in the chitlin' circuit was to buy a ticket and sit in the audience. That left us playing the sardine houses — the little out-of-the-way rooms where the crowd was packed in so tight that we could barely do our turns without slapping somebody upside the head.

Looking back, I don't know how we did it. If we cleared a hundred bucks a week between us, we thought we were rolling. But, back then, it wasn't about money. It was about the dream, the sensation. There was a joy, an excitement, a we're-in-it-together feeling that made everything bearable.

We loved performing and we loved each other. That's the only explanation I have for how we did the things we did. All I can do is shake my head when I think about some of the places we played. Crisscrossing Pennsylvania, New Jersey,

Maryland, Kentucky, and Virginia in the back of Mr. Montague's station wagon, we performed in places like the Elks' Home, the Wagon Wheel, roller rinks, and you don't even want to know how many firehouses and high-school gymnasiums.

The schedule was brutal. A lot of times we did double shows. A matinee and an evening performance. There was no such thing as a day off. As soon as we finished one show, the four of us piled into Mr. Montague's station wagon and drove to the next. For nearly four years, that's how we got from city to city, show to show. We burned up several station wagons burning up the highway. We were logging 80,000 miles a year. It didn't matter how many hours it took to get to a booking, two or twenty-two, we just drove until we got there. And we got there ready to blow.

Overnight motel stays between cities were almost always out of the question. For one thing, it was tough finding a motel that would even allow blacks. For another, even if we found one, we couldn't afford it. There was no time and even less money to spare. Our next performance was usually the next day. We'd have to drive all night just to get there.

It was grueling, but it was also glorious. We were so young and innocent and starry-eyed. And the way we saw it, it was just a proving ground. We knew all the small-time, small-town one-nighters were paving the way for the big-time, big-city headliners. They were making us tight. As friends. As performers. As artists. We knew our big break was coming. And when we got our pumps in the door we were going to kick that baby down. We never doubted it. We never questioned it. Not for a second.

That was the magic in our friendship — the shared belief that stardom was our destiny. *Failure* wasn't a word in our vocabulary. We were like the bumblebee. Scientists say that, with a body so big and wings so small, it can't fly. But nobody ever told the bumblebee. And nobody ever told us. The way we saw it, there was nothing to keep us from spreading our wings and soaring. The way we saw it, there was only one difference between us and all the big-name entertainers, only one difference between the sardine houses and the "chitlin' circuit." A hit record. And it was just a matter of time before we got one.

And, like so many of the breaks we had in the beginning, this one came sooner than any of us could have ever imagined.

Chapter Fifteen

It happened in Mr. Montague's basement. We were waiting for Mo to begin rehearsal. It wasn't like him to be late. But when he finally rushed in, we found out what the holdup was. He was excited. He had been approached by the president of a record company who had hired Mo to help produce one of his groups. "This guy is looking to sign a girl group," Mo told us. "And guess who I recommended?" The audition was set.

It was incredible. Our time had come. Our time to fly. As far as I was concerned, the audition was just a formality. There was no way the president of a record label could hear us sing without signing us. I had already dreamed us into our first gold record in the time it took Mo to give us the details. Who would audition us? When would it take place? The name of the record company president? *Harold B. Robinson?* This had to be some kind of joke.

Practically everyone in Philly knew who he was. It was hard not to. His ads were all over the place. But he wasn't selling records. He was selling cars. Harold B. Robinson was a big wheeler-dealer, all right. He owned a couple of Chrysler/Plymouth showrooms in the city. So, what did a car salesman have to do with making records?

Mo explained it all. Robinson was this rich white man who loved black music. He had formed two record labels — Newtown and Blue-belle — and built a two-track recording studio in one of his showrooms where he could audition acts before signing them and promoting their records. He had some of the most talented people in Philly working for him. Like Bobby Martin, a multitalented producer/arranger. Mo had the inside track with Bobby. After all, Mo had gained a lot of respect in the business that year when he wrote the Top 40 single, "Cry Baby Cry," for The Angels, the girl group most famous for their number-one smash, "My Boyfriend's Back." When Mo spoke, people listened. He told Martin and Robinson to look no further. He had the answer. He had the girl group. Sarah, Nona, Cindy, and me. They took his word for it.

Of course, Mo wanted to make sure he kept his word. Especially with Bobby Martin, the producer who would audition us. Mo told us we couldn't half-step with Bobby. He was a serious talent with a fine-tuned ear. Over the years, I would see for myself just how deep Bobby's talent ran. He went on to win three Grammys and produce or arrange dozens of gold records, including "TSOP" (The Sound of Philadelphia), the theme for *Soul Train.* Mo was confident, but he was also careful. He was sure Bobby would be impressed with our sound, but he wasn't about to take any chances. With the audition only a few days away, he drilled us like four GIs in boot camp.

Even so, there was no way I could have been ready for what I would experience at the audition.

Robinson's car dealership was located at 6600 North Broad Street. The recording studio was in the basement, under the showroom. It was small and cramped and, even though Bobby Martin had soundproofed the place himself, it looked exactly like what it was: a no-frills, bargain-basement setup. We just had no idea what a setup it was.

When Harold B. Robinson appeared, introductions were made all around. He was happy, excited, smiling. Until Mo pointed me out as the lead singer. Robinson's face changed instantly. Before we could sing a single note, Robinson turned around and headed back up the stairs with Mo following in hot pursuit. None of us knew what Robinson's problem was, and it would be years before I found out.

He was seriously ticked off with Mo. While we were cooling our heels downstairs, Robinson was upstairs reading Mo the riot act. Why was Mo wasting his time? Had he lost his mind? Didn't he know this wouldn't work? There was no way he was going to sign us. "That lead singer," he told Mo, "she's too dark and too plain." And everybody knew that a plain black girl couldn't sell records.

Mo didn't have the heart to come back downstairs and tell us our audition was over before it ever began. He asked Robinson if we could at least do one number since we had taken the time to come in. Robinson told him to do what he wanted, but it would be a cold day in hell before

he signed us. At the time, I remember wondering why Mo came back alone, but I was so pumped I didn't dwell on it. I was ready to wail.

Mo whispered something to Bobby, and Bobby put on a recording of the song he wanted us to sing. It was "I Sold My Heart to the Junkman." I knew it right away. The song had been around since the forties. Bobby had even recorded it on the Newtown label with one of Robinson's groups, The Four Sportsmen. But that wasn't why it was so familiar to me. Lately, I had been hearing it on the radio. It had just been released by a girl group and was getting a lot of air play. The song was strong. Just our style — tailor-made for Sarah, Nona, Cindy, and me. The beat was kicking. The harmony was smooth. The chorus was sharp. The lead singer even sounded a little bit like me.

If this was the test, I knew we were going to score. Big time. And we did. We tore it up. We worked it. Every note, every nuance. Every line, every lyric. I know we were rocking the place because, midway through the song, Robinson came running downstairs, followed by his whole accounting department. When we finished, Robinson wasted no time. We were signed. I guess when he saw "green," he got over his problem with "black."

A month before my eighteenth birthday, on April 8, 1962, Sarah, Nona, Cindy, and I signed our first recording contract with the Bluebelle Record Company. Actually, because we were still

minors, our mothers had to sign the contract, too, and "guarantee the artists' performance of and compliance with this agreement."

There were other changes. Along with the record deal, Robinson gave us something else. A new name. From then on, we would be called The Blue-Belles. He would later have a hand in renaming me, too. Robinson thought the name Patsy Holte wasn't exciting enough to front a group. After he talked it over with Bobby, Robinson rechristened me LaBelle. In French, it means "the beautiful." Ain't life funny. He looked at my face and thought "dark and plain." He listened to my voice and thought something completely different. A man who had staked his reputation on face value was forced to take a deeper look. The man who rejected me on sight became the one to name me "beautiful."

Chapter Sixteen

Many artists spend years in the recording studio before they turn out a single hit record. I had my first million-selling hit before I even laid down a single track. The story behind the record is a behind-the-scenes look at the sleazy, seedy, shady side of the business and the way black artists were manipulated and exploited in the early days.

When we signed with Bluebelle Records, Sarah, Nona, Cindy, and I thought we were the lucky ones. We had no idea just what a lucky break the deal was for Harold B. Robinson. I had assumed he renamed us The Blue-Belles after his record label. I assumed wrong.

Years later, I would discover the real deal. Bobby and Mo helped me put the pieces of the puzzle together. Robinson desperately needed a girl group to promote his record "I Sold My Heart to the Junkman," the song we sang at our audition. That song was already on the air, rapidly climbing both the pop and R&B charts. He had recorded and released that song by a girl group he *called* The Blue-Belles. But the girls who recorded "Junkman" weren't The Blue-Belles. The Blue-Belles didn't even exist.

Once *we* became The Blue-Belles, Robinson had the group he needed to promote "Junkman." I never questioned it since he was acting as if he owned all rights to the record. And no time was wasted getting us out there. Within days after we signed our contract, we got the word that we would be appearing on *American Bandstand*. National TV. Major exposure. A dream come true. At the time, the show was still based in Philly, at WFIL-TV down on Forty-sixth and Market Streets. On the way to the show, all I could think about was how just two years earlier, Dick Clark turned little Ernest Evans into Chubby Checker, an overnight sensation. I thought about how, just a few weeks earlier, The Blue-Belles were The Ordettes, and The Ordettes were singing in firehouses and roller rinks and now, what happened to Ernest Evans could happen to us. *Please, God, I prayed silently, let us be good. Let them like us. Let it happen for us today.*

We were dressed for the occasion. We wore the navy blue bell-bottom sailor suits that I believe Mrs. Montague had found in some surplus store. Our new uniforms. Our new signature. *Blue bells.* Things happened so fast — from the contract to the car ride to the cue to go on — that I really didn't have enough time to get nervous. Suddenly we were there, doing our routine, in front of a studio audience and all of teenage America. It was the biggest performance of our short career.

And it was all an act.

We lip-synched "I Sold My Heart to the Junkman" and instantly, all across the nation, Sarah, Nona, Cindy, and Patti became the faces behind the song, the voices behind the music, the girls behind the group. We were The Blue-Belles, the artists who sang "Junkman." That's what everyone who saw the show would believe. That's what Harold B. Robinson *wanted* them to believe. But hundreds of miles away, in a Chicago living room, sat a black woman who knew better. And she was watching the show.

A few weeks after our *American Bandstand* appearance, Robinson had Bobby Martin take us in the studio to record "Junkman" exactly the way it had been released. We were "covering" our own song. As it turned out, we were covering Robinson's ass. Now I know why.

Robinson knew what the lady in Chicago knew and what we couldn't possibly have known. In December of 1961, Robinson had The Starlets, a teenage quintet from Chicago, record "Junkman" for his Newtown label. The Starlets had been in Philly promoting their hit single "Better Tell Him No" when Robinson signed them to a six-month contract. But there was a problem. The group already had a contract — an exclusive contract — with Chicago's Pam Records. As I understand it, The Starlets weren't making a lot of money even though "Better Tell Him No" was a Top 40 release and they were opening for some of the biggest stars around. Who knows what Robinson told them to get them to record — that they could make a little extra money, that the deal was kosher, that he wouldn't release the record until their contract with Pam expired . . . Whatever he said, he convinced them.

With Phil Terry (later of The Intruders) producing, The Starlets recorded "Junkman" and the "B"-side tune, "Itty Bitty Twist." A few months after The Starlets pulled out of Philly, "Junkman" was all over the radio, but the name of the group on the record label was The Blue-Belles.

Now, if the song had flopped, like the single "You Better Move On," which The Starlets also recorded but which was released under the name of The Blue-Belles, there probably never would have been a problem. Then again, there probably never would have been any Blue-Belles, either. But it didn't flop. It was a smash — a Top 20 hit on both the pop and R&B charts. Of course, that meant there was lots of money being made. But, apparently, the only one making it was Harold B. Robinson. And that's where the problem started.

When we appeared on *Bandstand*, Jane Hall, the founder of The Starlets, got a frantic call at work. It was her mother. As Jane explained when we were trying to untangle the mystery for this book, her mother was at home sitting in her living room watching the show. She told her daughter there were four girls on Dick Clark calling themselves The Blue-Belles and singing her song. That's when all hell broke loose. By June, only two months after we signed with Robinson, lawsuits were flying right and left. I mean, everybody sued everybody. Carl Davis, the head of Pam Records, sued Robinson. The Starlets sued Robinson and us — Sarah, Nona, Cindy, and me. Phil Terry and Bobby Martin each filed separate suits against Robinson. All kinds of allegations were made — breach of contract, fraud, conspiracy — but basically it all came down to two things. Money and control.

Carl Davis asked for $50,000, claiming Robinson made The Starlets breach their exclusive contract with Pam Records and then had Sarah, Nona, Cindy, and me come in to rerecord "Junkman" to cover his tracks. The Starlets wanted a piece of the pie, too. In addition to money, they asked the court to forbid us from appearing as The Blue-Belles and singing and promoting the song. Phil Terry and Bobby Martin didn't have anything to do with Robinson's whole charade, but they wanted him to compensate them fairly for their work producing the songs.

At the time, I didn't know any of these details. In fact, one night not long after we had re-recorded the song, I was riding home from choir practice with Mrs. Chapman's daughter, Zara, and "Junkman" came on the radio. "That's my song, that's my group," I started screaming. Zara didn't believe it was me, and I couldn't convince her otherwise. Now, I don't know which of us was right.

Before it was all over, things got so confusing you would have needed a law degree just to keep up. But, there was one thing I knew for sure. Sarah, Nona, Cindy, and I had done nothing wrong. All we did was record "Junkman" under a legitimate recording contract. So what if the song had already been recorded? That was business as usual. Everybody knew Chubby Checker wasn't the first artist to record "The Twist." Hank Ballard and the Midnighters had turned it into a pop and R&B hit in 1959. But, when Hank Ballard couldn't appear on Dick Clark's show, Clark suggested that Checker cover the song. Checker's version went to number one. And the same thing that happened to me in the car with Zara happened to Hank Ballard. He once heard Chubby Checker's version of "The Twist" and thought it was *his*.

When we got sued, we were told not to worry about it; that the lawyers would handle it and everything would be all right. And I guess it was, even though, more than a year later, we were still in court. I don't know all the particulars, but somehow everything finally got settled. What happened between Carl Davis and Harold B. Robinson is still a mystery to me. But it was reported that The Starlets received around $5,000 each. Phil Terry and Bobby Martin went on to great things as artists and producers, taking the Sound of Philadelphia national. Harold B. Robinson? Well, controversy marked his life and followed him to his grave. A few years before the "Junkman" episode, the government sued him for failing to hand over thousands of dollars in state sales taxes. After he died in 1974, his lady friend got in a big legal fight with his family over his millions.

This was my baptism in the business. It taught me all that glitters isn't gold and that being in show business is as much about business as it is about show. I learned early that being an entertainer is more than just laying down a tune in a recording studio or laying out a crowd at a show. And there's more to a record deal than meets the eye — more than what you bargained for. It's not enough to read the fine print. You have to know how to read between the lines. There can be quite a few shadings between the "Whereas" and the bottom line. There can be quite a few shady people between the artist and the audience. As for The Blue-Belles, well, Sarah, Nona, Cindy, and I would never look back. The road ahead was bumpy enough.

Chapter Seventeen

We finally broke into the chitlin' circuit! With a hit record ("Junkman") and a hit TV debut (*Bandstand*), we got our ticket to some of the biggest stages around. We still had to do the small bread-and-butter gigs, but at least we had a few bright lights sandwiched in between. The Howard, the Uptown and, oh yes, the Apollo. It wasn't long before Mr. Montague told us he might be able to get us added to one of the hottest tours on the circuit: the James Brown tour. I thought, "Please, please, please!" James was music royalty — the king of R&B — and everyone paid him tribute. Wherever he went, he packed the house, and he only played the biggest houses around. When we got the green light, we were told to meet James in Los Angeles, and we would play our way through the West Coast, the Northwest, and then wind up with five back-to-back one-nighters in the Deep South.

As it turned out, getting on the bill with James Brown was the easy part. Getting to L.A. was the hard part. A real trip — it got off to a bad start and went downhill from there. In those days, there was no such thing as a cross-country plane trip for the Blue-Belles. There was no Motown bus either. We were still in Mr. Montague's station wagon and, because Mr. Montague was so strict and so protective, he had started bringing his wife along on road trips to be our chaperone.

So there we were, riding across the country in that old, raggedy station wagon jammed in there like french fries — six people, no air-conditioning, in the middle of summer!

It was agony. Three thousand miles of hell. Nona rode up front with the Montagues while Sarah, Cindy, and I sat in the back fighting like cats and dogs. The fighting started before we even got on our way. Which one of us was going to have to sit in the middle? Who had to ride the hump? Every time we'd make a rest stop, that fight would start all over again. After we got into a nasty, cursing fistfight over it, Mr. Montague made us draw straws. Short straw got the hump — and the numb butt.

If we weren't fighting over the hump, we were fighting over food. Who was hoarding it? Who was hiding it? Who was eating more than her share? In those days, a lot of restaurants wouldn't serve black people, especially six of them in a beat-up station wagon, and so we had to bring our own rations. Canned sardines, crackers, cookies, pretty much anything that didn't have to be cooked or refrigerated. And we had to make sure we packed enough to carry us through to someplace that would serve us.

Believe it or not, being cramped and hungry for three thousand miles wasn't the worst thing about that cross-country trip. We hit the desert out West in the middle of the afternoon, when the sun was at its peak. But, Mr. Montague kept right on driving. The heat was a killer. I've never felt anything like it. In no time, that station wagon became a clunky, funky, rolling sauna. It was smothering, stifling, sweltering. I was getting dizzy and light-headed. I felt as if I couldn't breathe, that at any minute, I was going to faint. Between the heat, the sweat, and the sardines, you can imagine what that car smelled like. Of course, opening the windows was unthinkable. We were stuffing everything in sight — napkins, pillowcases, stockings — in the cracks trying to keep that sweltering air from floating in. I hate the sun. And sleeping was impossible. At least for me. When I'm trying to sleep, if there is any light anywhere, you can forget it. Even today, I have special black-out drapes in my bedroom at home. On the road, I stuff towels at the bottoms of the hotel doors, tape garbage bags on the windows, and then put on a sleeping mask before I can drift off. So, in that station wagon, every time we passed a light on the highway, my eyes would pop open.

We weren't on the road long before I realized how important those rations were; how badly some people wanted to avoid serving us, never mind eating in the same room with us. The education of Patsy Holte was about to begin. It was touring America in the sixties that showed me I didn't know much about many things. Like racism and bigotry. Like how much and how deeply people can hate each other just because of the color of their skin. Growing up in the tight-knit community of Elmwood, what did I know about prejudice? In the Deep South, in the back of Mr. Montague's station wagon, I learned more about the insanity and inhumanity of it than I ever wanted to know.

When the sardine cans were empty, we had no choice but to stop, somewhere, to get something to eat. At some places, they were point-blank: "We don't serve coloreds." I wanted to say: "Fine, because we don't eat them." Others told us they would serve us, but only "carry-out" or I should say "carry-fast." To add insult to injury, we had to pick it up at the back door.

Once, at a restaurant in Texas, there were no warning signs. But there was something strange about the place, something mean in the air. We stood out like Pat Boone at the Apollo. Shortly after we placed our order, in strutted ten cowboys in their ten-gallon hats. They took one look at us and their conversation turned real foul, real filthy, real funky, real fast.

"I don't know what the hell they do up North, but we don't allow our niggers to eat with us."

It was that kind of thing. We just ignored them. They refused to be ignored. When we didn't get the message, two or three of them got up from their table and headed for their trucks. A few minutes later they came back in wearing big grins on their faces — and big guns on their belts. It didn't take long for it to sink in. Mr. Montague paid for our food, then quietly told us to look straight ahead and walk quickly to the car. I can still hear the spiteful, self-satisfied laughter of those cigar-chomping, beer-chugging, foul-mouthed cowboys as we left the restaurant and hurried to the car.

A few hours after we had eaten our food, my stomach felt like it was on fire. I was nauseous and dizzy. I got the shakes, the chills, and a mean case of Montezuma's revenge. One by one, we all got sick as dogs. It was the food. I don't know how they did it, but I do know those people in that restaurant poisoned it. Looking back, I don't think I want to know exactly how.

Not long after that incident, Mrs. Montague, our chaperone, thought we needed a little more protection. She started packing a piece. Everywhere we went, she wore a thirty-eight strapped across her chest. She didn't tell me about until years later but, even if she had, I don't know how secure it would have made me feel. Late one night, when we drove by a Ku Klux Klan rally in a field just off the road, I saw this huge burning cross and I was terrified. I thought, "Oh, shit." All I could see was a bunch of rednecks in white sheets jumping in their pickup trucks and chasing us down the highway. No one would ever know what had happened to us. But once again, Mr. Montague kept his cool. He told us to look straight ahead and he just kept on driving. I looked straight ahead, all right. Straight down at the car floor with my head between my knees. I stayed that way until we had left that field of demons far behind.

There were times, however, when we couldn't

avoid the hatred and the racism no matter how hard we tried. To escape the "whites-only" motel scene, we would often wash up in the rest rooms of national parks. When that ice-cold water hit my back, I would have paid Grandmother Ellen for one of those middle-of-the-kitchen baths she used to have to force me to take. At least her water was hot. And nobody treated me like I was committing bloody murder, either. Years later, Mr. Montague told me that our very presence in one park had put white people in a state of shock. They were horrified. And it wasn't over seeing four little naked black butts. It was seeing the four little black wigs we left hanging on a tree. They swore to the state troopers there were some colored girls up there in the woods scalping people!

There was yet another lesson to learn while touring in the early sixties. It wasn't as painful as learning about racism, but it was just as revealing. It was a lesson about the competitive nature of great artists and the depth of the ego that drives them, a fact I would see played out throughout my career. Many a night, for example, while we were touring with James Brown, we would get hand-clapping, foot-stomping roaring ovations. I don't know whether they were too long or too loud, but they were too something because James clearly had enough of them and he thought we did too. Night after night, while the crowd was cheering us, the Godfather of Soul had the curtain closed on us — while we were in mid-bow.

Then there was the time I was performing back East at a resort in Delaware and closing the show with the Dinah Washington hit "Where Are You." The audience loved it. I loved it. Dinah herself was performing nearby in Wildwood, New Jersey, and she sent me a message. I was thrilled. The Queen of the Blues had heard of me! And I couldn't wait to hear what she had to say. Then I got the message. "Stop singing my damn song."

Dinah Washington gave me one of the great lessons of my life that night, though it didn't sink in until many years later. You shouldn't try to dim your light to let other people shine. It doesn't help them, and it only makes you unhappy. Throughout my career, people have often tried to push me out of the spotlight or lower the curtain on me. I can't tell you how many times I've been asked to tone it down, to hold back, to give less Patti, to step aside. I have bent over backwards so that other people wouldn't get bent out of shape. But not anymore. When I'm singing, I'm not trying to outshine or upstage anyone. I'm just doing what I can't help doing. Singing what I feel with all the pain and passion that powers it. My voice is a gift from God and I must use it as God intended. With all the love and energy that flows through me. I can't hold it back. It's the same way I try to approach everything in my life. Chubby always told me, if it's worth doing, it's worth doing right. And if it's not, don't do it. If I was a street sweeper, I would sweep streets the way Michael Jackson moonwalks, the way Michael Jordan flies to the hoop, the way Michaelangelo painted heaven on earth. I happen to sing and once the lights go on, so do I. Once I put on my five-inch fever pumps, there's no half-stepping. I'm committed to my art and my audience and it's complete, it's total, it's absolute. Body and soul. My voice is a blessing. And no matter what other people say, I can't block it.

Chapter Eighteen

Celebrity egos. Rednecks and racism. The seamy, sordid underbelly of the music business. Fortunately, those weren't the only things I was learning about in the early sixties. I was also learning about love. After high school and before I got married, I had three serious boyfriends.

Kermin was my first serious, grown-up romance. He was several years older than I and training to become a professional boxer. I can't remember his last name, or even how we met. But I do recall the most important thing about our brief relationship: He came into my life at just the right time. I was a young, confused, inexperienced eighteen-year-old with so many hang-ups and conflicted feelings about sex. I was becoming a woman with a woman's desires. But after the abuse I had suffered at the hands of one of Chubby's boyfriends, I saw those desires as something shameful, something foul and filthy.

Kermin helped me sort out my confusion without even knowing it. Because of him, I started to understand that sex isn't sinful or wicked or wrong. He helped me see that, when it is shared by two people who truly care for each other, it can be a tender, gentle, wonderful experience. After what happened to me in Chubby's basement, I didn't know any of that. And I really, really needed to.

It happened at my house late one night when I thought everyone was sleeping. My first time. I wasn't sure I was ready, but there was something about the way Kermin told me I didn't *have* to that made me know it was okay if I *wanted* to. When he told me to take all the time I needed, that he would wait for me as long as it took, something inside me shifted. I still have a vivid picture of his face when he said it. Looking into his eyes, I knew he wouldn't hurt me like Chubby's boyfriend. I knew I could trust him.

Holding hands, we tiptoed to the back of the house, the two of us trying not to make a sound so we wouldn't wake up Chubby or my sisters who were sleeping upstairs. It was over quickly — within minutes. I had been so tense about this moment that, when it finally came, I felt an overwhelming sense of relief. I couldn't hold back the tears. I started sobbing like a baby. It was a confusing moment for both of us. Poor Kermin. Thinking he had hurt me, he took me in his arms and tried to comfort me. He kept apologizing over and over.

"No, no, no," I told him, shaking my head. "You didn't do anything wrong." That's all I could manage to say.

My heart sat in the middle of my throat, blocking the words. I couldn't tell him what was really going on inside me. It would take decades before I was able to tell anyone that. So we just sat there, holding each other tight in the darkness.

After several months, Kermin and I broke up.

It wasn't bitter. It wasn't hostile. It wasn't painful. Like our first intimate moment, it just happened. Time can be a friend or an enemy, depending on the situation. It's been my experience that when the situation is a romance, it's usually an enemy. It was for Kermin and me. With all my touring, we rarely saw each other. And that got old fast.

Within a short time, I started dating Jim "Mudcat" Grant, an award-winning pitcher for the Cleveland Indians. Mudcat and I met in Cleveland, at a club called Leo's where he had come to hear The Bluebelles sing. (Somewhere along the way, Robinson had dropped the hyphen in "Blue-Belles" and we became Patti LaBelle and the Bluebelles.) Mudcat was a big music fan. In fact, in addition to being a baseball star, Mudcat also had a great voice. During the off-season, he would perform with his group, Mudcat and the Kittens. When we met, I thought he was a nice guy, but no fireworks. The sparks wouldn't come until later when we saw each other in New York at the birthday party of a mutual friend. We clicked and ended up talking the whole night. We left the party together and walked the streets of New York arm and arm singing to the moon and each other. It was the start of a lovely, but brief, romance. As with my relationship with Kermin, this one collapsed under the weight of conflicting schedules and busy careers. Again, the breakup was friendly. In fact, long after we said our good-byes, Mudcat still came to visit Chubby whenever he had a game in Philly. They were fast friends.

She taught him the trolley routes in the city, and he took her to baseball games. Chubby loved Mudcat more than any of my suitors, except for the man I would eventually marry.

After Mudcat came another star, but this one was in the music business. A singer who will always be special to me. After all, you never forget the first man who asks you to marry him. In his autobiography, Otis Williams says we met while out on tour together. That may be so, but I remember our meeting differently. It was the last weekend in April 1963, a date I'll never forget and you'll see why when I tell you about it. It was one of those rare times when The Bluebelles had a night off and the house was quiet. Barbara and Jackie both had dates over, and I was looking forward to getting into a hot bubble bath with an ice-cold beer and turning in early for the night. As I was saying good night to Chubby, there was a knock at the door. It was late, but I figured it was somebody looking for one of my sisters since nobody knew I was home. I was right. It was Armstead Edwards, looking fine in a suit and looking for Barbara. The situation threw me for a minute. I knew he was crazy about Barbara. Always had been. From the early days when we all sang together in church in the Young Adults Choir. But I knew they couldn't have a date. Barbara's date was already there.

As we sat talking in the kitchen, Armstead told me the whole sad story. He was celebrating his twenty-first birthday. He wanted it to be a special night, a night he'd never forget, so he had gone all out. He had reservations at the hottest club in town, the Showboat down on Lombard Street. The Temptations were performing that night, and everybody wanted to be there. Well, almost everybody. Apparently, Armstead's date, who lived in the neighborhood, wanted to be somewhere else. She stood him up. He told me he just couldn't face going back home; not yet, not barely an hour after he had left. He knew Chubby's house was always full and, even if he didn't catch Barbara, he knew there would be somebody home to keep him company. Poor thing. Not only was his date a no-show but Barbara's date was already there. That left me.

As I listened to his story, all I could think about was my bubble bath, my beer, and my bed. But, I felt so bad for him. As the bubbles started bursting in my head, I heard myself saying, "Would you settle for me?" That's how I ended up at the Showboat the night The Temptations were performing. And they were awesome. In the sixties, The Temps had the baddest steps, the baddest suits, and the baddest sound in soul music. But, on that night, it wasn't the group that held my attention. It was their founding member who kept tempting me. Through much of their performance, I sat in the audience making eyes at Otis, winking and blinking at him from across the room. When The Temps finished their set, I told Armstead I wanted to meet him. But, I had a problem. I knew Otis would never come over to the table and talk to me if he thought I was with Armstead. I mean really *with* Armstead. So, I did the only thing I could. I asked Armstead to introduce us.

Now, don't get all bent out of shape. Armstead didn't mind. In fact, he was totally cool with it. He knew we weren't a couple. The whole time he was driving to the club, I kept teasing him. Nonstop.

"You know you're going to owe me big-time for this one since you know this is strictly a mercy date."

As I sat at the table chatting with singer Dee Dee Sharpe, Armstead hooked the whole thing up. The next thing I knew Otis was standing at our table and we were exchanging phone numbers. By the end of the year, Otis and I were a couple. In February of 1964, his career took off like a rocket when The Temps' single, "The Way You Do the Things You Do," charted pop and R&B. Though it was their seventh single, it was their first big hit. And after that, things got crazy. Between his touring schedule and mine, the only time Otis and I saw each other was when he got to Philly — if I was there. That's where he proposed, in Philly, sitting on Chubby's sofa. And I wish you could have seen that diamond ring he gave me. Honey, that thing was so big I could have used it as a headlight. But it was the light of his personality that had hypnotized me. The way he did the things he did. Our romance had been a whirlwind of brief encounters. It had been exciting. And I looked forward to a lifetime of excitement. I said "yes."

Otis and I had a lot of good times together. But, the more we discussed our future, the more I began to feel things might change. I got the impression that Otis wanted a very traditional home life once I became Mrs. Williams. Rightly or wrongly, I honestly believed he wanted me to leave Philly and move with him to Detroit. Worse, I was convinced he wanted me to slow down my singing career. I couldn't see myself doing either. Philly was my home and music was my life. This was going to be a problem. A big problem. Part of me wanted to be married, but most of me didn't want to give up anything to do it. I didn't know how to tell Otis, and so I started confiding in Armstead. Since the night he introduced me to Otis, we had become good friends. I loved his conversation and his company. He was funny, kind, sensitive, and smarter than anyone I had ever met. He was about to graduate from Cheyney College with a B.S. in education. But as comfortable as I was talking with him, one night he shocked the fool out of me. I was crying on his shoulder about Otis again, when he took my hand in both of his, looked me straight in the eyes, and said it.

"Well, Pat, if things don't work out between you and Otis, I'm here for you."

I remember thinking, "Did he just say what I think he said? Was Boyfriend trying to throw me a hint that he is interested in me?" It sure *sounded* romantic but, as fine as he was, Armstead had never so much as even flirted with me before. And I had never given much thought to all those times he had come by whenever Otis was visiting even though it kind of looked like he was trying to outsit Otis. After all, since our days growing up in Elmwood together, I always knew he was interested in Barbara. I decided I must have been misreading the whole thing, blowing the whole situation out of proportion. What he really meant was that he would always be there for me whenever I needed a *friend*.

Not long after that conversation, I worked it all out in my head and my heart. I told Chubby I didn't think I could marry Otis and I was planning to break the news to him soon.

"You have to follow your heart," she said. And I did. When Otis and I finally talked, he seemed to understand my feelings and wished me well. As for the ring, I didn't feel right wearing it so I gave it to Chubby. To this day, I don't know what happened to it.

What I do know is that when I told Armstead I had broken my engagement, he seemed unusually happy. I was still feeling guilty about the breakup and sometimes, not often but sometimes, I wondered if I had made the right decision. It wasn't just that I had broken up with a great guy who treated me well. Let's be real here: Otis was one of the most eligible bachelors in the country, rich, famous, and internationally adored. Part of me thought I was crazy. Armstead's support helped me get through it. He said the same thing Chubby did — that I had to follow my heart — but he took it one step further.

"You can't live your life for other people," he told me. "You have to be true to yourself."

There are turning points in everyone's life, though we usually don't recognize them until later. But somehow I knew that Armstead would always be a part of my life. The whole experience deepened our friendship. When the dust finally settled, whenever either of us needed a shoulder to cry on, a hand to hold, or a sympathetic ear, we were there for each other. It was a relationship that would grow stronger and stronger over the years. And I would replay his advice — "Be true to yourself" — over and over in my head.

Chapter Nineteen

After "Junkman" went gold, we recorded about a dozen more songs for Robinson's Newtown label. Besides being the label's CEO, Robinson fancied himself a hands-on producer. When I say hands-on, I mean just that. He thought he had the magic touch. We'd be in the middle of a recording session when Robinson would stop me cold.

"The song needs more soul, Patti," he would declare, shaking his head and walking toward me.

"Soul?" I thought to myself. "What does this middle-aged white man know about soul?" And he would proceed to show me just what he knew.

When I think about it now, I crack up laughing. But, at the time, I thought it more strange than funny. Robinson always went through the same ritual. First, he'd pull a perfectly folded white handkerchief from his suit pocket. Next, he'd make a big production out of shaking and smoothing it out. Finally, he'd wrap the handkerchief around the microphone and place his free hand on the small of my back.

"Try it now, Patti," he'd whisper. "This will release your soul."

I'd sing the song the exact same way but, with his hand squeezing my back like a lemon and his handkerchief covering the mike, somehow Robinson heard something different. I guess he thought he was squeezing the soul out of me.

As much as he loved making records, Robinson loved making money more. When the right deal came along, he sold his record label. I don't know if it was an offer he couldn't refuse or if he had taken such a hit after that whole "Junkman" episode that he had to get out of the business. Whatever the reason, in November of 1963, we had our last hit song on Newtown Records when our single "Down the Aisle" made the Top 40.

Fortunately, we were pretty well known in and around Philly, and it was only a matter of months before we inked a new deal. It was with Cameo/Parkway, Philly's leading independent label and the company that released all of Chubby Checker's early hits. Though we only recorded three singles for the label — "You'll Never Walk Alone," "One Phone Call," and the Irish classic "Danny Boy" — it was a hectic time for us. Even when we didn't have a hit record, we were always in demand as a live group. We toured constantly, without letup, at least 320 days a year. In September, we toured for a few weeks with the "Iceman," Jerry Butler, who was on his own after getting his start with Curtis Mayfield and the Impressions. On Jerry's tour, we did double duty. We were his warm-up and backup.

Of all the places we played, my favorite was the Apollo in New York, although the conditions were hardly ideal. The schedule was punishing — four shows a day, six days a week. The neighborhood was rough — Harlem's 125th street was not a place where you wanted to be walking around at night. Inside the theater, things weren't much better. Even though the Apollo had always been a shrine for black entertainment, by the time we got there, it was an ancient shrine. In a word, it was funky. The dressing rooms were spread over four floors. They were cramped and filthy and filled with "surprises." Leslie Uggams's mother was known for putting a roach bomb in her daughter's dressing room before either of them would set foot in it. And, as her mother said, unless you wanted to take some "pets" home with you, you had better shake your clothes out long and hard before you left the place.

When Sarah, Nona, Cindy, and I started playing the Apollo, we were the new kids on the block. That meant we were always put in a top-floor dressing room, way up on the fourth floor. Everybody who played the Apollo started there. As you worked your way up the record charts, you worked your way down the Apollo stairs. Down to the preferred dressing rooms on the lower levels. Only the superstars got placed on the first level off the stage.

The Apollo's audience was the toughest in the country, too. The place seated 1,600 and, if you didn't have your stuff together, they would boo your behind off the stage fast, quick, and in a hurry. So you're thinking what's to love, right? For one thing, the fans. Even though they were tough, when they loved you they let you know it every way they could. Our first fan club was started at the Apollo by two fresh-faced teenagers who used to go to extremes to see us. One of them would cut school to catch our show, until the day his mother showed up for the same performance and pulled him out of the Apollo by his ear. But that didn't stop this kid. Luther Vandross was determined to be on the scene. Luther and his friend, choreographer Bruce Wallace, were members of Listen, My Brother, a workshop sponsored by the Apollo for artistic youth. That membership got them into the theater free whenever they wanted and, when we visited one of the workshop's meetings, it also got them to meet The Bluebelles up close and personal. But that wasn't enough for Luther. When I was writing this book, he told me he made up this whole long story to get a personal audience with us. Luther told Peter Long, the Apollo's public-relations director, that he had to do a school report on The Bluebelles. If he didn't get an interview, he said, he would flunk. Peter bought it and, though I was running an errand at the time, Luther got his "interview" with Sarah and Nona. Not long after that, Bruce and Luther founded the Patti LaBelle and the Bluebelles Fan Club. Bruce was the first president with Luther serving as his vice president.

In addition to the fans, I loved the feeling, the atmosphere, the spirit of the Apollo. The theater was history. It was *the* place for black entertainers. The big time. The height of prestige and achievement. The greatest entertainers in the world played there: Ray Charles, Ella Fitzgerald, Otis

Redding, Billie Holiday, Sam Cooke, James Brown, Dinah Washington, Smokey Robinson and the Miracles, The Supremes, Gladys Knight and the Pips, and so many others. It was an honor just to be there. As the head of Atlantic Records put it: "It was like going to Mecca."

The show backstage could be better than the one out front. There was a little catwalk up in the ceiling that hung over the stage, and Gladys Knight was known for going up there and dropping chicken bones on people's heads while they were performing. Me? I preferred the basement to the catwalk any day. In the basement, you could always find a card game. It seemed like half of Motown's male stars were down there playing and gambling — Smokey and the Miracles, Marvin Gaye, David Ruffin to name a few. Of course, whenever there was a bunch of guys around a card table, there was money to be made. And when there was money to be made, I was sitting at the table. A lot of times, I was the only girl in the game but, thanks to Daddy, I could hold my own. Poor Chuck Jackson, I used to win *all* his money. I lost my fair share, too. Once, when they cleaned me out, I had to borrow ninety-nine cents from Cindy to buy a basket of fried chicken wings. After that incident, I devised a plan. In the morning, I would buy myself two hot dogs from the stand on the corner. To keep them warm throughout the day, I would lay them across the bare lightbulbs in the dressing room. That way, even if I lost all my money, I wouldn't

157

go to bed hungry — I had my dinner. I don't even want to tell you how many lightbulbs burst when my hotdog grease dripped down on them.

In those days, the wolf was always at the door. In more ways than one. But losing money at the gambling table and losing weight living on two hot dogs a day wasn't the worst of it. When you're young, when you're new at the game, there's always somebody lurking out there waiting for the perfect moment to take advantage of you. That moment came when I least expected it. We were appearing at a theater in Brooklyn on the bill with America's heartthrob, Jackie Wilson. In his prime, Jackie was The Man. He was known as "Mr. Excitement," and if you ever saw him perform you'd know why. From the moment he stepped onstage in his sharkskin pants, Jackie drove the women crazy. He was a former Golden Gloves champ and had the world-class footwork to prove it. It was just like Beverly Lee of The Shirelles said: "He was like a slinky, powerful leopard onstage. There was nothing he couldn't do there."

Jackie could move like James Brown — the splits, the spins, the slides. And he could sing like Sam Cooke — that pure, clear, amazing voice. With his back-flips, his knee-drops, and his golden voice, he would drive the women so wild they would literally rip the shirt off his back just trying to touch him. Like everyone else, I was in awe of him. I worshiped the stage he moved on.

My adoration changed to hatred in a dark corner of Brooklyn's Brevoort Theater one terrifying night.

Just as I always did, I had gotten dressed early. Not so much to check out the crowd before show-time, although I was still doing that. But, since we started performing with some of the biggest names in show business, I had another reason for getting dressed early. I wanted to show off — my wigs, my makeup, my clothes. I wanted to look cute for the big-name headliners before I started singing and sweating and looking like a man. Being noticed by these great stars always made me feel special. Once, when I was passing Sam Cooke's dressing room, he hollered out, "Girl, you're looking good tonight." I looked around to see who he was talking to. When I realized I was the only person there, it felt like somebody had given me a million dollars. Sam Cooke thought I looked good? Little Patsy Holte? I thought I had died and gone to heaven.

On this night, though, I got a very different reaction. This was to be no pleasant surprise — it was a terrifying shock, one of the most frightening experiences of my life. I was making my way down a dark corridor headed for the stage when it happened. Somebody reached out and grabbed me from behind, pinning my arms against my sides. Before I could scream, a large hand covered my mouth. That's when I realized there were two people. Out of the shadows came a familiar voice.

"I've been wanting you for a long time."

It was Jackie Wilson. He started kissing my neck, and I could smell the liquor on his breath. As I struggled to free myself, Jackie's accomplice started dragging me backwards. I was kicking with all my might, but I was no match for him. Here I was, this little five-foot-three-inch girl up against this 250-pound sweaty, funky gorilla. Suddenly, he stopped dragging me. I heard a door shut. It was the sound of doom. I was their prisoner. No one knew I was in trouble. It was Chubby's basement all over again. Only this was worse. Much worse. Now there were two of them.

Jackie went first.

He took his hand away from my mouth and started touching my breasts. When he reached down to lift my skirt, I did the only thing I could. I started screaming. In the distance, I could hear the audience screaming out front. It was time for Patti LaBelle and the Bluebelles to take the stage. But no one could hear me screaming for help. *Please, God, I prayed, let somebody hear me. Let somebody help me.*

I thought about Chubby fighting back. I didn't have a knife, but I did have my voice. I started screaming even louder, at the top of my lungs. And I can scream every bit as loud as I can sing. It worked. Suddenly, they backed off. They let me go. I ran as fast as I could in the direction of the lights. I had to find help. I found Sarah and Nona, who had been looking for me. I told them what had happened, but I swore them to secrecy. Who was going to believe that Jackie Wilson, the

160

man who could have any woman he wanted for the asking, would have wanted me? Who would have believed I wouldn't have wanted him, too? Who would have believed he was about to rape me?

Though, after the nightmare, I would see Jackie on the circuit from time to time, I never spoke to him again. For years, before I learned the power of forgiveness, I hated that man. I couldn't bring myself even to look at him. I never could understand why a man who was so loved would try to force himself on a young admirer. In 1975, Jackie Wilson suffered a heart attack onstage while singing one of his early hits, "Lonely Teardrops." He spent the last eight years of his life in the hospital in and out of a coma. In January of 1984, Jackie Wilson died. Three years later, in an extravaganza at New York's Waldorf-Astoria, he was inducted into the Rock and Roll Hall of Fame. Some of the biggest names in the business celebrated his extraordinary talent. Everyone recalled the remarkable things he could do in the spotlight in front of an audience. But no one ever knew what he did in a dark corner in the back of the Brevoort Theater.

Chapter Twenty

By 1965, the British Invasion had turned the music industry on its head. Four white boys — John, Paul, George, and Ringo — led the revolution that totally changed the American music scene. Their success was so awesome it left a lot of black artists and their record labels scrambling to survive. That whole period was just so wild to me. I have never understood it. I don't to this day. Just think about it for a minute. The most popular English groups of the time — The Yardbirds, The Animals, The Rolling Stones — were white boys who loved playing black music. Even The Beatles covered hits by black artists. (Remember their big hit "Twist and Shout"? The Isley Brothers hit with it first.)

Over in England, British teenagers couldn't get enough of black artists and their music, which was one of the main reasons The Rolling Stones asked Ike and Tina Turner to open for them when they toured England in the fall of 1966. But back here at home, a lot of brilliant black musicians, the artists the British groups were *imitating,* couldn't get arrested. Don't ask me to explain it. All I know is that, just as the old folks say some people think "the white man's ice is colder," when it came to selling records, it seemed like a lot more people thought the white man's *cover* was hotter. Some of the biggest black acts were hit hard. As Hank Ballard put it, "People were so caught up in The Beatles, they forgot about us."

We were lucky. Though our record label didn't survive the Invasion, Sarah, Nona, Cindy, and I were never at a loss for work. Money was another matter. We were working all the time, but it was for peanuts. In the mid-sixties, for example, we did a week in Kingston, Jamaica. Three shows a day for $2,000. Split four ways. You do the math. With the help of the William Morris Agency, where Wally "Famous" Amos handled our account before he became the "cookie monster," cashing in his chocolate chips, Patti LaBelle and the Bluebelles hitched a ride on the British Bandwagon.

In the fall of 1965, we got our ticket to ride with the bad boys of rock, The Rolling Stones. And what a ride it was. We thought we were living in the lap of luxury when, a few months earlier, Mr. Montague got us our own minivan. Then we found out what luxury *really* felt like. The Stones had their own plane — a sleek, forty-seat, twin-engine Martin. And they invited the artists on the tour — a male quintet called The Vibrations and Sarah, Nona, Cindy, and me — to fly with them. I took my first plane ride courtesy of Mick Jagger, Keith Richards, Charlie Watts, Bill Wyman, and the late Brian Jones. As happy as I was to be out of Mr. Montague's wheels, I can't say I loved flying. It's just never been my thing. I do it because I have to but, even now, every time I get on a plane, I still get nervous. I'm not as bad as Aretha Franklin. Girlfriend hasn't set foot on a plane in Lord knows how many years. But I always make somebody — my husband, my son, my best friend — fly with me to cool me out if the ride gets bumpy.

On the Stones tour, I had Sarah, Nona, and Cindy to give me courage. With them, I always felt safe. With them, I could psyche myself into doing almost anything, including flying nonstop for six straight weeks. Nerves aside, though, there was one thing about flying that I just couldn't handle: that dull, tasteless, airplane food. Two shows into the tour, I found the perfect solution. More than thirty years later, I'm still using it. Hot sauce. The tangy, spicy make-your-eyes-water-your-nose-run-and-steam-shoot-out-your-ears kind. I'm telling you, if you get the right hot sauce, it will wake up your food and clear out your sinuses. Plus, it's cheap, compact, and portable. Since that tour with The Stones, I have never gone out on the road without at least two bottles in my purse. Of course now, whenever I tour, I pack a lot more than hot sauce. You open my suitcase, and you'll see my garlic powder, my seasoning salts, and my electric pans right alongside my gowns. After a show, I always go back to the hotel and cook. A lot of times, I'll fix enough food for the whole band and they'll come by my room and pick up a plate before calling it a night. Cooking relaxes me. It takes me out of my head and helps me come down from the high I'm on after a show. But the first time I pulled my hot sauce out of my purse, The Stones' photographer,

Gered Mankowitz, damn near fainted. And when he saw how much I put on my food, he really tripped out. I told Gered to just chill. I had to add some soul to that food just like Sarah, Nona, Cindy, and I were doing for this tour. I guess my seasonings appealed to Mick and the boys. Sixteen years later, in the fall of 1981, when they opened their umpteenth sold-out U.S. show at Philly's RFK stadium, Mick called me at home. "Patti, how about cooking us one of your absolutely fabulous meals?" The Stones ate real good that day.

Flying made me nervous but, other than our near-misses in the Deep South with racists and rednecks, I never had to worry about safety on the ground. Since the Ordette days, Mr. and Mrs. Montague had always watched over us like hawks. They were so strict and protective, you would have thought we were their daughters. It had taken months for us to convince them to let us wear makeup and wigs. When it came to Sarah, Nona, Cindy, and me, the Montagues had a reputation on the circuit as human pit bulls. They were not to be messed with. I can't say the reputation wasn't well deserved. When he had to leave us alone for so much as an hour, Mr. Montague would get one of the older artists in the show to look after us. When we played the Apollo, he was always asking Sam Cooke to keep an eye on us. When we were still underage, we'd have to sit outside in the station wagon between sets in places that served alcohol. And if Mr. Montague thought we were going to try to sneak out to hang out, he wouldn't hesitate to lock us in our room. Many nights, when I tried to do just that, I found the door locked from the outside. Of course, he forgot about the window, but I didn't. The Montagues had more rules than a Catholic girls' school, and they would fine your butt in a heartbeat for the slightest violation. We couldn't be even five minutes late for rehearsal. We'd better not show up with a single wrinkle in our dresses and Lord help us if we missed curfew. On this tour, we were caught between The Stones and a hard place. Mr. Montague was watching us like a hawk. He knew the group's reputation. Who didn't? Before we set foot on the plane, he laid down the law: No hanging out with Mick and the boys. No exceptions. No kidding. The fine for breaking this law would not be the usual two or three bucks. Oh, no. The fine for any violation of this law would be major money. And it's not like we had any to spare!

With all these rules and regulations, you can imagine my shock when, a few years ago, an unauthorized biography about Mick Jagger implied that, during this tour, the two of us had a steamy affair. That was news to Mick and me. Between performances, the only excitement we had was a hot card game with the group backstage. And I had to halfway sneak to do that. But it was worth it. I won all their money. I made more at the card table than I did onstage!

Most of the time, we weren't even staying in

the same hotel. We may have been flying with The Stones, but Jim Crow brought us all back down to earth. Our booking agent knew the lay of the land and where and when we had to be split up. It was usually in the South, where a lot of white folks didn't even want black folks drinking out of the same water fountains, let alone staying in the same hotels. You never get used to that kind of ignorance, but at least we had dealt with discrimination before. But for Mick, Keith, and the rest of the guys, it was a whole different movie. They were shocked and offended, but there was nothing they could do about it. You can see why it never bothered me one bit when I heard about them trashing their hotel rooms or peeing in the sinks. I took it as a statement.

I guess the bad boys of rock did have some kind of influence on us. I'm not sure, but I think it was on this tour that Cindy and I had our first and last fistfight. Good thing it only happened once, because once was enough. It was a knock-down-drag-out affair. For some reason, Girlfriend decided to play a practical joke on Sarah, Nona, and me. She concocted this whole complicated story about us having an appointment downtown to do a radio interview with a really popular deejay. Cindy let us take our showers, put on our makeup, get all dressed up, and start heading out the door before she fessed up. "Psyche," she yelled, collapsing on the bed in a fit of laughter. I couldn't believe it when she told us she had made the whole thing up. I was so ticked off, I couldn't see straight. I picked up a bag of peanuts and started throwing them at Cindy, one by one. That's when Sarah jumped in it.

"Leave her alone, Pat. It was just a joke."

As soon as Sarah said that, Priscilla came out. "This is between me and Cindy, so mind your own damn business," I shot back in my I'm-not-taking-any-shit-today voice. Sarah kept right on yapping. "This *is* my business, and don't you forget it" and on and on. When she wouldn't shut up, I picked up a glass and threw it against the wall. Glass flew everywhere. Sarah got cut, saw blood, and started screaming bloody murder. I guess Cindy took her nickname seriously because the next thing I knew, "Mom" was all over me. Furniture was falling. Wigs were flying. And we were rolling on the floor. Biting, scratching, kicking, and screaming. Suddenly, we heard this frantic banging on the door. It was Mick.

"Cut it out in there," he yelled. "You girls are going to wind up hurting each other."

At the time, none of us had any idea how prophetic his words would turn out to be.

After our flight of fancy with The Stones ended in December, we were back on the ground, back on the chitlin' circuit, back to back-to-back one-nighters. The twelve months following our tour with The Stones were full. Full of changes, full of challenges, full of surprises. We'd been flying all over the country with Mick and the boys, but it was back in Philly, right in our own backyard, where we got the biggest break of our career. We were playing with a big R&B revue at the Uptown Theater when a couple of executives from Atlantic Records caught our act. They loved everything about us — our look, our style, our sound — and, after the show, they approached us about signing with the label. We didn't think about it twice. After all, this was the "House that Ruth Built." That's what Atlantic Records was called in the fifties, when Ruth "Miss Rhythm" Brown was turning out hit after hit for the company. At the time, it was the home to many of the biggest black acts in the business — Aretha Franklin, the Queen of Soul herself; Otis Redding; Wilson Pickett; The Drifters; and Solomon Burke. Atlantic Records was definitely the big league — a major national label with major money to match. And they made it clear that they wanted to spend a lot of it promoting us. The day we signed the contract, I had that it's-really-about-to-happen-for-us feeling. To our surprise, we learned we weren't the first Bluebelles to be signed at Atlantic. In the mid-fifties, a female quintet had used the name to record their only single, "The Story of a Fool." I knew that *our* Bluebelles were going to write a different story, the story of fame and fortune.

Almost immediately, we were put in the recording studio, where we cut the first of the dozen singles we would do for Atlantic. We even sang backup for Wilson Pickett on his number-one

R&B hit "634-5789." The same year, 1966, we toured with Otis Redding, who treated me like gold. He even took me to his home to have dinner with him and his wife, Zelma. They had a fabulous home with a beautiful swimming pool. Otis tried to teach me to swim, but that was a hopeless cause. Despite his best efforts, I couldn't even float. Still can't. It broke my heart when, in December of the following year, Otis was killed when his plane crashed into an icy lake less than three weeks after he had recorded his signature song, "Dock of the Bay."

It was while we were on Atlantic Records that we launched our own "American Invasion" of the U.K. They sent us to London, where I met the person who was going to shape my future in ways unimaginable to me then. We played the club circuit catering to British teenagers, and we appeared on the hugely popular TV show, *Ready, Steady, Go,* the *American Bandstand* of England.

I liked the show's producer, Vicki Wickham, from the moment we met. She had this warm vibe about her, as if she really cared about the person behind the performer. In her autobiography, Tina Turner says that when she was touring London with Ike in the mid-sixties, it was Vicki who took her to see a woman who read cards and foretold her future: "You will be among the biggest of stars . . . and your partner will fall away like a leaf from a tree."

Back then, Vicki was meeting all the big stars. She was booking everyone who was anyone on her show — The Beatles, The Kinks, The Who, Jimi Hendrix. It is a point of pride with me that we were the first and only group she ever booked to appear two weeks in a row. Before we left London, Vicki and I exchanged phone numbers, and over the next several years the two of us would stay in touch.

London was such a high for me that, when our tour was over, I didn't want to leave. It wasn't just the audiences, who packed our shows night after night and showed just how deep their love of black music ran. Even the musicians were fans. At the beginning of the tour, we hooked up with this fierce English group, Bluesology, that was working as a backup band for a lot of visiting American R&B artists. After our shows, they would come over to our place and a bunch of us would get drunk and play cards. The piano player, Reggie Dwight, could play keyboards like no other white boy I have ever heard. For some reason, he thought he could play cards like he played that piano, and he wouldn't give up until I had won what little money he had.

"Come on, Patti," he would say in his cute British accent. "One more game of tonk and I'll win back all my pounds."

Of course, the only thing he ever won was my sympathy. I might have sent him home with an empty pocket, but I never let him leave with an empty stomach. After I won all his money, I cooked Reg the biggest, spiciest dinner he'd ever tasted. After we ate, we sat around and talked —

about music, about the States, about his dreams. I learned that Reggie had won a piano scholarship to the Royal Academy of Music when he was only eleven years old. It was clear he was talented and he didn't want to be a sideman forever. But he wondered about his chances of breaking in big in an industry that worshiped matinee-idol looks. He would ask me, "How can I start? How can I get to sing like you?" I said, "Baby, if you have it *in* you, it will happen *for* you. You've got the fire inside; I can feel it. As determined as you are, it will probably happen for you before it happens for me." When the Bluebelles left London, we promised to keep in touch. I guess Reggie really got to me. Before he left, I packed up a big bag of food and sent him home with all the leftovers. Boy, could that kid eat. And I wanted to make sure he didn't lose any more pounds, since I had won all the ones he had in his pocket.

I was really surprised a few years later when Reggie called me at home. He was in Philly, and he invited me to a concert at the Spectrum that night.

"Oh, Reggie that's great," I said. "Who are you playing piano for?"

Long pause. "Well, Patti, I'm playing for myself."

"No, baby. I mean who are you *opening* for?"

Longer pause. "Patti, you didn't know?"

"Know what, Reggie?"

"I'm Elton John."

Chapter Twenty-one

There were no warning signs. How can you tell when a friend, someone you think of as a sister, is about to betray you? You can't. At least I couldn't. Up until the day it happened, I would have sworn on my life that Sarah, Nona, Cindy, and I would always be together. Sure, we had our stupid little fights. But they never affected our friendship. At the end of the day, we knew what the deal was. We weren't just another girl group. We were family. As far as I was concerned, our bond had never been more secure. There was nothing and no one that could come between us. As many an outsider found out, you messed with one of us, and you messed with all of us.

While I never felt any serious tension with Sarah, Nona, and Cindy, there were times when I did feel it from members of other girl groups. It had started early on at the Apollo when the crowds wouldn't let us off the stage without doing a couple of encores and the manager, Bobby Schiffman, dubbed us "the Sweethearts of the Apollo." For a while, we were closing our set with "You'll Never Walk Alone," and it always drove the crowd nuts. Our standing ovations got to be so loud and so long that a lot of other girl groups had second thoughts about going on after us. At the height of her popularity, Veronica "Ronnie" Spector, the drop-dead gorgeous lead singer of

The Ronettes, "freaked out," as she put it in her autobiography, when she learned they would be following The Bluebelles onstage to sing their signature song, the million-selling number-one single "Be My Baby."

"When Patti hit the last refrain, the part where she goes, 'You'll nev-VERRR,' she must have held that note for about two minutes," Ronnie remembered. "The people in that theater went nuts — every wig in the place hit the ceiling. And now these three little half-breeds are supposed to walk out on that stage and sing, 'Be my little bay-bee'?"

For a long time, The Shirelles ("Will You Love Me Tomorrow," "Soldier Boy") and The Bluebelles were like oil and water. The four of us were always having some kind of friction with the four of them. On more than one occasion, the arguments went from verbal wars to knock-down-drag-out fights. We fought over everything — from coming into our dressing room without knocking to men. Once, when we all were per-forming on a Murray the K show at the Brooklyn Fox, Nona and Micki of The Shirelles got into it over Chuck Jackson. They both had a huge crush on him and they were kicking and scratching and pulling wigs so hard, I thought they were going to kill each other. I had to jump in the middle to break it up.

The fights I remember most, though, were with The Supremes. Actually, they were only with The *Supreme* — Diana Ross. Before we went onstage, she used to come in our dressing room to see what we were wearing. I guess she sent somebody out to buy The Supremes the same outfits, because the next thing I knew, Florence Ballard, Mary Wilson, and "Miss Thing" were onstage wearing our drag. It took me a little while to get hip to what was going on. But about the third time it happened, I figured out it wasn't just by chance. It got to be a real problem, too. We only had a couple of outfits to our name, so it wasn't like we could just change into something else. And we sure couldn't buy anything new. The few outfits we did have came from Lerner's or Woolworth's and even they took all our little money. To straighten the whole thing out, I tried to talk Bobby Schiffman into putting us on ahead of The Supremes. I sure didn't want people thinking *we* copied *them*. But, when switching the program around didn't work, I decided to have a little talk with Diana. I was so mad I could hardly see straight. Diana knew it, too. She was acting so nervous, I think she thought our little heart-to-heart was going to turn into a hand-to-hand. It didn't, but I told her straight out, if she was smart, she wouldn't show her face in our dressing room again.

As it turned out, The Supremes, or the "suits" behind The Supremes, raided The Bluebelles for something I loved far more than any outfit. Something that would never be replaced.

I knew something wasn't right the minute Mr. Montague got the call from Cindy. We had a club date in New York in a few hours, and she said she wasn't going to make it. She wouldn't say why. All she would say is that she wasn't sick and we shouldn't worry about her. But worry was all I could do. The only time Cindy had ever missed a show was the year her father died and she went home to handle the arrangements and grieve for him. But then, everything had been worked out in advance. Until Cindy returned, Sandra Tucker, the singer Cindy had replaced in The Ordettes, came back and filled in for her. But this was different. This was strange. Something was definitely wrong. I wouldn't know just how wrong things were until I got the news. From the press. Cindy had left us for The Supremes. Berry Gordy, the legendary head of Motown, had sent one of his lieutenants to recruit her to replace Florence Ballard when Flo's drinking became a problem and the friction between Flo and Diana came to a head.

As I found out from Cindy only recently in preparing this book, the folks at Motown went all out to woo her. They wanted her for a lot of reasons. They loved her voice, but they also loved the way she looked. Like Flo. The night before our show, they flew her to Detroit, promising they would get her back to New York in time to make our engagement. Once in Detroit, she met with Berry Gordy and the pressure was on. Motown needed her. And The Supremes were the hottest girl group of all time. They had a string of number-one hits that no one could match, and they were on TV as much as the record charts. She had to make a decision. It was now or never. She chose The Supremes. Flo was out. Cindy was in. And we were left behind.

Sarah, Nona, and I were the last to get the word. It felt like someone had put a knife in my heart. No, it was more like a knife in my back. It was bad enough that Cindy abandoned us. What made it worse, what turned the knife over and over, was that she never even told us. She didn't even say good-bye. After six years of sharing everything — our dreams, our secrets, our sardines, our makeshift beds on Chubby's living-room floor — she just up and walked away.

At first I was hurt, but then I got pissed. In interviews, whenever people asked *me* about *her,* Priscilla answered.

"Cindy who?"

I said a lot of mean and ugly things, things I regret, but I just wanted to forget her. Remembering was too painful. Cindy's defection had another effect on me. It made me feel even closer to Sarah and Nona. We were all we had left, and we circled the wagons. Cindy appeared on stage as a Supreme for the first time in July of 1967. And from that day forward, The Bluebelles were a trio. As the saying goes, The show must go on.

About a year later, when we were performing in L.A., Cindy came to our hotel room and apologized. I knew she meant it, but it would be many more years before I could really forgive her. I was polite, but that's all. I told her I had forgiven her, but I think she knew better. Chubby always told me one of the secrets of happiness was to learn to forgive and forget. Now, I know she was right. But at the time, I couldn't forget how much I had to forgive. The wound was too deep and too fresh.

It took me a lot of years to see that I was hurting myself as much as I was hurting Cindy, probably more. I know now that, in leaving The Bluebelles, she was only making a move she thought would improve her life. But I know something even more important about myself. Holding on to anger and resentment is a waste of time and energy. It blinds you to the beauty and joy in your life. It's like putting a vise on your heart, surrounding it, squeezing it, stopping the flow of love. Blocking your blessings. Think about it. How can you enjoy the present if you keep reliving the past? You can't. But when you forgive, you let go of your anger, and all those other toxic feelings that it breeds. When you let your anger go, it and the person causing it lose all power over you.

It's just like someone once said: We should think of hatred as a clenched fist. When it's closed and tightened up, your hand can't receive anything *from* anyone and can't offer anything *to* anyone else. Just like your hand, your heart has to be open to give and receive. I'm happy that Cindy and I eventually reconnected.

Chapter Twenty-two

The three years after Cindy left the group were good ones for me personally. I met the woman who would become my closest friend and married the man who would become my rock. But, professionally, those years were rough, to put it mildly. The Bluebelles were stuck in neutral, and we were going nowhere fast. Though Sarah, Nona, and I recorded six more singles for Atlantic, not one of them charted. In fact, we never again had a hit record as The Bluebelles.

Though we weren't selling records, at least we were working. We had no trouble getting live work with bookings by two agencies — William Morris and Queen Booking, the agency Dinah "Queen of the Blues" Washington started with a five-hundred-dollar loan she used to rent office space in the CBS building. As a matter of fact, we were working all the time, more than three hundred days a year. But the pay was so low we were barely getting by. It seemed like everybody got a piece of our pie and we were left licking the plate. We learned the art of survival. We had to. We made it any way we could, though there is something I did in those days that I'm not proud of. I stole. We all did.

It all started one afternoon when Sarah, Nona, and I were shopping in some exclusive New York department store. I don't remember which one, but it was on Fifth Avenue. Shopping is probably not the right word for it, since not a single one of us could afford so much as a pair of stockings in the place. We were playing the Apollo that week, and all I wanted to do was look at the fabulous clothes and dream a little. I had been browsing for about ten minutes when nature called. I saw a sister working on the floor and tapped her on the shoulder to ask directions to the closest ladies' room.

"You're Patti LaBelle!" she screamed. "I just saw you at the Apollo."

"Yeah, well, that's great," I said. "But I really have to pee."

Her name was Norma Harris, and from the moment we met the two of us clicked. I can't explain it, but it felt like I had known Norma my whole life. She offered to let me use her employee discount to buy a dress I had been eyeing.

"Honey, even with your discount, I can't afford the zipper on that dress," I told her. "The Blue-belles shop at Woolworth's and lately we can't even afford that."

Things were so bad, I told her, I couldn't even afford a new pair of pumps from Baker's. They couldn't stand up to our intense performance schedule. The first or second time I'd wear them onstage, the heels would break right off. Every time it happened, I took those babies right back to Baker's for a replacement pair. Of course, when I showed the manager the broken heel, I didn't mention I was wearing them onstage for four shows a day.

On her days off, Norma told me, she moonlighted as a hairdresser, and she offered to do The Bluebelles' wigs whenever we were in New York. By the time I left the store, we were tight girlfriends, and we have been ever since. It is Norma, in fact, who created all my outrageous eighties hairdos from the "bucket" to the "fans" to the "broom." She does my hair today. And it all started that day we met in the designer department of that chi-chi store.

I invited Norma to our show and when she came backstage a few days later, she was bearing gifts.

"Here," she said, handing me a shopping bag. "A surprise for The Bluebelles."

And what a surprise it was. Inside the shopping bag were the most beautiful designer dresses I have ever seen. It was like looking in Vivian's trunk. Only now there were three of everything — one for Sarah, one for Nona, one for me. They were the dresses I had been looking at the day Norma and I met.

I know Norma was only trying to help three sisters she saw struggling to make it. But, however good her intentions, I also know she shouldn't have taken those clothes and we shouldn't have accepted them. Let me be real clear here. I am not about to make an excuse for what we did. There isn't one. But I can offer an explanation. The fact is, we were desperate. We had been wearing the same tired outfits night after night, show after show. At the Apollo, we were doing several performances a day and we barely had enough clothes to do a wardrobe change between *days,* never mind between *shows.* Those dresses were like food to a starving man. And so we took them from Norma just like Norma took them from the store.

Then we took it a step further. On our next trip to New York, Norma told us to come down to the store and she'd work out a good deal for us. Sounded good to me, so I told Chubby.

"Shopping in New York?" she said. "I'm coming, too."

The four of us went through those racks like locusts through a field. Norma was ringing up everything — dresses, skirts, scarves. Only she wasn't charging us full price. Actually, she wasn't even charging us half price. Some outfits made it into our shopping bags with no charge at all. But the way Norma was working that cash register, you would never be able to tell it. I had a shopping bag full of designer drag, and my total bill was next to nothing. When it was time to leave, Sarah, Nona, and Chubby were cool as cucumbers. Nona and Sarah picked up their shopping bags and strolled out of the store like they owned the place. Ice queens to the tenth power. Me? I was sweating bullets. I was sure somebody knew what was going on and I was going to get caught. I panicked.

"I gotta get out of here," I told Norma and

headed for the back stairwell. Of course, the back stairwell was where the electronic sensors were located.

"Pat, no!" Norma screamed.

She knew what I had no way of knowing. Two steps farther and I would have set off every alarm in the place. Now, people were really starting to stare. Before I could do anything stupid, Chubby came to the rescue. She calmly took my shopping bag out of my hand and said, "Let me handle this, Patsy."

I nodded. As she strolled away with the shopping bags, I ran down the stairs. Through the grace of God, none of us got caught. While our wardrobe problem was solved, for weeks, every time we went onstage I was looking over my shoulder, terrified that somebody was going to drag me off in handcuffs.

Sarah, Nona, and I had so many escapades in our years together. Unlike the one at that Fifth Avenue department store, most of them were funny and harmless. Once, when we were playing the Apollo, we pretended Nona was having an epileptic fit and we let Bobby Schiffman call the ambulance before we told him it was just a gag. Another time, we had just finished performing at some convention, when an old white man propositioned us in the elevator. I know we were wearing our wigs, our stage makeup, and our tight dresses, but what did he think we were, anyway? We decided to teach him a lesson. We pretended to go along with the program, took him to our hotel room, and told him to get undressed. As soon as he did, we threw him out in the hall with nothing but his drawers and a warning: "The next time you see a black woman in a hotel, don't assume she's a hooker." The three of us laughed all night over that one.

We might have been poor as church mice but, God, we had so much fun with each other. We did *everything* together, from the silly to the sacred. When Sarah married Sam Reed, the sax player in The Bill Massey Band, Nona and I stood with her. Nona was a bridesmaid and I was maid of honor. Sarah had this big church wedding back in Trenton, and I remember thinking how beautiful she looked — like a fairy-tale princess. As I watched her saying her vows, I didn't realize that the next wedding I attended would be my own.

I will always be grateful to Sarah and Nona for talking me into getting married. They saw what I didn't see. They helped me see what they saw. If it hadn't been for them, I don't think I would have taken the plunge.

After I broke off my engagement to Otis, Armstead and I became close friends. He had just graduated from college and was studying at night for his master's degree in urban education. Whenever I came to town, we'd go to the movies or dinner or just hang out at Chubby's. I don't think either of us had any intention of falling in love but, what can I tell you? As the friendship grew, so did our feelings for each other. I knew Armstead cared about me. But, that eternal-forever-spend-the-rest-of-our-lives-together kind of love? I just didn't see it. And I sure didn't see his marriage proposal coming. Even now, after twenty-seven years of marriage, Armstead's so cool with his feelings, it's hard to read him. So you can imagine how shocked I was the first time he popped the question. We'd been seeing each other about a year when, out of the blue, he turned to me and said it.

"I want you to marry me, Pat."

My gut reaction was to scream, "You want to do *what?*" But screaming was out of the question. Making any noise was out of the question. We were at his parents' house, and no one was supposed to know I was there. Neither of us had an apartment of our own. So, whenever we wanted to spend some intimate time together, Armstead would sneak me through the back door of his family's home, and I would tiptoe up the staircase to his bedroom. We thought no one knew, but now I wonder. It was certainly possible, if not likely, that Armstead's parents knew exactly what was going on. For one thing, no matter how many times Armstead reminded me not to do it, I always did it anyway. I wore my favorite perfume — Jungle Gardenia: "the call of the wild." It had an unforgettable scent, and even if you *wanted* to forget it you couldn't because it hung in the air long after I sneaked back out of the house. In addition to the trail I left, somewhere in the middle of that staircase were these two steps that screeched like a hyena on speed the moment you stepped on them. For the life of me, I could never remember which ones they were and, more times than not, I would step over the silent stairs only to hit both of the creaky ones. Between the Jungle Gardenia and the squeaking stairs, Armstead's parents must have known exactly what the deal was. But they never said a word. And I am eternally grateful to them for that kindness.

While I was flattered that Armstead wanted to marry me, I turned him down cold. I didn't think I was the marrying kind. My career was everything to me, and I didn't see room for a husband and a home life. I had already thought the whole thing through in my experience with Otis. But, it was more than that. A lot more. Like I told Armstead, it would never work between us. We were opposites in every way. I was an artist; he was an intellectual. I was hotheaded; he was cool. I was Saturday night; he was Sunday morning. I was New Year's Eve; he was Christmas Day. I was fire; he was ice. Armstead listened patiently as I ticked off all the reasons it would never work between us. When I finished, he didn't say a word. He just nodded. He didn't seem hurt or upset in the slightest, and I thought the subject was closed forever. And then a funny thing happened about three months later. It was November of 1967 and Armstead proposed again. This time, he flew to Montreal where Sarah, Nona, and I were taping a popular TV show and this time he came armed with two things he didn't have the first time he asked me to marry him: a hell of a

186

rationalization and a hell of a ring.

"For over two years, neither of us has seen anyone else and neither of us wants to," he said in that calm, collected, ultracool, tone of his. "We're good together, Pat. If you want to, we can make this work."

What can I say? I'm a sucker for a diamond ring. No, really. On the serious side, I realized Armstead had a point. We *were* good together. We understood each other. We wanted the best for each other. We were opposites, all right, but whatever we had going was sweet. This time, I said "yes."

When we got home from Canada, the first thing we did was tell Chubby the news. She was overcome with emotion, all right. She had a *hissy* fit. She was against the whole thing. Chubby loved Armstead like a son. He had practically grown up in our house, and she didn't want to see him get hurt. She was convinced that I was bound to do just that. Hurt him. Not intentionally, she said. But Chubby didn't think I had sown my wild oats yet and one day I would want to. She thought that, after a few months of playing house, I was going to wake up this suburban schoolteacher's wife and think: "This ain't me. I'm out of here." She thought I was like Daddy — too much gypsy in me to settle down, especially with someone like Armstead, someone so grounded and centered and stable. At twenty-three, she warned him, I wasn't ready for the Ozzie and Harriet life. Chubby and I had talked about this when I got engaged to Otis, and she reminded me it was the reason I had decided not to get married then.

Armstead told Chubby he was willing to chance it, and he went about the business of laying a foundation for our future. He moved out of his parents' house and rented a charming one-bedroom apartment on Johnson Street. Then he tried to teach me to drive so whenever he had night classes, I could get back and forth to rehearsals. That was a big mistake. I'll spare you the ugly details, but by the end of the day, I had done serious damage to his beautiful, brand-new Thunderbird. Since that day, I have never been behind the wheel of a moving car.

I tried to make it up to Armstead at Christmas. I gave him a special gift, which I buried at the bottom of a huge box that I had filled with apples and oranges. "Merry Christmas," I said, pointing to the gift-wrapped crate. When Armstead opened it and saw all the fruit, I could tell he was totally confused but he kept his cool.

"Oh thanks, Pat," he said. "Is all this for me?"

"All that and more. But you have to dig for your surprise."

At the very bottom, hidden under pounds of apples and oranges, Armstead found it. The tiny gift-wrapped box with the diamond ring. I could tell the moment he saw it, he was really touched. "Put it on," I told him. "If I have to wear a ring that tells everybody I'm taken, so do you."

That was one of the best Christmases I've ever had but, as the whole marriage thing started getting real to me, I started getting scared. Chubby's words had put something on my mind, something that terrified me. What if she was right? What if I *wasn't* ready to settle down? What if marriage made me miserable? The last thing I wanted to do was to hurt Armstead. We had known each other since junior high school, and we had never been closer. I felt like I was losing my mind. Half of me wanted to run away and elope that minute and half of me wanted to call the whole thing off. I didn't know what to do, so I took the coward's way out. I did nothing.

Whenever Armstead asked me to set a wedding date, I put him off. For almost two years, he would ask me once, sometimes twice, a month. Every month. And every time he asked, I always had a "Pat" answer.

"I'm not sure yet. I need some more time to think about it."

And then one day, he had enough. After I'd given him yet another lame excuse, he gave me his most serious look and said, "You will never have to worry about me asking you again."

He didn't yell, he wasn't angry, but there was something about the way he said it that sent chills up my spine. Something in his tone made me know he meant what he said. And from that day forward, Armstead never brought up marriage again. I told myself that this was what I wanted, that I was happy that the pressure was finally off. But as the weeks passed, I could feel Armstead pulling away from me. Little by little, I could feel him disconnecting. I was losing him. And it scared me to death. Just the thought of it hurt like hell. As I imagined my life without him, I felt like someone had kicked me in the stomach. It was an ache I couldn't shake.

When I told "Doctor" Nona and "Doctor" Sarah, they diagnosed the problem right away.

"Girl, you're lovesick. And you've got it bad."

And then they prescribed the cure.

"If you don't think he's going to propose to you again, then you ask him."

I knew they were right. I also knew if I was going to do it, I had to do it right then, before I lost my nerve. Sarah rode with me in the taxi to Armstead's apartment to keep me calm and hold my hand. When we drove up, Armstead was coming down the stairs. I got out of the cab and as it pulled away, I heard Sarah's parting words: "Good luck, girl. You can do it."

"Do what?" Armstead asked.

"We need to talk," I said.

For the next several hours, that's all we did. All night long and into the morning. I told Armstead everything. Why I had been stalling so long. Why I wouldn't set a wedding date. Why I was so scared. I couldn't bear it if what happened to Chubby and Daddy happened to us. But at the same time, I couldn't imagine my life without him. I closed my eyes and said the words: "Will you marry me?"

Armstead took a deep breath. "I don't know, Pat."

I could feel my heart shattering into a thousand tiny pieces. I had waited too long. It was too late.

"Just give me a little time to think about it," he said.

Now I knew how he felt all those times I said those words to him. Even though Armstead didn't make me wait a year and a half, it felt like it. I proposed to him on Friday. He finally said "yes" on Sunday evening. On July 23, 1969, five days after I proposed, we eloped with Chubby's "mixed" blessing. As she put it when she kissed us good-bye, "I think you both are crazy, but since you're bound and determined to do it, you must be crazy about each other."

It was pouring down rain when Mr. Montague drove us to the airport. I didn't want a big, fancy ceremony, so we flew to Maryland where Armstead's cousin, Joan, graciously offered to find us a justice of the peace and let us crash in her guest room for a night. Her husband picked us up from the airport and witnessed the brief ceremony in a Virginia courthouse, while Joan stayed home and prepared a huge celebration dinner. After we stuffed ourselves, we all toasted our future and drank champagne. I was on my second glass when it hit me. I was in Maryland — home of the best hard-shell crabs in America. When I told Armstead I wanted a dozen, he looked at me like I had lost my mind. When I told him the honeymoon wouldn't start until I had some, he came to *his* senses and ran out and got them. After I finished the crabs, we had each other for dessert.

The honeymoon was very short, but very sweet. The next morning, we flew back to Philly and within days, I was on a plane with Sarah and Nona headed for Germany where The Bluebelles were booked for several performances. This would be the first of many farewells I would have to bid my husband because of the demands of my career. As our plane took off, I wondered if our marriage would be able to stand the pressure of constant separation. Only time would tell. As I watched the city disappear below my window, the only thing I knew for sure was that I missed him already.

RIGHT: *Me and Richard "Bird" Glenn at the John Bartram High prom. (Photo courtesy of Martha Glenn)*

BELOW: *Armstead, age fifteen, trying to look suave. (Photo courtesy of the author)*

Me (standing on the box) with my sisters of the spirit —
(left to right) Nona, Sarah, Cindy. (Photo courtesy of
Cindy Birdsong)

LEFT: *My beloved oldest sister, Vivian. You can see why I called her "the countess of cool!"* *(Photo courtesy of the author)*

MIDDLE: *My beloved sister Barbara — she was the prettiest bride you ever saw! (Photo courtesy of the author).*

BELOW: *My beloved baby sister, Jackie. (Photo courtesy of the author)*

ABOVE: *Me with Keith Richards, Mick Jagger, Cindy, Nona, and Sarah (seated). Thanks for my first plane ride, guys! (Photo courtesy of The Rudy Calvo Collection)*

BELOW: *The Bluebelles in a publicity still from the mid-sixties — and you thought I had big hair in the eighties! (Photo courtesy of the author)*

LEFT: *My wedding day, July 23, 1969 — right before I sent Armstead out to get those crabs! (Photo courtesy of Joan Groce)*

BELOW: *Labelle and friends — fooling around in Central Park, 1971. For once, Armstead had more hair than I did! (Photo by Bob Gruen)*

ABOVE: *Nona, Sarah, and me — after Cindy left we were like three peas in a pod. (Photo courtesy of The Rudy Calvo Collection)*

BELOW: *Me singing with Sarah, Nona, and Laura Nyro — who saved my sanity in the weeks after Zuri was born. (Photo courtesy of The Rudy Calvo Collection)*

LEFT: *Labelle wearing some of the outrageous drag designed by Larry LaGaspi. (Photo by Bob Gruen)*

BELOW: *Nona, Elton, and me — by this time he was rich enough to buy his own food and lose at the card table to me! (Photo courtesy of The Rudy Calvo Collection)*

TOP: *You can see why I named my baby Zuri — "beautiful" in Swahili — that's him at five months. (Photo courtesy of the author)*

ABOVE: *Me and Jackie with Henry Holte, the coolest dad on the block! (Photo by Matthew Pearson, Jr./Courtesy of the author)*

LEFT: *Hanging out with my babies, Armstead and Zuri — Sweden, 1979. (Photo courtesy of the author)*

ABOVE: *Fooling around at home with Stanley and Dodd. (Photo courtesy of the author)*

LEFT: *Doesn't Zuri look just like his mother? (Photo courtesy of the author)*

ABOVE: *Me singing with Gladys Knight and Dionne Warwick on our HBO special,* Sisters in the Name of Love. *(Photo courtesy of The Rudy Calvo Collection)*

BELOW: *Jackie and me putting on a brave face the night she told me she had cancer. (Photo by Rachel Cobb)*

ABOVE: *Singing with the golden-voiced Luther Vandross — as a teenager, he cofounded the first Patti LaBelle and the Bluebelles fan club. (Photo courtesy of The Rudy Calvo Collection)*

BELOW: *Armstead and me showing off our boys at the Parents Anonymous of New Jersey Special Achievement Award Dinner —* (left to right) *Stanley, the Harvard Law graduate; Zuri, the Temple University student; Dodd, the head of his own sports-apparel company. (Photo by Rachel Cobb)*

*My handsome boys — Stanley, Zuri, and Dodd —
Christmas 1993. (Photo courtesy of the author)*

RIGHT: *One of the proudest moments of my life, with Zuri and Armstead at the dedication of the Patti LaBelle star on the legendary Hollywood Walk of Fame. (Photo by Rachel Cobb)*

BELOW: *Whoopi, my Aunt Joshia Mae, and Aunt Hattie Mae came out to celebrate with me. (Photo by Rachel Cobb)*

ABOVE: *Another lifelong dream come true! Me and Armstead at the opening of my own 300-seat cabaret theater, Chez LaBelle, October 6, 1994. (Photo by Earl W. Edwards/Courtesy of the author)*

RIGHT: *Me and my boy, Z, 1995. (Photo by Moneta Sleet, Jr./ Reprinted by permission of Johnson Publishing Co., Inc.)*

RIGHT: *Me with Norma Harris-Gordon, my closest friend, and Sam Fine, makeup artist extraordinaire. (Photo courtesy of the author)*

BELOW: *Hey, does this mean they have to call me* Dr. *Patti now? Receiving my Honorary Doctorate of Music from Berklee College of Music, an honor I share with Duke Ellington, Dizzy Gillespie, Tony Bennett, Sarah Vaughan, James Taylor, and Quincy Jones, among others. (Photo courtesy of Berklee College of Music)*

The day I never thought I'd live to see — my 50th birthday party at LA's House of Blues. (Left to right) My niece Stayce, Armstead, the birthday girl, my nephew Billy. (Photo by Rachel Cobb)

Chapter Twenty-three

Not long after I got married, The Blue-belles began the transformation that would change our name, our look, and our sound. Remember what I said about The Bluebelles having tough times in the years after Cindy left? Well, by the end of 1969, we were so far down we had to look up to see bottom. As the sixties ended, it seemed like everything was also coming to an end for us. Our record contract with Atlantic. Our management contract with Mr. Montague. Even our popularity with the public had begun to slide. We were only in our twenties, and we were already being booked as an oldie-but-goodie act. At a time when we should have been soaring, we were sinking.

We went looking for help in all the wrong places. After Sarah's marriage to Sam Reed broke up, she started seeing a sweet-talking, slow-walking, smooth operator who I'll call Leroy Lily. While Mr. Montague had done a lot for us, he never had a lot of money to put behind us. Leroy Lily, however, always seemed to have serious bank. I don't know where his money came from. I don't know what he did to get it. All I know is he had plenty of it. After my experience with Harold B. Robinson, I probably should have asked how he earned his living. I should have, but I didn't. Instead of asking questions, I took it on faith that Lily had the answers to our problems, starting with his promise to give us all the backing we needed — from money to contacts to management. Lily said he had a plan. He said with him as our manager, we would soon be on top. Whether we should have or not, we believed him. We were desperate, and we were ready to believe anyone who promised us the moon and said he could make us stars.

After several months under Lily's "management," it started to dawn on me that his mouth had written checks his skills couldn't cash. If anything, we were in worse shape than before. We still didn't have a hit record or a new record deal. As for our live shows, nothing had changed. We were still performing on the chitlin' circuit for chicken feed. The clubs Lily *did* manage to book us in looked like gangster city. Some nights, I'd be onstage singing and when I looked at who was in the room, I had to start praying: "Lord, please don't let anybody in here pull out his piece and start shooting."

I knew we couldn't go on like this; I just didn't know how to deal with it. Before I could figure out how to get us away from Lily, things got really scary. Lily turned violent with Sarah. He'd bought her all kinds of expensive gifts, including furs in every color of the rainbow, and I guess he thought that meant he owned her. I will never forget the night we were at his apartment in Brooklyn and Lily's temper turned deadly. I can't remember what he and Sarah were arguing about, but I will never forget what he said.

"Bitch, I'll kill you."

I could tell by the way he said it, he meant it. But it wasn't just his tone that made me know he was for real. Lily had picked up his gun, and he was holding it on Sarah. I don't know what came over me, but the next thing I knew, I was in the middle, between Sarah and Lily and a loaded pistol. Even though I was unarmed, he was outmatched. I might have been scared, but I wasn't going out like that. And, if I had anything to say about it, Sarah wasn't either. Chubby had set the example for me when she stood up to Daddy. Only this time, it was the man who was holding the weapon. I don't know what I thought I was going to do, so I did the only thing I could. I prayed to God, and then I started talking — fast and furious.

"If you shoot her, you're going to have to shoot me, too."

Lily shrugged. "If that's how its gotta be."

My mind started swirling. What was I going to do now? How was I going to get us out of there alive? And then God answered my prayers.

"If you shoot both of us, you're not going to have a group," I told Lily. "And if you don't have a group, who will you manage? We'll all lose."

That seemed to get his attention, so I kept on talking. "And there's a damn good chance you will end up in jail."

He looked at me, then he looked at Sarah. "I'll deal with you later, bitch," he said to her. And then he walked out.

There were other ugly incidents before Sarah, Nona, and I were finally able to sever our ties with Lily. It took an overseas connection to do it. Her name was Vicki Wickham, the London TV producer we met a few years earlier when we appeared on her show, *Ready, Steady, Go.* Vicki and I had kept in touch over the years, and she had always said she wanted to produce an album with us. When we were still signed to Atlantic, she had even approached Jerry Wexler, the label's renowned vice president and the man who coined the term "rhythm and blues" for what used to be called "race records." Vicki asked him to let her produce a few songs for us, but Wexler turned her down cold. I never understood why since he was devoting so much of his time and energy to Aretha Franklin, producing some of her greatest releases starting with "I Never Loved a Man (the Way I Love You)." In the meantime, The Blue-belles were not getting the attention or the push we thought we deserved.

In late 1969, Vicki and I hooked up again when she was in New York working with Kit Lambert and Chris Stamp who were managing the English rock group, The Who. I told her we were out of our contract with Atlantic and asked her if she was still interested in producing us. To my delight, she said absolutely, but first she had to talk to Kit about financing the project on his new

London label, Track Records.

Kit was a trip I'd never taken before. Boyfriend's middle name was "eccentric." He spent money like it was going out of style. The best food, the best champagne, the best of everything. He would wear a shirt once and then throw it away. (A few times, I took those shirts home to Armstead.) One night, Kit came riding up to the Apollo in the longest stretch limo I have ever seen. Vicki had brought him to catch our show. Afterwards, when he gave Vicki the green light to sign us to his label, I knew we had taken our first step away from Leroy Lily. The next step was convincing Vicki to manage us. When Nona and I asked her, she was reluctant. Her plan was to produce one album with us and go back to London. Besides, she argued, she didn't know a single thing about managing a group. Maybe she didn't, but I knew Lily didn't either, and we had to get away from him before somebody got seriously hurt. So I kept badgering Vicki until she finally agreed. When Lily found out, he went ballistic. He made it clear he had no plans to let anyone move in on his territory. Lily threatened to put Vicki "at the bottom of a river." We took him seriously. After all, I had been there when he pulled the gun and threatened to use it. Vicki had to get her lawyer involved before we could break free.

Once Vicki agreed to manage us, she was full of ideas about the direction we should take. It was going to be bold, brash, brazen. It was going to be revolutionary. Though I didn't know it at the time, it was going to shake, rattle, and roll the world of rock — and rock my world in the process.

Chapter Twenty-four

The fights started early. And from day one they were intense. Even before Vicki started managing us formally, she began telling us her ideas about the direction she saw the group taking. Vicki is a visionary. And her view was radical. She saw us doing things that I had never even imagined. The more she revealed, the more I thought Vicki was way off base. The changes she proposed were so drastic and so extreme, I was afraid our fans, all the people who had followed us for nearly ten years, would turn away from us. And so I fought her tooth and nail.

Vicki wanted to do a complete makeover — our material, our appearance, and our performance. She wasn't talking about a remodeled Bluebelles. She was talking about a revamp. Basically, she wanted to change us into a female version of The Rolling Stones. The bad girls of rock. Not bad as in evil — bad as in hot, happening, cutting edge. Everything would be different. Even our name. Patti LaBelle and the Bluebelles, with our cute little matching dresses and our come-back-home-Daddy-please-don't-leave-me love songs, would be over, history, a thing of the past. Our future, as Vicki saw it, was rock and roll. But rock and roll with an edge, a message. Our music would be political, progressive, passionate. Vicki saw us as Labelle, three black women singing about racism, sexism, and eroticism.

Nona shared Vicki's vision. From the beginning, they saw eye to eye. That left Sarah in the middle. She became the buffer, the shock absorber and the peacemaker. I didn't want to give an inch and Vicki, Nona, and I were miles apart. When I tried out Vicki's concept on other people I knew, their reaction was the same as mine: "You can't be serious." But Vicki didn't want to hear any of it. She said the sixties were over and a new decade was dawning. For Vicki, it wasn't about keeping up with The Supremes. She wanted us to be pacesetters, pioneers. She wanted Sarah, Nona, and me to change the face and future of women in rock music. And she had a plan to do it.

The first step was taking us out of the country. Vicki felt we needed to get away from everything and everybody if we were going to focus on a new day, a new concept, a new us. I think, as much as anything else, she wanted me to get away from all those people who agreed with me when I disagreed with her. She wanted a new environment, away from all the reminders of the way we were so that we could focus all our energy on the way we were to be. I wasn't convinced, but I was outnumbered. At Vicki's insistence, we left everything safe and familiar — our families, our friends, our fans — and headed for London where, over the next few months, we would become what we became.

We rented a huge flat in a ritzy section of London known as Belgravia. We brought our piano player, Gene Casey, a gifted musician who could play anything and everything. Every day, the five of us rehearsed new songs and went through endless material. And every night, a bunch of us got drunk on the wine we always kept in the flat. Cases of it. Between the drinking and the rehearsing, Vicki and I fought constantly. We had some real knock-down, drag-out arguments over the look of the future. Our first album cover as Labelle would give the world a glimpse of things to come. Vicki wanted us to lose the empire dresses and wear jeans. *Jeans.* She wanted us to imitate the scruffy, don't-give-a-damn look of white rock groups. The jeans would be bad enough. But then she told me about our next fashion statement — Nona in jeans, Sarah in skirts, and me in boots and knickers.

I damn near died. "Vicki, are you tripping? I don't *feel* boots and knickers." I would have worn anything — even those little Woolworth's dresses, tiaras, and matching gloves that The Bluebelles used to wear when Cindy was still with us — anything but boots and knickers. The more I argued, the more Vicki dug in.

She always said the same thing: "Pat, I see you in boots, luv."

I gave in, but I was not happy. Every time I would pull a knicker up my leg or a boot on my foot, I would be as mad as the last black widow spider. I was not cute.

It wasn't just the clothes that I had a problem with. I fought Vicki on every single change, from the new name she wanted us to use to the music she wanted us to sing. Eventually, I just got tired. Eventually, they just wore me down. Over the years, people have asked me what finally convinced me that the changes were right. The honest answer is nothing. I just made up my mind that I wasn't going to argue about it anymore. If they wanted to do this, I would give it a try and if it didn't work, well, I'd cross that bridge when I came to it. Or I should say I would jump off that bridge when I came to it.

The truth is, Vicki and Nona were stronger than I was. I felt all alone, and everything seemed to be spinning out of control. Before, it was Sarah, Nona, and me against the world. Now, it seemed to be us against one another. What had happened to the good old days when we used to go out drinking and dancing at New York clubs like Nepenthe? Many a night, we closed those clubs down and Nona would practically have to carry me home when I'd done a little too much drinking and partying. We were so close then. Inseparable. Now I missed all that. I missed *us;* the way we used to be and never would be again. In London it was Sarah and Nona hanging out at the discos, leaving me alone at the flat. At first I begged them not to go. But then I just got used to being by myself. How had we gotten to this point? Halfway around the world and even further away from each other?

By the time we left London, I felt like a rag doll that had all the stuffing kicked out of her. I was so tired of fighting. I was worn down and worn out. And I didn't know what to do about it. I knew in my heart that I didn't want to make Vicki's changes, but I didn't think I had a choice. It never occurred to me to leave the group. I had been with Sarah and Nona my entire professional career. In the end, I didn't have the strength to keep fighting all of them. And so I just caved. I gave in to everything. I didn't realize then that I wasn't just losing a fight. I was beginning to lose myself. And, for me, things would get worse before they got better.

Chapter Twenty-five

Maybe our first performance as Labelle was a sign of things to come. In the summer of 1971, we toured the U.S. opening for the British rock group The Who and promoting our new album, "Labelle." The tour opened at Forest Hills Stadium in New York and we took the stage in a raging thunderstorm. It was nothing compared to the stormy clashes on the horizon for Labelle.

Not long after we got back from our London retreat, I had started feeling better, stronger, more like myself. Of course, that meant I felt like I could speak up, talk back, take on Sarah, Nona, and Vicki all over again. Some of our biggest arguments were over our new material.

After Kit Lambert lost interest in producing us, Vicki managed to get us signed to Warner Brothers Records, where we released our first two albums as "Labelle." The first single release was an example of Vicki's vision. Hers was a vision of women who would never shy away from anything, no matter how controversial. I still didn't share that vision. "Morning Much Better" was a song about sex, specifically how good it is in the morning. I just could not see myself standing on a stage in front of hundreds of people belting out " 'cause I like it so much in the morning." Just the thought of it made me shudder. Vicki, Sarah, and Nona didn't see the problem. Especially

Nona. She didn't have a conventional view about sex, as she told me many times.

"I like appealing to both men and women," she told me. "I have no preferences. I don't limit myself. I'm all sexes. I don't know what a heterosexual or a homosexual or a bisexual or a monosexual is. I don't understand the differences."

Personally, I didn't have a problem with any of that. I judge people by who they are not who they love, which is what I told Nona the day she told me her relationship with a member of our entourage was more than professional. Years later, I would have a similar conversation with Jackie's daughter, my niece Stayce. She had gone through a painful breakup with her partner, a woman she loved dearly. "I love you like a daughter," I told her. "And nothing will ever change that." But as for that song, I just didn't know if I could get onstage and sing about sex in such an open, explicit way. Recording "Morning Much Better" for the album was one thing, but performing it live, well, that was a whole different movie. I just couldn't bring myself to do it.

One night, as the four of us sat around a friend's apartment in New York, things came to a head. I had been drinking gin and orange juice and, when the issue was brought up again, I gave Vicki, Sarah, and Nona an ultimatum. If they insisted that I sing the song, I would quit the group. They insisted. I quit. I couldn't believe I had said the words. I couldn't believe I was ready to make good on the threat. After all those years together, I was about to walk. Maybe I had just been pushed too far. Maybe it was the gin. All I know is that I grabbed my coat and stormed out into the freezing New York night. The snow was coming down, the hawk was howling, and the gin was wearing off. My plan was to get to Penn Station and catch the train back to Philly, but I didn't make it more than a few blocks. When that wind cut through my coat, I sobered up fast. Chubby didn't raise any fools. When I walked back into the apartment, I told Sarah, Nona, and Vicki, "It's too cold to quit tonight." They had a good laugh over that one.

"Labelle" wasn't the only album we recorded in 1971. That summer, we sang backup for singer-songwriter Laura Nyro on her classic album, "Gonna Take a Miracle." You ever meet somebody who you feel an instant connection with? Well, that was Laura and me. From the day we met at her apartment on the Upper West Side of New York, we clicked. It felt like we were old friends meeting for the first time. I owe it all to Vicki. Back then, she was writing for a British music paper, *Melody Maker*, and when she told me she was interviewing Laura for a profile, I tagged along. As I used to tell Laura all the time, she is a black woman in a white girl's body. Her music is so soulful. And she can write her butt off. Everybody who is anybody — from Frank Sinatra to Aretha Franklin — has recorded her songs. It was Laura who wrote the 5th Dimension's big hit, "Stoned Soul Picnic."

Before Vicki's interview was over, Laura and I were sitting at her piano singing all the old R&B hits she loved. As a kid growing up in the Bronx, one of her favorite groups was Patti LaBelle and the Bluebelles. Since she was a teenager, she'd always dreamed of recording with us and when she asked me if Labelle would sing backup for her on an album of R&B oldies, I wanted to scream "Yes, yes, yes!" This was *my* music. To my surprise, Vicki was all for it and Laura and I headed off to her kitchen to celebrate our upcoming collaboration by doing the two things we both love almost as much as singing. Cooking and eating.

To produce the album, Laura chose Philly hit-makers Kenny Gamble and Leon Huff. They had produced some of her favorite songs from their nationally famous soul factory, Sigma Sound Studios, where the crew of musicians, MFSB, was known as one of the baddest backup bands in the business. I couldn't wait to get started.

Rehearsals were a breeze. They started in Laura's New York apartment, then moved to Philadelphia's Bellvue Stratford Hotel where Laura stayed during the recording sessions. It wasn't until we got in the studio that we hit a snag. Laura insisted on playing the piano with the band, but they weren't used to her pacing or her rhythm. At the end of two weeks, Sarah, Nona, and I still hadn't laid down our vocals. I was fit to be tied. Unlike most artists, I do not like going in the recording studio. Never have. For one thing, there is no audience, a major problem for me since I work off the love and energy of the crowd. I just do not feel it from studio equipment and recording machines the way I do when I'm on stage. For another, producers are always asking me to hold back, an even bigger problem because I sing it the way I feel it. And I want to do it right away. When I have to go into the studio, I want to be in and out. Let me lay down my tracks and go home. On the Laura Nyro album, we'd been sitting around for two weeks when Kenny called and said he and Leon would start adding our parts that day. *Start* adding our parts? I went off.

"We're going to start *and* finish this album today because I am not coming back in this studio," I said.

"You wanna bet?" Leon asked.

"How much?"

"A thousand dollars," he said.

Did Boyfriend think that was going to scare me, the gambler's daughter?

"You're on," I said.

Four hours and thirty minutes and ten songs later, the album was finished and I had a thousand-dollar bonus. That was easier than winning all of Reggie's, I mean *Elton's,* pounds at the card table.

After the album was released, we did a few shows with Laura around the country. But the show that I remember most was at the end of the year. Christmas Eve at Carnegie Hall. It wasn't just that it was my first time on that hallowed stage. The show itself was amazing. The audience had no idea we were there, and Laura told us to come onstage after her third encore. I remember thinking, "How can she be sure she is going to get *three* encores?" Sure enough, Girlfriend knew what she was talking about. As Sarah, Nona, and I waited, as Laura took her bows, as the crowd kept calling her back, I kept count backstage. Once. Twice. Three times. We came out on cue and sang songs from the album, songs like "I Met Him on a Sunday" and "Dancing in the Street," and "You Really Got a Hold on Me." By the time we finished our program, the audience was going wild.

For me, it was heady stuff. Patsy Holte at Carnegie Hall? I was living my dream. But, as much as I loved performing with Laura, our best times together were out of the spotlight. We formed a strong bond. In the early seventies, Laura used to come and stay with Armstead and me in our tiny apartment on Johnson Street. We'd spend all day in the kitchen singing, harmonizing, and trying out new recipes. Sometimes she'd stay for weeks and, even then, she never wanted to leave.

"Patti, I want a place just like this," she would tell me.

That always tripped me out since Laura had more money than God. "Honey, you can buy twenty of these," I'd say. "What's the problem?"

The problem, she said, wasn't *buying* the place. The problem would be *filling* it with the same spirit. She said she felt a warmth and happiness flowing through that apartment that had a lot to do with the nature of my relationship with Armstead.

"I want what you two have together," she confided. "I want a husband like Armstead and a place like this."

"It will happen for you," I promised her. "Soon."

And I really believed that. Laura gave so much joy to everyone else, I knew love would soon find her. And it did. It wasn't long after those talks in the kitchen that Laura got married. In October 1972, she and her husband, David, planned a trip to Japan to celebrate her birthday and she wanted Armstead and me to join them. *Join* them? In *Japan?*

"Honey, on my money I can't even afford to pay attention," I told her. Why did she think my wedding gift to her had been a couple of my secret recipes? Money was funny and change was strange. A trip to Japan was definitely not in the plan.

Laura wasn't fazed in the slightest. She offered to pay for everything since Armstead and I had never really had a real honeymoon. I was packing my bags before I hung up the phone. The trip was too fabulous. But nothing could match the magic of the first night. We had saki and Armstead socked it to me. Of course, I didn't know it until weeks later but, before the clock struck midnight, I conceived my son. He was literally made in Japan. But when the magical moment was just a memory, reality began to set in.

Back at home, when the doctor told me I was pregnant, I burst into tears. I couldn't believe it. At twenty-eight, a baby was not in my plan. I didn't even know if I wanted to be a mother. What would having a child mean to my career? Would I have to stop singing? If not, who would take care of the baby when I had to go on the road?

And how would we be able to afford it? I was scared and confused. And, as I would soon discover, while my pregnancy was a surprise to me, it was an even bigger one to some of the people who were closest to me.

Chapter Twenty-six

It took me awhile to calm down, but once I did and talked things over with Armstead, he helped me realize that this baby was a blessing. How many couples were aching to have children and couldn't? I had a supportive husband so, while balancing a career and motherhood might be tough, it wouldn't be impossible. As he reminded me, black women with a lot less had been doing it for years. And who had more love to give a child than we did? After I thought about it, I realized Armstead was right. How could I have been so blind? This baby was a gift from God. And from the moment I recognized that, I really got into the idea of being a mother.

The immediate problem was space. That tiny little apartment that Laura Nyro loved so much was way too small for Armstead and me, let alone a baby — while I knew that, on a rational level, I still had trouble letting the place go. Armstead and I had so many wonderful memories there. It was where everything started for us. It was where I asked him to marry me. It was where we had spent those first few years, growing together. It was hard to leave. We found a lovely ranch house for sale with a backyard pool on Vernon Road in the Mount Airy section of Philly. I loved it but, even with Armstead's teaching salary and my income, the house was beyond what we could afford. After thinking about how wonderful it would be to raise our baby there, Armstead and I decided to do whatever we could to get the house. He borrowed money from his father for the down payment and I got Vivian to co-sign our loan application so we could qualify for the mortgage.

As it would turn out, the move to Vernon Road was one of the few things about my pregnancy that would go smoothly. Since we signed with Warner Brothers, Labelle hadn't been selling a lot of records. Like our first Labelle release, our second album, "Moonshadow," was critically acclaimed but a commercial disappointment. Nona had written half the songs and, while her work was getting a lot of well-deserved praise, it wasn't translating into airplay. It was time for another change. We signed a new deal with RCA, and we had to turn out a new album soon. The pressure to get a hit was mounting but, even so, I did not expect the reaction I would get from Sarah, Nona, and Vicki when I told them the news. Maybe it was the *way* I told them. Maybe they could sense that I had been struggling with the whole thing myself. Whatever they were *thinking*, it was what they *said* that shook me to my core. They asked me if I had thought about getting an abortion.

At first I didn't think I had heard them right. But then they said it again. As we talked, it became clear to me that they were concerned that my baby might interfere with our career. I felt like someone had kicked me in the stomach. My impulse was to jump up and run and never look back. But I didn't. I think that moment will be etched in my mind forever. At that moment, a little voice inside me kept whispering, "Something is terribly wrong here. Sarah, Nona, and Vicki have very different priorities." I wasn't ready to hear any of that. So, instead of listening to my inner voice, I ignored it. I rationalized the whole thing away. They weren't worried about themselves, I told myself. They were worried about me. Of all people, Sarah and Nona knew what singing meant to me and they were afraid I hadn't thought this decision through. Having a baby was not in my plan and I had never even mentioned the possibility to them. I had been worried about the pregnancy myself until I talked it over with Armstead. How could they know how much I wanted this baby now? How could they be certain I knew exactly what I was getting into? They were only looking out for me. I desperately needed to believe that, and so I convinced myself without too much trouble. And then I did what I had always done since I was a little girl. I tried to make *them* — the other people — feel better so they wouldn't be mad at me. It didn't matter what I had to do or what it would cost me. All that mattered was that they didn't stop liking me. I promised Sarah, Nona, and Vicki that nothing would change because I was pregnant. I'd still do all the shows, make all the recording sessions, meet all our professional commitments. Even when the baby came, I told them, I wouldn't miss a beat. We talked it through. We worked it out. The "A" word was never mentioned again. Later, my sisters of the spirit would become my baby's spiritual parents. Sarah and Nona agreed to be godmothers.

I pushed my pain, and my nagging inner voice, to the deepest, farthest corner of my mind and continued on as if nothing had happened. When I was pregnant, we performed everywhere — from the Continental Baths to Carnegie Hall. It was Bette Midler, who calls herself the "White Patti LaBelle," who told us about the Baths, the gay men's club in New York where, with Barry Manilow as her musical director, she developed her world-famous routines in the early seventies. When I think about some of the things that happened to me at the Continental Baths, I have to laugh out loud. There was, for example, the night when I dropped my change in the vending machine and bought what I thought was a fancy pack of bubble gum only to rip it open and find a fancily wrapped condom! Another time, I brushed my teeth with what I thought was toothpaste, but it turned out to be Desenex. Ugh! That was some nasty-tasting powder. Of course, Sarah and Nona thought the whole thing was hilarious, and they teased me about it for weeks. That's why I showed Nona no mercy the night her false teeth came out onstage. To her credit, Girlfriend picked them right up, popped them back in her mouth, and never even missed a beat. I don't think the audience even noticed. But nobody missed the scene I created the night I came on-stage half dressed. Well, sort of. I had all my clothes on, but somehow I had put both of my legs inside one leg of my pants. I don't know what I thought that was hanging in front of me. I didn't really think about it until the audience started laughing so hard that Sarah and Nona stopped to tell me to go backstage and get dressed. And this time use a mirror!

After that show, it might have taken me a little longer to get dressed, but I made sure I never missed a performance. Even at eight months, I was still singing and dancing in my five-inch fever pumps. When we headlined at Carnegie Hall, we put together a show that included flashbacks to our glory days as Patti LaBelle and the Bluebelles. Before we did our new Labelle thing, we showed film clips from some of our early performances. Then, as if we were stepping off the screen, we stepped onstage and took the crowd on a trip down memory lane. I stuck out — literally — or at least my stomach did. But I didn't care. Wearing the new drag that was designed especially for this performance, we sang "I Sold My Heart to the Junkman" and "Over the Rainbow," show-casing our three girls, three gowns, sixties glamour. It was great.

Strange as it may sound, all the performing we did while I was pregnant didn't really bother me. What really took its toll on me, both physically and emotionally, was recording our first and only album on RCA, "Pressure Cookin'." For one thing, the baby was performing too, kicking up a storm, especially when I got to this one line, "Keep the lid on." I told Armstead, "He's probably saying, 'No way, Mom. Take the lid *off*. I'm ready to get out of here.' "

For another thing, the recording sessions were in New York. That was fine for Sarah, Nona, and Vicki. They all lived there. But I had to commute in from Philly. I was singing lead *and* doing the background vocals with Sarah and Nona, as I did on all the Labelle albums. Since I was coming to term, I was hoping Sarah and Nona would offer to come to Philly to record the album, but they never did. And, after what happened when I told them about the baby, I didn't want to ask them. By the time we finished, I was dragging. After those recording sessions, I was so tired I could barely make the last train back to Philly.

Armstead always insisted on picking me up. It wasn't just that the baby was due any day. But the station was in a seriously rough neighborhood. When my train pulled in, he was standing there on the platform waiting for his babies. He didn't want us to take two steps off that train without him.

He wasn't quite as brave when it came time for me to deliver. We were at home when my water broke around one in the morning. Armstead calmly got me down to the car and helped me squeeze into our little Volkswagen — a Karmann-Ghia. But when we got to the hospital, that was a whole different movie. As they were rolling me into the delivery room, Armstead did an about-face.

"Where are you going?" I asked him. "Aren't you going to come with me and watch the baby being born?"

He shook his head. "It's probably better if I don't. But I'll be right outside if you need me."

I let him off the hook since I couldn't take it, either. I had told my doctor early on that natural childbirth was not for me. When that first contraction hit, I told him to put me under. *Twice.* After nine hours of labor, our son was born on July 17, 1973 — nine months to the day after he was conceived on our trip to Japan. When the nurse put him in my arms, the first thing I noticed was his hair. Thick, black curls covered his little head. He was the prettiest little thing I have ever seen, which is why we named him Zuri, Swahili for "beautiful."

When I left Temple Hospital a few days later, Zuri was doing fine. It was after I brought him home that all the trouble started. Zuri cried all the time. I don't mean like normal babies. I mean *all* the time. Hour after hour. Day in and day out. Almost nonstop. Nothing I did could quiet him. Not rocking him, not singing to him, not even nursing him. It almost drove me crazy. I felt so useless, so helpless, so sad. I didn't want to do anything except sit by the window and stare outside. Every time Zuri cried, I thought this was God's way of telling me I wasn't cut out to be a mother. Armstead got so worried, he called

Chubby and asked her to come stay with us for a while. For the first two weeks of Zuri's life, he spent more time with his grandmother than with his mother. Finally, we learned why Zuri was crying. Poor little thing was starving. When the doctor analyzed my milk, he discovered it didn't contain the right nutrients. As soon as we put Zuri on formula, he was fine. After that, he was a healthy and happy little baby. The only time he cried was when he was hungry and when Armstead and I played the new release, "Pressure Cookin'." We could play the whole album and Zuri wouldn't so much as whine. He seemed to really like the song "Open Up Your Heart," which Stevie Wonder wrote especially for Labelle. But the minute he heard *the song* — "Pressure Cookin' " — and *the line* — "keep the lid on" — he would cry his little heart out. And he wouldn't stop until we turned it off.

While Zuri got better, my sadness only got deeper. In 1973, I had never heard of post-partum depression. I had no idea that, in the weeks after they give birth, many women experience feelings of grief and helplessness. I thought it was just me. I thought I was crazy. I was sure that there was something wrong, something unnatural, about the way I was feeling. I could hardly stand to hold my baby and, even when I did, I couldn't make the little guy stop crying. I didn't know what to do, and I couldn't tell Sarah and Nona. Desperate, I turned to Laura Nyro. She was living in Massachusetts and, when I called her, she simply said, "I'm on my way."

For the next several weeks, Laura was Zuri's nanny and my psychiatrist. Armstead didn't know what was going on. He'd come home from work and find me sitting in the window staring out at the yard where Laura sat rocking and singing Zuri to sleep in the shade of this huge oak tree. Laura even took care of Armstead's cousin, Joan, from Maryland. She's the one who had put us up when we eloped and she had come to Philly hoping to pull herself together after a devastating breakup with her husband. After Laura put Zuri to sleep, she would play the piano for Joan, then talk me into singing with her to try to shake me out of my funk. I don't know what I would have done without her and Chubby. With their help and Armstead's patience, I gradually pulled out of my depression. The day Laura left, I told her I'd never be able to repay her.

She just looked at me and smiled. "That's what friends are for." She kissed me on the cheek and waved good-bye.

Chapter Twenty-seven

When Zuri was only a few months old, I went back out on the road with Labelle. At the time, Armstead was teaching at Temple University and studying there in the evening for his master's degree. Every morning, he would drop Zuri off at his sister's house, then pick him up after his evening class. I knew Mary was taking great care of Zuri, but I felt a lot of guilt for not being there. When I called home, I could hear Zuri cooing in the background and that *really* did a number on my head. I ached to hold him. It was a long-distance longing. Now I had two reasons to miss home.

At least out on the road, some things were getting better. My problem with the boots and knickers had been solved. The year before, in 1972, we were playing the club circuit in New York's Greenwich Village and we were drawing a large following of gay men. When we did a show at the Village Gate, we met an innovative designer, Larry LaGaspi, who had followed our career since we were The Bluebelles. Larry was a true fan and a true original. He told Vicki our sound was cutting edge, but our look was yesterday's news. He convinced Vicki to let him design some clothes for us, and people have been talking about his creations ever since. It was Larry who conceived the whole Labelle look, designing and sewing that unforgettable drag that writer Jamaica

Kincaid once described as "a Puerto Rican's idea of Negroes from Mars." The silver, the cabling, the breastplates, the feathers, the platforms, the space suits, the helmets, they all were LaGaspi originals. Camp vamp. His friend, Richard Erker, added the finishing touches with his jewelry designs. Thanks to Larry, Labelle went from grunge rock to glam rock in the blink of an eye. A stitch in time. With those outfits, Labelle revolutionized the look of rock and roll. (Larry went on to do special designs for the rock group Kiss and Nona's old friend, Dr. Funkenstein himself, George Clinton.) From the day we stepped out onstage in those outrageous outfits, people would never see girl groups the same way again. We broke the three-girl-three-gown mold wide open. Uniformity was a thing of the past. Individuality was Labelle's future. And our message.

To everybody's surprise, no one had to talk me into this change. I melted right into that drag. I am the original *drag* queen. Whenever Larry brought his sketches by, I thought, "This is me, baby!" Once Larry told me the concept behind the outfits, I loved them even more. He said his space suits did not mean we were from outer space or spaced out, but that Labelle was futuristic, miles ahead of all the other girl groups. Thanks to Vicki's vision, we were about *inner* space. A head trip.

It might have taken me awhile to see eye to eye with Vicki and even longer to get with the program but, eventually, I did. Vicki was right. Not only did people accept us as Labelle, they began to hear the message in our music. Larry's clothes got their attention and Nona's songs put something on their minds. Starting with our second Labelle album, "Moonshadow," Nona was writing a lot of our material. By the time we recorded "Pressure Cookin'," Nona was cooking. One of my favorite songs is one she wrote for that album. She said a lot of the inspiration for "Can I Speak to You Before You Go to Hollywood" came from me. She knows I can't stand it when people get grand and let their egos get out of control. I could always see it coming a mile away. Before folks could get too deep into their I'm-better-than-everybody bag, I would stop them cold and say, "Excuse me, can I speak to you before you go to Hollywood?" Most black folks knew exactly what I meant. Going to Hollywood meant you were ego-tripping. I never do it, and I can't stand it when I see people try to. To me, it's a sign of ignorance and insecurity. We're all God's children.

Nona's songs spoke to that truth in a number of ways. If she wasn't criticizing people for going to Hollywood, she was appealing to them to make the world a better place. Nona didn't have any time for the usual woman-done-lost-her-man-and-can't-live-without-him girl group lyrics. Her songs didn't ask "Where did our love go?" Nona wanted people to think about where humanity was going. Labelle's songs were about empowerment, about taking control of your life, about politics, revolution, and liberation. Things that no other girl group had ever sung about. And we weren't just *singing* about independence, we were trying to *live* it by taking charge of our future, our finances, our fate. With Vicki's advice and guidance, we had our own production company (Bubbling Under), our own management company (Paleface Productions), and our own publishing company (Gospel Birds, Inc.).

Before Vicki, we had allowed men to control everything. They told us what to do and how to do it. We didn't do any thinking for ourselves. Now we were doing it all — thinking, planning, and speaking up for ourselves. And for others. It was clear people were getting the message. After one performance, a woman told me how much she appreciated our having the courage to say the things we were saying in our music. She said we were singing for anybody whom society had discriminated against because of who they were — blacks, women, gays. She paid us one of the highest compliments anyone ever could. It was so touching and real, I just started crying.

Not everyone appreciated our messages, I'm afraid. We took a lot of heat for some of the things we sang about. Especially the Gil Scott-Heron song, "The Revolution Will Not Be Televised." Some people said we were promoting violence and encouraging people to go out and raise hell. As I said then, I thought we were encouraging people to raise their consciousness.

If we weren't making people uptight with our

social comments, we sure got under their skin when we sang about sexuality. The year after we released "Pressure Cookin'," we went to New Orleans where we turned out our biggest single, the song that would become the disco anthem of the seventies. With its steamy lyrics, it got Labelle up on the charts, our fans up on their feet — and our critics up in arms.

Chapter Twenty-eight

It wasn't long before Vicki announced we had another project. Despite our so-so record sales, in June of 1974, Vicki managed to get us signed to Epic Records and we had to go to New Orleans to record our first album on that label. I felt like I was being torn in half. For the first year of Zuri's life, Armstead had been both mother and father to him. Because I was out on the road so much, I had already missed my son say his first words and take his first steps. He was growing and changing by leaps and bounds and I was missing most of it. Armstead's sister, Mary, was caring for Zuri most days. He had started calling her "Mi Mi Mommy." He couldn't pronounce "Mary." But that only explained the "Mi Mi" part.

The thought of being away from Armstead and Zuri for what I knew could easily turn out to be several weeks was sheer agony. But, I had an obligation to Sarah, Nona, and Vicki. I had made a promise that the group wouldn't suffer because of my decision to become a mother. And so far it hadn't. I wasn't so sure I could say the same thing for my family. Labelle was scheduled to go into the studio with the genius songwriter-pianist-producer Allen Toussaint and, since I couldn't be in two places at one time, I headed for New Orleans.

Everything I had heard about Allen was true.

He had style, flair, dash. Not only is he as fine as he wants to be, Allen knows how to live. Inside the music business, he is known for his talent and his champagne-and-caviar lifestyle. Dressing like he just stepped out of a magazine, tooling around the French Quarter in his Rolls-Royce and, my personal favorite, getting a pedicure every day. While Labelle was recording "Nightbirds" at his Sea Saint Studios, Allen even had his own cook, a woman everybody called "Pots." Every evening, Pots would come down to the studio on Clematis Avenue and bring us the best, spiciest Creole cooking you ever tasted. If the truth be known, Pots's cooking is the only reason I didn't go stir-crazy while we were in New Orleans. Allen is gifted, but he does things in his own time. He does not rush himself for anything or anybody. And he took his sweet time producing us. He'd keep us sitting around the studio for hours at a time while he worked in his office. Every now and then he'd speak to us over the intercom. Since we never saw him, we used to joke it was like hearing the voice of God.

As I've explained, I hate long recording sessions. But what made this one almost unbearable was the thought of all the time I was wasting just sitting around that I could have been spending with Armstead and Zuri. I complained all the time, but I have to give Allen his due. When it was finally over, I loved the result. The minute we heard the Kenny Noland and Bob Crewe-penned ode to Creole ladies of the night, we knew. We had a hit on our hands. We just didn't know how big it would become. Allen's Creole creativity produced Labelle's first and last million-seller, "Lady Marmalade," the single that became the disco anthem of the seventies and had everybody in America singing the sexy French lyrics, *"Voulez-vous coucher avec moi ce soir?"* (Translation: Do you want to sleep with me tonight?)

Suddenly, we were in demand everywhere. Labelle was hotter than Pots's dinners. The Sweethearts of the Apollo became the Darlings of the Big Apple. Just a month after we released "Nightbirds," Labelle made history. On October 6, 1974, we played the Metropolitan Opera House at Lincoln Center, the first time a black vocal group had ever appeared at the historic New York City venue. Vicki went all out to make the Sunday evening show an affair to remember. I, for one, will never forget it and I don't think anyone in the audience will either.

The hype started long before we took the stage. Ads for the show were placed everywhere, and they all carried the same instruction: "Wear something silver," our fans were told. And did they ever. The glitterbugs came out in force. When Vicki first told me the idea, I thought we would see a few silver earrings, bracelets, and maybe even a silver shirt or two. But what I saw was a whole different movie. The silver screen for real. Some of the outfits were better than ours. People paraded up the Met's red-carpeted white-marble stairs wearing silver from head to toe. Silver hats, silver skullcaps, silver eyelashes, silver Afros, silver capes, silver jumpsuits, silver body paint, silver Christmas tinsel, silver studs spelling out "Labelle." I even saw a silver jockstrap. The crowd was truly colorful. And they came ready to be part of the show. They brought tambourines and maracas and bought silver whistles that were being sold outside for a dollar a pop. Hundreds of people had to be turned away at the box office because we had sold the place out. Good thing. We had to recoup the $27,000 it cost to rent the place with ticket prices that started at $4.50 and peaked at a *whopping* $10.00. Chubby and my sisters came from Philly to see the show. My mother was so nervous, it seemed like she stayed in the rest room forever. But I think Sarah was even more nervous than Chubby. Her father, the minister, was in the audience, and it would be the first time he ever saw Sarah perform with Labelle. What would he think when we got to "Lady Marmalade" and heard "Would you like to sleep with me tonight?" Everybody who was anybody was at the Met that night — from Bette Midler to Jackie Onassis. But we were the attraction. The main event. Labelle of the Ball.

At eight P.M., when the houselights went down and the chandeliers were raised into the Met's high ceiling, Sarah, Nona, and I gave the sellout crowd a night to remember. Butterfly McQueen introduced us, and the cheers of the crowd told us they were ready to party. We divided the show

245

into two acts. Act One, which we called "Prelude in Silver," opened with us singing "Space Children" from our new Epic album. And, thanks to Larry LaGaspi, we looked every bit the part. Nona wore a tight silver spacesuit with platform boots. Sarah had on a loose silver gown with a matching silver hat. I had spray-painted my hair with streaks of silver to compliment my metallic silver leggings. We sang to the cheering crowd as we opened the show singing:

> *Space children, universal lovers*
> *Space children, are there any others?*

We ended Act One with what for me was one of the most moving moments of the show. Singing with The Mt. Vernon Gospel Chorus, a choir of black youths who walked onstage from the youngest to the oldest, the shortest to the tallest, singing, clapping, and moving in time. They were wearing T-shirts and jeans and singing what to me is one of Nona's most stirring songs, "I Believe That I've Finally Made It Home." I remember standing onstage with Sarah and Nona and all these black kids singing the line "I'm all right" over and over. It almost made me cry when I heard the way those kids were *singing* that message, because I knew they were *getting* that message. Too many black kids think they're nothing special, but at least that night those kids knew the audience and Labelle thought there was a winner in each and every one of them.

Then came Act Two.

Following intermission, we began the second half of the show, "Nightbirds," with an entrance people are still talking about. Somebody said we looked like African goddesses ready for some erotic ceremony. The gold curtains behind the band opened to reveal Sarah, her back to the crowd, standing atop a staircase wearing black feathers everywhere. The crowd stood up and cheered as she turned to face them and slowly descended the stairs. As she walked, she was singing Nona's composition "Nightbirds," and the audience went wild. The crowd had barely settled back into their seats when Nona came out dressed in a formfitting white spacesuit with silver studs at her breasts and crotch. On her head she wore a huge white feather headdress, and she too began singing "Nightbirds." Once again, the crowd was on its feet. When the cheers died down, the audience saw what one writer described as "a glowing orange bird-goddess descending from the ceiling." It was me, being lowered to the stage inch-by-inch by invisible rings and wires, my arms stretched out to showcase a twenty-foot train of black and orange feathers. When I touched down, I dropped the feathers to the floor and turned around to show the copper spacesuit I was wearing underneath. It was pandemonium. "Lady Marmalade" had the crowd dancing in the aisles, and Sarah's father didn't disown her after all. In fact, he became one of our biggest fans.

That night we didn't just sing the last song of

Act Two, "Can I Speak to You Before You Go to Hollywood?" We performed it as a miniplay. By the time we reached the fifteen-minute encore, "What Can I Do for You?" I was pumped. I ran out into the audience touching, hugging, and shaking hands. After the performance, Epic Records hosted a party for us at the Grand Tier. I had never felt closer to Sarah and Nona or more excited about our career. When the reviews came out the next day, we were the new divas of the music world. Labelle could do no wrong. As *Rolling Stone* magazine put it: "Labelle owns New York. The city which is supposed to be the performer's ultimate conquest bows in unashamed surrender any time the group takes the stage."

Shortly after our triumphant performance at the Met, we took our show on the road doing a ten-city tour of the country. When I left home, I had no way of knowing that our sellout performance at the Met was more than a personal high point for me. It was the professional peak for Labelle. And it would be all downhill from there.

Chapter Twenty-nine

Almost a year to the day after I was flying high with Labelle at the Met, I had to deal with what, at that point, was the most painful thing I had ever faced. October 1975 was one of the darkest periods of my life. Three years earlier, the doctors had told my family that my sister Vivian would be all right. But they were all wrong. When, late in 1972, Vivian was diagnosed with lung cancer, we were all terrified of what it might mean. But after the operation that removed the cancerous spot from her lung, the doctors were full of good news. The surgery was a complete success. Vivian would beat this thing. She would make a full recovery and everything would be all right. For a while it was. After she got out of the hospital, Vivian bounced back pretty quickly. It seemed to take no time before she was back on her feet and back to work at her job at Gulf Oil. I didn't think much more about it. I just thanked God for making my sister okay. Two years later, Vivian's nagging cough returned. This time, the doctors found cancer in her other lung. This time there would be no speedy recovery. After a second operation, Vivian was too weak to go home, and so she moved in with Chubby. She stayed with my mother for two months after the surgery, until she felt strong enough to move back into her duplex. But she still was much too weak to go back to work. Vivian had her good days and her bad days. Thank God for her neighbors, Eula Taylor and Catherine Webber, and for Chubby, Aunt Verdelle, and Vivian's boyfriend, Charles. The five of them took care of her when she couldn't take care of herself. Especially Charles. She had always called him "Old Faithful," and he proved no one was more deserving of the nickname. During their seventeen years together, even Chubby came to see how devoted he was to Vivian and the two of them made their peace. More surprisingly, Charles's wife and Vivian came to know and accept one another and each other's place in his life. When Charles's wife had a child, Vivian would sometimes baby-sit and a few times she and Vivian would even go shopping together on South Street. Whatever other people thought of the situation, it worked for Vivian, Charles, and his wife. As far as I was concerned, their opinions were the only ones that mattered. The whole situation reminded me of Katharine Hepburn and Spencer Tracy.

I'm grateful to Charles. He was there for Vivian when I wasn't. While I was out on the road with Labelle, "Old Faithful" was home watching over my sister. Every weekend, he would leave his family in New Jersey and drive to Philly to be by Vivian's side. It was his compassion and humor that helped her get through some of the toughest times — when the morphine couldn't ease the wracking pain and when the chemotherapy ravaged her body. Like the day she was sitting on her bed brushing her hair and with each new stroke, she lost more and more. First a few curls, then a cluster, until it was coming out in thick, huge clumps. When she looked in the mirror, she couldn't believe her eyes. Her beautiful, beloved hair sat in piles all around her. She was bald. It was as if she had shaved her head. Vivian couldn't take it. She broke down crying. Charles just held her tight. He told her that, with or without her hair, she would always be beautiful to him. Later, he made her laugh about it. He took her bowling, but on the way to the alley, he gave her a warning:

"Don't sit too close to the lanes. I don't want to mistake your head for a bowling ball."

Vivian laughed harder than Charles at that one. No matter how bad things got, she never lost her sense of humor. When Charles bought her an expensive color TV she took one look at it and said, "Now I know I'm dying."

Vivian was so brave. And she wanted the rest of us to face her illness with courage, too. She didn't feel sorry for herself, but she didn't want people to pretend she wasn't sick, either. She wanted her family to come to grips with the fact that she had cancer. She wanted us to use the C-word. She never let us soft-pedal the situation. She fought with all her might, but the cancer was just too much for her. At the end, Vivian was in so much pain she couldn't even eat and her hourglass figure had wasted away to skin and bones.

On one of his regular weekend trips to Philly, Charles took one look at her and knew she needed more help than he could provide.

"You're going into the hospital now," he told her.

He spent the next weekend by her side. After he left to pack for his return to New Jersey, he got an urgent phone call. It was Chubby. She was at Vivian's bedside. Charles hadn't been gone much more than an hour before Vivian started calling his name. He came back. He always did.

That was the last time he saw her alive. A week later, Vivian was gone. On October 8, 1975, five months before her forty-fourth birthday, my oldest sister died. I wasn't there with her at Philadelphia's Osteopathic Hospital when she passed away. As usual, I was out on the road with Sarah and Nona. It has taken me a long time to forgive myself for not being there and, to tell the truth, I'm not sure that I really have. At least not completely. Not just because I wasn't there for Vivian when she was sick or by her side at the end. That's just part of it. The other part haunts me even more. I never told her all the things I should have. All the things she deserved to know — how much I loved her, that she was my idol and my inspiration. From the time I was a little girl watching her sitting on Chubby's sofa singing "Sweet Sixteen" and breaking into her trunk to steal her clothes, all I wanted to be was like her. Beautiful. Poised. Courageous. I never told her any of those things. And now I never would.

Four days after my sister's heart stopped beating, we held her funeral at our family church, Beulah Baptist, the church where she was baptised and the church where she came to hear me sing. Chubby was beyond grief. She had dealt with tragic, untimely death before. When he was in his late thirties, her older brother, my Uncle David, drowned when he had a heart attack while he was out boating. Chubby's only sister, my Aunt Martha, and her baby brother, my Uncle Pizell, pulled together with Chubby to get through the shock and pain of losing their brother. But Vivian's death was different. We are not made to bury our children, and Vivian was my mother's first-born daughter as well as her friend. They had practically grown up together. Chubby didn't wail, she didn't scream, she didn't shout. She just looked to me as if *her* heart had stopped beating, too.

I knew Chubby was in no shape to handle all the details of burying Vivian, so my brother and sisters and I tried to carry most of the weight. Like a lot of black families, we were having an open casket at the funeral service and so, before the funeral service, Butchie — Vivian's son — and Charles, Barbara, Jackie, and I went down to view the body to make sure things were as Vivian would want them. I dreaded even the thought of it. Vivian had always been so beautiful and full of life, and I had no idea how I would react to the sight of her lying in a coffin — cold, still, lifeless. But I knew what I had to do. However hard it was, I had to make sure people saw my sister then the way they had always seen her before. Before she had become deathly ill. Before the cancer had robbed her of everything but her courage and her dignity. I had to make sure she was presented in death the way she always presented herself in life. Immaculate dress. Flawless hair. Perfect nails. The morticians had done a good job, a morticians' job. But it wasn't Vivian. They had painted her nails a pale, soft pink. Anyone who knew Vivian knew she was fire-engine red. Her wig was all wrong, too. Too traditional, too conservative, too old-fashioned. As I looked at my sister lying in the coffin, I said a silent prayer and asked God for the strength to do what I had to do. And He guided my hand. First, I removed the pale pink polish and re-painted my sister's nails "Vivian red." Next, I redid her hair in her chic, elegant style. When we were all satisfied that Vivian was ready to be seen, I had to make sure I was ready. Ready to bear my burden and the burden of others who needed me. Many of the things that happened at Vivian's funeral come to me now as if from a dream — hazy, fuzzy images that haunt my memory. Chubby's anguished, muffled moans, Charles's unselfish attempt to stay in the background and at the same time somehow say good-bye.

After all he had done for Vivian, I saw no reason for Charles to have to sit in the shadows. Earlier, when he tried to send Vivian a heart-shaped wreath of roses, he was informed they would only be accepted if he sent them anonymously. He did. But I felt he deserved to be recognized. More important, I knew Vivian would want Charles where he belonged. With the people who loved her most. With her family. When they called us up to the casket to say our final good-byes, I turned and scanned the pews until I found Charles. I motioned for him to come with us — it was the least I could do for my sister — then each of us bent to kiss her good-bye.

This was just the first of many painful good-byes I would have to say in the coming years. When I left the church that day, I deliberately separated myself from my guilt and my grief. While I found comfort in my family, I found escape in my music. It had always been my refuge, my retreat. And now it was going to be my absolution.

Chapter Thirty

If I ever needed an escape from the things that were going on in my life, it was after we buried Vivian. For a long while after she died, I was numb. To make matters worse, things between Armstead and me were strange. The constant separation, not to mention that whole sex, drugs, and rock-and-roll lifestyle that surrounded Labelle, was beginning to take its toll on my marriage. And Armstead was doing everything he could to make me see it. But he knows what he was feeling better than I do, so I'll let him tell you what he was going through.

"This is something I'm not proud of at all," says Armstead, "but it's real, it happened. Because Pat went back to work when Zuri was so young, not even three months old, he came to see me as his primary caretaker. When I got off work, I would pick him up from my sister's house in my Hornet station wagon and it would be just the two of us. Our bond became incredibly strong, and I'm ashamed to say I used it against Pat. If, for instance, Zuri fell down when we were both there, Pat would hold her arms out toward him, and he would run right past her to me. And I did everything I could to keep that going. Not because I wanted my son to love me more, but because I wanted Pat to realize what her absence was doing to all of us. This was precious time in

Zuri's life, time we could never get back. Zuri was only going to say his first words and take his first steps once. And I thought Pat should be there. But I didn't want to *say* it. I wanted her to *see* it. For herself. For Zuri. For me. Looking back, I realize it was the coward's way out. I should have told Pat what I was feeling so we could have worked it out together. But at the time, I had to wonder if Chubby knew her daughter better than I did when she tried to warn me Pat wasn't ready to settle down."

Out on the road, things weren't much better. In the seventies, drugs were everywhere, especially in the music business. Dope was so much a part of the rock-and-roll culture that, at our concerts, people in the audience used to toss all kinds of drugs up onstage. People have always assumed I got high, that there is no way I could give those high-energy performances unless I was on something. Music has always been the only high I needed, and so I would pick up all that dope — the pills, the powders, and the funny cigarettes — and throw it all back. This drove a lot of folks around us crazy. If I didn't want the stuff, I was told on more than one occasion by more than one person, the least I could do was pass it on to those who did. There were plenty of people who did. And plenty of people who still wanted me to want it, too. Once, when I fell to my knees onstage at New York's rock palace, the Palladium, an audience member shoved amyl nitrite under my nose. Luckily, I was able to back off in a hurry — missing the kick without missing the note.

Another time we were in the studio in L.A. recording "Moonshadow" and I was tired, my head was hurting, and I just couldn't seem to get my rhythm. Somebody passed me a pill and said, "Try this. It will make you feel better." I thought nothing of it, assuming it was just some extra-strength pain reliever. It turned out to be mescaline and it was a trip — a very bad one. I felt like I was coming out of my body. It took me a long time to calm myself down enough to finish the session. If you listen closely to that cut, you'll hear me say, "It took me awhile, but I think I'm finally there." Now you know why. That was my first and last experience with drugs.

I'm not trying to imply I was some kind of angel. I wasn't. Far from it. While I didn't do dope, I drank a lot of booze. So did Armstead. For a while, he was smoking reefer, too. Sometimes, we would drink until we got so drunk we were sick. I think part of it was trying to forget our problems and part of it was trying to keep up with the Joneses. People around us were doing so much more — mescaline, cocaine, acid — that we drank to be part of the crowd. Stupid, huh? Tanqueray and orange juice was my drink until I graduated to Courvoisier. I was into beer and wine, too. It was during this period that we started hanging out at the Roundtable, a neighborhood bar, whenever I was home. I was a serious little barfly, too. I told Armstead no sitting at the tables; I wanted to be right there at the bar sitting on one of those swivel stools where I could talk to my favorite bartender, Tootsie. It was just like that TV show *Cheers*. In between drinks, Armstead and I told Tootsie all our business. And while we were pouring out our hearts, he was pouring out the booze. Tootsie always gave us the top brands — double, sometimes even triple shots. More often than not, "happy hour" went well into the night. I would hate to have to guess how many times Armstead and I closed that bar down.

I knew people around me were doing more than drinking. We had a huge entourage, not to mention groupies, and drugs were everywhere. There were people who spent all their money on drugs and would come to me for a loan until payday. I gave the money, but first I made them listen to a lecture. Once, when we were in New Orleans working with Allen Toussaint on one of our Epic albums, I caused a major commotion when I walked in on some people sitting around some nice, neat little lines of white powder in our hotel. I knew what they were doing, and so I picked that stuff up and threw it in the air. Why did I do that? All of them started yelling at me as if I had stolen their money.

"Pat, are you crazy? Do you know what you just did?"

"No, I'm not crazy. I don't understand why you all need to keep doing that," I scolded.

I don't know how much of my lecture they

heard, since all of them were down on the floor on their hands and knees trying to scoop up what little cocaine they could salvage from the carpet.

More and more I was feeling left out. Like there was one long party going on and I wasn't invited. It was more than the constant drugging scene. Sarah, Nona, and I were singing together as always. But, our personal lives had gone in completely different directions. For one thing, Sarah, Nona, and Vicki all lived in New York City, while home for me was a quiet neighborhood in Philly. For another, all three of them were single and childless while I had a husband and a young son. That meant while it was no problem for them to work on various holidays — Easter, Father's Day, Christmas — it was a big problem for me. And I always felt guilty for even thinking about a day off. I didn't know how to communicate my confusion, fear, and loneliness, so I just withdrew deeper into myself. It landed me in deep water. Literally.

We were out in L.A. and staying at the Sunset Marquis when it happened. Nona, Vicki, and some other friends were all sitting around the pool having a good time while I was in my room with my dear friend, Rudy Calvo. I don't know what came over me. As I've already explained, I hate the sun and the water but the next thing I knew, I was asking Rudy to come with me out to the pool. We were only out there a few minutes when I did it. I had been staring into the cool blue water when everything seemed to go into slow motion. All the laughing, the talking, the poolside patter, it all just faded away. The movement of the water was so gentle, so soothing, so tranquilizing, I couldn't take my eyes off it. It hypnotized me. It called me.

Before I knew what I was doing, I ran full speed toward the deep end and jumped.

The minute I hit that water, I knew I was in trouble. I couldn't swim. As I had told Otis Redding when he tried to teach me, I couldn't even float. I panicked. I was swallowing water and sinking fast. Just when I thought it was over, I felt an arm around my waist. Someone was trying to pull me up, but I was so scared, I kept clutching and grabbing and pulling until we both started going under. Somehow, my rescuer managed to pull me out of the water. It was Nona. She knew I couldn't swim, and so she jumped in and saved my life. Was I trying to commit suicide? I've asked myself that question a hundred times and the honest answer is no, I wasn't. I don't really know how to explain my bizarre behavior that day. Maybe I just wanted some attention. Maybe I just wanted to feel like part of the gang again. Maybe I was feeling so lost and alone that, for that split second, I just wanted out.

It wasn't always that bad, though. There were also some magnificent moments. In March of 1975, when we returned from a triumphant tour of London, Paris, Madrid, and a few other European cities, "Lady Marmalade" was the number-one single in America. That same month, when we were performing at the Santa Monica Civic Auditorium, we got the surprise of our lives. Not only did the stars turn out to see us — Martha Reeves, Ryan and Tatum O'Neal, the late Rosalind Cash, to name a few — but so did two very special men from my past. Otis Williams, who looked like he hadn't aged a day since I last saw him, was there and so was the surprise of the night, my old friend, Reggie Dwight, now known the world over as the fabulous Elton John. I was so happy to see him, and so was the crowd. He came onstage to introduce us and, at the end of the show, when we did our encore, Elton came back onstage to help us bring the house down. The four of us sang "What Can I Do for You?" as we paraded through the aisles like a bunch of kids at a carnival.

Two months later, in May, Labelle had another high point when we did a week at the Harkness Theater, the highbrow venue on Broadway usually reserved for ballet. We were the first rock group to perform there, and what a performance it was. While we basically did the same show we did at the Met, Larry LaGaspi designed all new costumes that were, if you can believe it, even more outrageous than the ones we wore at the Met. They had to be. We sponsored a special contest where the best-dressed person in silver would get to come backstage after the show and meet us. Think Nona in silver short shorts, silver halter top attached to wings that shoot out from the back, short silver boots, and silver elbow-length gloves. Sarah was every bit as sexy in a slithery silver skirt and matching top attached by chains to her silver gloves. Yours truly wore a silver jumpsuit with matching helmet. And that was just Act One. After intermission, Sarah came out in a floor-length pale blue all-feathered cape that covered a hot-pink ensemble complete with silver breastplates. Nona was lowered from the ceiling wearing a white feathered headdress and white feathered cape. I was in turquoise lamé from head to toe. At the end of the concert on opening night, I spotted Laura Nyro in the audience, pulled her onstage, and made her sing "Lady Marmalade" with us. Afterwards, Sarah, Nona, Vicki, and I were each presented with a gold record for "Lady M." We closed the show by dancing in a conga line into the audience. Oh, what a night.

Three months later, on August 9, we returned to the Santa Monica Civic Auditorium for the widely watched Rock Music Awards. In 1975, the Rock Awards was as big as the Grammys or the American Music Awards are today. Co-hosted by Diana Ross and Elton John, it was carried live by CBS. We were nominated in four categories and when "Lady Marmalade" won for the best R&B single, I don't think any of us could believe how far we had come.

Unfortunately, the good times were becoming fewer and farther between and would not be enough to sustain us. In the end, there would be nothing that could hold the dream together and keep it from becoming a nightmare.

Chapter Thirty-one

I was struggling.

By the summer of 1975, Labelle was hotter than July. When, in the early seventies, Andy Warhol's *Interview* magazine predicted that Labelle would be *the* group of the decade, nobody paid much attention. But, now that "Lady Marmalade" was the hottest single in America, everybody wanted a piece of us. And the folks at Epic Records were anxious for us to repeat our mass success. So was I. After all, this was it. The Big Time. What Sarah, Nona, and I had always wanted — what we had worked the sardine houses and the chitlin' circuit to reach. But, as happy as I was about our success, I also felt like I was being torn in half. In show business, you have to strike when the iron is hot, and that meant I had to leave Armstead and Zuri yet again so we could return to New Orleans for a second recording session with Allen Toussaint. I didn't know how long this one would take, but if our last experience was any indication, I knew I would be gone for weeks. And that was only half of it. Once we finished recording the new album, we would have to tour the country to promote it. When I told Armstead, he didn't say much.

"This is your decision, Pat."

Of course, that made me feel even worse. If he had fussed and cussed and screamed and yelled, at least we could have fought about it and I could have left in a huff. But he was so damn cool, I left on a guilt trip.

By the time we returned to New Orleans, Nona was writing most of our material and she had a concept for our new album. When Nona wrote "Nightbirds," she was inspired by Janis Joplin — a bird of the night who soared to great heights but died too soon. For our follow-up album, the focal point was the title song, "Phoenix: The Amazing Flight of a Lone Star." Nona wrote it, she said, as an extension of "Nightbirds." While "Nightbirds" is about a bird that dies, "Phoenix" is about resurrection. Just like the mythical bird that was consumed by fire and then rose from the ashes, Nona said our "Phoenix" was about re-birth. The rebirth of the spirit.

Of course, once we released the new album, we had to come up with a whole new stage show — one that would have people buzzing the way they had for our "Nightbirds" extravaganza. Our New York debut was at the Beacon Theater, which was broadcast live on the *King Biscuit Flour Hour* syndicated radio show. And, once again, we gave our fans something to talk about. While our "Nightbirds" shows featured spacesuits, this one featured feathers, with costumes designed by Dorian Blakely. While "Nightbirds" showcased me fluttering down to the stage suspended by invisible wires, "Phoenix" put me in the spotlight, raised high above center stage by an 1,800-pound hydraulic lift, while Sarah and Nona sang:

"Open your eyes; rise, Phoenix, rise."

Even though our live shows were always full-house affairs, after "Lady Marmalade," none of our record releases caught the fire of our stage performances. A lot of it had to do with the tunnel vision of the music industry. Radio programmers didn't know what to do with us. Their airplay lists pigeonholed musicians into R&B (black music) or rock (white music). We were just not as simple as black and white. Labelle was neither. We were innovators who combined soul with rock. That meant we couldn't be put into neat little categories. We were too black for pop, too rock for rhythm and blues, and our unique sound — an ahead-of-its-time soul-rock fusion — made airplay hard to come by. The *Village Voice* summed up the whole problem this way: "It was OK for a white group to sound 'black,' but for a black group, especially a 'girl group' to sound 'white,' well — it just wasn't done."

That wasn't our only problem. Many of our songs were political and made people uncomfortable. Women in general and black women in particular weren't supposed to be making social and political statements through their music, and they sure weren't supposed to be singing about compassion, humanity, and sexuality. Girl groups were supposed to stand onstage wearing the same dresses and the same wigs and singing the same tired refrain: "Baby, please come back home."

There were times when people even tried to censor us. When we did the *Mike Douglas Show*, for instance, we had to eliminate "Lady Marmalade" at the last minute because President Nixon's daughter, Julie Eisenhower, was on the show that day. While we got to sing it on the Cher show, the network executives insisted that we change the lyrics. "Voulez-vous *coucher?*" was changed to "Voulez-vous *danser?*" From "Do you want to *sleep* with me?" to "Do you want to *dance* with me?" More than a few parents' groups even tried to get "Lady M" banned from the radio.

It wasn't just the risqué lyrics that caused an uproar. When we appeared on an NBC music special, we were told the only way we could sing "The Revolution Will Not Be Televised" was if we changed the words. We decided to drop the song instead.

Despite all the touring to promote the "Phoenix" album, it didn't match the success of "Nightbirds." Neither did the final Labelle album, "Chameleon," which included a number of new songs written by Nona and showcased all new costumes designed by Norma Kamali. Worse, recording "Chameleon" was a nightmare. For me, that session was the straw that broke the camel's back, the project that signaled the end for Sarah, Nona, and me as a group. Before we went into the studio to record it, things were already tense. To add to the stress of being away from Armstead and Zuri, Chubby had been diagnosed with diabetes, the disease that would eventually claim her brother and sister. I couldn't even escape through the music anymore. As I told Sarah, Nona, and Vicki, I didn't mind singing the rock and soul songs, but I also wanted to include some of the music I loved — the ballads, the standards, the torch songs, that have always touched me so deeply. They didn't want to hear it. At first, they didn't even want to include the one song I really wanted to record on the new album: "Isn't It a Shame." The only person besides me who was pushing for the song was David Rubinson, our producer. But he and Nona had such different visions for the album that she wanted him off the project.

Once again, I gave in. I backed off and left David to win the fight all by himself. But it kept gnawing at me. At one point I thought I had come up with the perfect solution for all of us. Since Sarah and Nona didn't want any part of recording any ballads, I could record a solo album when Labelle had some downtime. That way everybody would get what they wanted. When I told Sarah, Nona, and Vicki my idea, they made me feel like a penny waiting for change. You would have thought I had suggested we go onstage buck naked and sing "Surfin' U.S.A." There would be no solo album.

Instead of standing up for myself, I kept all my anger inside. Until I got home. I took out a lot of my hurt and frustration on Armstead. It almost destroyed my marriage. It almost destroyed me. It almost destroyed my family. Once again, I found myself attacking my sister Barbara. It happened one day when I was visiting Chubby's house. I noticed something was out of place and tried to straighten it out. Barbara was still living there at the time, and she reminded me that I wasn't. I had no business coming into "her" house moving things around. Why did she have to say that? Here was somebody else telling me what I could or couldn't do. As we stood there screaming at each other, I *heard* Barbara but *saw* the faces of Sarah and Nona and Vicki. One thing led to another and I left Barbara, black and blue, lying on the floor.

There were other fights at Chubby's, mostly with Jackie, my baby sister. It was always hot, always physical, always over nothing. And the only person who could ever pull us apart, the only person who could make peace with us again, was Claudette Henderson Grant, who had been Jackie's best friend even before she became mine and one of Zuri's godmothers, along with Sarah and Nona.

After that fight with Barbara, I started doing some real soul-searching. I couldn't keep fighting the people I loved. I had to ask myself some hard questions. And I wasn't even sure I was ready to hear the answers yet. Why was I putting myself through this? What was it costing me? Was it worth it? Why did I care so much about what everybody else thought? Why was I so hung up on everybody liking me? Why couldn't I stand up for myself with anybody other than my sisters? The tension kept growing until everyone around us could feel it. There was a time when Sarah, Nona, and I shared the same dressing room even when we were assigned three separate rooms. Even at the Met. There was a time when we ate breakfast, lunch, and dinner together. There was a time when we all even wore the same fragrance — Halston. But those times were behind us. Things came to a head one night in December of 1976 when we were doing a show in Cincinnati. Nona and I had a knock-down-drag-out fight in the hotel. I'm still not ready to talk about it, but suffice it to say it was ugly. Norma Harris consoled me after the fight. She had been handling our hair and wardrobe practically since we met in the designer department of that posh Fifth Avenue store. More important, she had become as close to me as my friend Claudette.

Something happened to me that night I fought with Nona. I knew I couldn't go on that way. I knew *we* couldn't go on that way. We owed it to our fans not to go on if we couldn't bring them all the love we had always brought to the stage.

"That's it," I told Armstead. "I can't take anymore. I'm quitting."

I don't know if he believed me, since I had often told him I didn't know what I would ever do without Sarah and Nona. While I wanted to do a solo *album,* I never once thought of leaving the group and pursuing a solo *career.* By the time we left Cincinnati, everyone had heard about the fight and the rumors were flying. We had a show in Baltimore the next day and it was there, at Painter's Mill Theater-in-the-Round, that everything fell apart.

We were about to sing our next-to-last song, "Can I Speak to You Before You Go to Hollywood?" when it happened. The band was playing the introduction, and Sarah was standing there waiting for Nona to sing her opening line. The band kept coming around to her cue, but Nona never took it. She was just standing there, leaning on her mike stand as the stage slowly turned around and around. I was sitting at the piano, since my part didn't come until much later in the song. At first, I thought Nona was just adding more drama to our most dramatic number. But when she looked up, and then suddenly walked off the stage and out into the audience, I knew something was wrong. I looked at Sarah, Sarah looked at me and, flustered, I finally spoke to the audience.

"This isn't my part, but I'm going to give it a try."

Somehow, Sarah and I got through the song and headed backstage to wait for the encore, "Lady Marmalade." The next thing I knew, Vicki was out on the stage. At that point I was really confused. Vicki never took the stage. And then I heard her say it.

"Ladies and gentlemen, this concludes tonight's performance."

I couldn't believe what I was hearing. I grabbed Ken Reynolds, our road manager, and started screaming.

"What does Vicki mean the show is over? It's not over. What's going on? Where's Nona? What happened out there? Why can't we do the encore? I'll sing it myself if I have to."

Ken shook his head. "It's too late. The lights are up and the audience is leaving."

I was in shock. I didn't know what to do. All I knew was Nona was acting weirdly and, with no explanation, Vicki had just pulled the plug on the show. I didn't know what to think. I knew something really bad was happening, but I just couldn't handle another crisis right then. I had to get out of there. I grabbed a couple of the band members, we jumped in the limo, and went to get something to eat.

It wasn't until later that I found out what Ken meant when he said it was "too late." When Nona suddenly left the stage, Ken was alarmed. He sent Dicky, our stage manager, out into the audience to find her. Once Dicky got her backstage, Nona disappeared into the dressing room. That's when they heard the pounding. When it first started, nobody knew where it was coming from. Then they heard it again, only louder, and it was coming from Nona's dressing room. Ken tried to open the door, but it was locked. They called for Nona to let them in, but she wouldn't open the door. She didn't answer at all, and the pounding just got louder and louder. Ken had a roadie break open the door, and that's when they saw it. The blood. Nona had been banging her head into the wall. They had to call an ambulance to take her to the hospital in restraints.

That night, everything collapsed. We fell apart.

Nona had some kind of breakdown. I flew home the following day. Vicki later told me, after that horrible night, Nona went away to get some help. Vicki called a month or two later to say Nona was doing great. I couldn't have been happier for Nona but there was a sadness, too. We all knew we couldn't go on. Labelle was finished. I felt like I had lost another sister. Two of them, really. And I had no idea what I was going to do with the rest of my life. A life I had never pictured without them.

Chapter Thirty-two

In the months following Labelle's breakup, I was a basket case. I went into a serious depression. I couldn't eat or sleep, and I felt this overwhelming sense of sadness that I couldn't seem to shake. Suddenly, everything had just stopped. All the performances. All the plans. Our next album, "Shaman"; a Broadway revue, "Nile Women"; a TV pilot; an international tour of Europe and the Far East. None of that would happen now. I felt as if I were going through an ugly divorce where everything — and everyone — had to be split up. Vicki would continue to manage Nona and Sarah and our lawyer, Ina Meibach, chose to stay with the three of them. Norma Harris wanted to stick with me. So did Budd Ellison, our musical director and piano player since the early seventies. I wasn't convinced that was a good idea for them. I didn't have a clue how things would turn out. I had never even considered a solo career. As much as I loved to sing, just the thought of going onstage all alone — without Sarah and Nona — terrified me. Funny, but without really thinking about it, in the months following the breakup, I almost always wore black. I was in mourning. I had suffered a real loss in my life. I felt as if someone had died. And something inside me had died, too.

Once again, I started taking my frustrations out on Armstead. Our relationship was already shaky and, day by day, it got harder to live together. I had gone from hardly ever being at home to being home all the time. I was so miserable thinking about my career, I'd find any little thing to fight about. It didn't matter how silly the point. I was ready to argue it down into the ground, and many a day I let Armstead have it, with both barrels. When he refused to fight with me, which was 90 percent of the time, I got even more frustrated.

After one particularly ugly argument, he couldn't take it anymore. He told me that he didn't know if we were going to make it. But, before we made any permanent decisions, he felt we should get some professional help. We needed counseling as a couple to sort out our marital problems, and I needed some one-on-one analysis to help me deal with my depression. When Armstead first suggested that we see a psychiatrist, I was skeptical. I didn't think some stranger who didn't know anything about us could do anything to help us. How could he possibly tell what was wrong with my marriage or with me? But, Armstead felt so strongly about our getting professional help, I'll let him tell you why he was convinced it was the only way to save our marriage.

"Things had gone so far that I felt the only person who could help us was a trained professional," he says. "It couldn't be a close friend or relative; it had to be an objective and impartial outsider. So we went to a psychiatrist. We had to hear, together, that one of us was absolutely wrong or that both of us were. We had to be told the truth, and we had to confront whatever was going wrong after all these years."

I have to admit, I learned a lot from my one and only visit to the shrink. He told us that a large part of our problem was that we had permitted other people to invade our private domain; that I had let other people and other things take priority over my family. With the breakup of Labelle, we both knew that wasn't going to be a problem anymore. And so, while it wouldn't be easy, Armstead and I agreed that rebuilding our marriage wouldn't be impossible if we both really wanted it to work. Dealing with my paralyzing insecurity, however, was a whole different movie. I honestly believed that I would never be able to build a career without Sarah and Nona. My self-doubt was just too ingrained, too deep. I looked at it like this: I was no spring chicken, and I was working in an industry that worships youth. I was thirty-two years old and, if I was going to sing again, it would be the third time around the block for me. The Bluebelles, Labelle, and, now, if I risked it, just me. Patti LaBelle. Flying solo. Without backup. Without a net. Whenever I thought about trying to make it on my own, I kept coming back to those two old sayings: "Third time is the charm" and "Three strikes, you're out." I didn't know which one would wind up being true for me.

I did know my insecurity was something that no stranger could help me with. If I was ever going to step on a stage again, I would have to work through my fear and self-doubt on my own. No family. No friends. No shrinks. At least not right away. I had to sort it all out myself before I could talk to anyone else. So, while Armstead continued to see the psychiatrist, I stopped going. It was time for me to do some deep soul-searching. I started praying for strength and guidance. I started thinking it through. When I felt a little stronger, I started to really open up to Armstead about my fears. And one day he said something that really struck me.

"Look, Pat, this breakup can be whatever you want it to be. It can be a devastating ending or a wonderful beginning. Just as waking is an end to sleeping."

Something about what he said helped me summon the courage to take the plunge. Up until that moment, I had been the master of playing it safe. I had been with Sarah and Nona so long — since I was sixteen years old. I knew I couldn't even think about forming another group. That meant if I wanted to sing again — and I did, God, I did — I had to go it alone. I had been a night bird, a phoenix, and a chameleon. Now, I had to be myself. And I wasn't even sure who that was. If there was any question left in my mind after hearing Armstead's advice, something else he said gave me the answer I needed to move forward. Armstead would take a one-year leave of absence from his job to help me put my solo career in motion. If he was that dedicated to me, if he believed in me that much, there was no reason for me not to be committed and not to have faith.

The people at Epic Records were thrilled about keeping me on the label as a solo artist. They wanted me in the studio right away. That was fine with me, because I wanted to get back in there and get busy again. I needed to have something to occupy my time. Right away, I started looking for new material for the album. I chose David Rubinson to produce my solo debut since we had really connected during the recording sessions for the last Labelle album. Budd left New York and moved in with Armstead and me in Philly. That gave the three of us the chance to work on material for the new album every day. David brought in fifty possible songs and, while I only selected a few, I could tell by the feel of the material that I had chosen the right producer. I knew David understood what I wanted to do when he suggested a song I have loved since childhood, "Since I Don't Have You." From Day One, it was clear his head and mine were in the same place.

Though I loved David's suggestions, none of them could ever match the song on that album that became the most special to me, and to Chubby. It's one of Armstead's favorites, too. And not just because he, Budd, and I wrote it standing in my kitchen one night. What makes it so special to Armstead is the song's inspiration: Zuri.

During the months that we were drinking heavily and hanging out at the Roundtable, Armstead was also smoking reefer. One night, after too much booze and too much smoke, he lay sick and out of it on the couch. Zuri was only a toddler, but he knew something was wrong with his dad. And so he tried to comfort him.

"It's okay, Daddy. You my friend," he said over and over, as he gently patted his father's forehead.

Zuri was repeating what his father had been telling him from the time he was a baby. "You are my best friend." Armstead was so moved, he never touched another joint again. And he never forgot that moment or those words of reassurance from his son — out of the mouths of babes. He was so inspired, he not only recorded the incident in his journal, as time went on, he kept adding thoughts, lines, and phrases to Zuri's words. One day, Armstead left his journal out and Budd and I did something I knew we shouldn't — we read it. As we were going through the pages, Armstead walked in on us. He went nuts, and there was nothing I could say because he was absolutely right — we had no right to invade his privacy. Later, when Armstead cooled off, we all wound up agreeing that his words were the makings of a beautiful song. While I was in the kitchen cooking, Budd was at the piano composing. By the time we finished dinner, the three of us had finished the song Zuri inspired: "You Are My Friend."

Recording the album went smoothly. David wanted us to do the session on the West Coast at the Automatt studio in San Francisco. At the time, it was one of the most modern and fully automated recording studios anywhere in the country. This time, I didn't have to worry about Zuri crying when I told him I was leaving. This time, I felt free to bring him with me.

After we released the album, called simply "Patti LaBelle," Epic was eager for me to go out on the road to promote it. They wanted to kick off this promotional tour at their upcoming international convention in London. That meant a live performance. In front of hundreds of people. I freaked out. This was a huge event for Epic and its parent company, CBS Records. It was where CBS gave everyone a preview of many of its upcoming releases and the artists who were performing them. More than a thousand people from around the world would attend. I told Armstead I couldn't do it. I hadn't been on a stage, period, in seven months and I hadn't been on a stage without Sarah and Nona in sixteen years. Worse, Epic was Labelle's label. The label where Sarah, Nona, and I had had our greatest success. The people who had promoted us were the same people who were going to be sitting in that audience. And I was sure they were blaming me for breaking up the group. I was torn. While I was terrified of having to entertain at the CBS convention, I also felt grateful to the people at Epic for their willingness to keep me on their label as a solo artist. The folks at Epic had been there for me when I needed them, so how could I turn my back on them when they needed me? I couldn't. And so I said yes.

The night of the performance, I had a panic attack. The show was at London's exclusive Grovesnor House Hotel, and a few minutes before showtime I was in the bathroom throwing up. I had barely gotten myself together when I heard the forty-piece orchestra go into my intro. I said a silent prayer, and slowly stepped into the light. I was wearing my Cinderella pumps. The ones that were specially made for this night. The ones with the solid-gold spike heels. I could see it was standing-room-only in the main ballroom. My nerves were so bad, I couldn't even make it through my second number. I had just started singing "Joy to Have Your Love" when I felt like I was losing my voice. I asked for a glass of water, swallowed hard, and looked around for Sarah and Nona before I realized they weren't there. I think the only thing that kept me from running off the stage was seeing David, who was there conducting the orchestra, and my musical director, Budd Ellison, who was on keyboards leading my rhythm section. After a reassuring glance at the two of them and a gulp of water, I sang my heart out. All the songs I had been aching to sing for so long — "Since I Don't Have You," "When I Think About You," "Dance Swit Me," and, as a bow to Sarah and Nona, our last hit single, "Isn't It a Shame."

How is it that two people who cling together and dream together sometimes end up all alone? . . .

282

Isn't it a shame, my friend, sometimes such a love must end?

By the time I did my encore, Armstead and Zuri's song, "You Are My Friend," I knew everything was going to be all right. I had come out onstage thinking the audience was going to throw rotten fruit at me, and I would leave with the only standing ovation of the night. As I stood onstage fighting back tears of relief and gratitude, I felt I had a real chance of making it. I knew I had done the right thing in stepping out on my own. Somewhere in the distance, I heard my mother's words rising above the cheers of the crowd: "You can love somebody with all your heart. But sometimes, to save yourself, you just have to walk away." That evening, I said farewell to the ghost of Labelle. And I said hello to a brand-new me. Never again would I look over my shoulder for Sarah and Nona. In fact, I would never again look back.

Chapter Thirty-three

I had made peace with myself. Now it was time for me to make peace with my family. In the Labelle years, everything was centered in New York. When we weren't out on the road, I had to commute into the city almost every day for something — to rehearse, to sign papers, to discuss tours, to plan albums, sometimes to record them. Now that I was in control, I made sure everything was located nearby in Philadelphia. For the first time in years, I was home for dinner every night, spending quality time with my babies — Armstead and Zuri. Sometimes, I even took Zuri to rehearsals with me. And I could go to functions with Armstead, events that were important to him. Events that I had always missed before. Reconnecting with my family produced another benefit for me, a most amazing and unexpected one. I began to love performing even more because I was no longer torn. When I did go out on the road, there was no guilt, only joy and excitement because I knew I wasn't sacrificing my family for my career.

Shortly after I went solo, our little household began to expand. We hadn't planned to have any more children, but we hadn't planned to have Zuri, either. And, as I have learned throughout my life, sometimes there is a master plan for us that we know nothing about. That certainly was the case with Dodd and Stanley

Stocker, two teenage boys who lived across the street with their mother and three other brothers. We met Dodd, first. One day he just showed up on our doorstep.

"Mr. Armstead, can I come over and swim in your pool?"

Coming over gave way to eating over, sleeping over, and bonding with Zuri. It wasn't long before Dodd started bringing his younger brother, Stanley, with him. Both of them were so good with — and good to — Zuri. All of a sudden my only child had not one, but two older brothers. Zuri wasn't the only one who started thinking of Dodd and Stanley as family. They were in and out of our house so much, Armstead and I started to feel they belonged there. When tragedy struck their lives, we tried to be there for them.

Dodd and Stanley were just teenagers when their mother died of pneumonia at age thirty-nine. Dodd was about to go away to college, and Stanley was having trouble dealing with his mother's death. His whole world had changed. His mother was gone forever, his father had moved back into the house, and he was about to start high school. He was so young and so wounded, he had trouble handling it all. While he had always been a straight-A student, his grades took a nosedive. Dodd told Armstead he was worried. He was leaving for college soon, and so he asked if we could look after his brother. Pretty soon, Stanley was spending more time at our house than at his own. After school, he'd come by and I would cook his dinner, Armstead would help him with his homework, and he would play with Zuri.

The next year, when Armstead and I decided we needed a bigger house, we asked Stanley if he wanted to come with us. Armstead and I didn't want him to feel pressured into leaving his family but, at the same time, we had come to love him and Dodd like sons. Stanley talked it over with his father and brothers and decided to move with us to the Philadelphia suburb of Wynnewood and into the house where we still live. By the time we thought about formalizing our commitment, Dodd and Stanley were both over eighteen and too old to be adopted. So Armstead suggested we do the next best thing: give the boys our name. And that's what we did. A few months later, in an emotional hearing in Montgomery County Court, their names were officially changed to add our name to theirs. Dodd and Stanley Stocker-Edwards. They didn't come from my womb, but it sure feels like it.

Our household grew even larger shortly after we moved. Claudette had always been a part of our family. Since the Elmwood days, Chubby had always treated her as if she were one of her daughters. She had become best friends with my sister Jackie, first. But, over the years, she had become my sister. Armstead loved her that way, too. So, when she needed a place to stay for a few months, we didn't have to think twice about her moving in.

There were still a lot of obstacles in getting my solo career off the ground. James Brown may have had the curtain closed on The Bluebelles, but at least I had a chance to get on the stage. After my London solo debut, I got a few bookings around the country but not nearly as many as I had hoped for. When I found out what the problem was, I don't know if I was more hurt or shocked. It seems nobody wanted me for an opening act because the feeling inside the music business was that my high-energy concerts were a hard act to follow. Too much intensity. Too much power. Too many standing ovations. Things got really tough after the reviews came out when I opened for Al Green at New York's famous Radio City Music Hall. The critics raved about my performance, but they were less than kind to Al.

"The question that practically everyone left asking was simply who deserved to headline the show," one writer noted.

After that, I couldn't *buy* an opening spot from a headlining singer. Somebody once described my shows as "one part revival, one part nervous breakdown" and, while I can't disagree, it did hurt me to my heart to learn that other artists refused to perform with me just because I give my all to my audiences. In fairness, I have to say a lot of the people who refused to tour with me were newcomers, one-hit wonders with big heads and small minds. Just thinking about their pettiness made Priscilla come out. (I called them "rats" which is "star" spelled backwards.)

We don't always know God's plan and, fortunately, my problem with the "rats" turned out to be a blessing in disguise. Chubby's diabetes had gotten worse and, since I was rarely out on the road, I was able to spend time with her. I thank God for those days with Chubby, especially since I regretted that I hadn't been able to take time with Vivian. And there wouldn't be much more time left. My manager, Murray Schwartz, was close to Richard Pryor's manager and, in the summer of 1978, when Richard decided to go out on a four-month national tour, Murray suggested that I open for him. Richard, God bless him, agreed. And believe me, he didn't have to. In the seventies, Richard Pryor was already a living legend. As I learned on that tour, he is as kind and generous as he is funny. He used to give me gifts all the time. And I mean expensive ones. His first gift was a sauna. He didn't even tell me about it. His girlfriend did. He just had it shipped to our new house in Philly. I had been telling him how excited I was about the move, and he thought this was the one thing the house was missing.

"Patti," he said, when we finally talked about it, "you work so hard on that stage every night, I want you to have something to help you relax when you get home."

When I told him my mother wasn't feeling well, he started sending her flowers — every day!! Then Armstead called with bad news. Chubby had taken a turn for the worse, and she had to be hospitalized. When I told Richard my mother needed me, he had a blunt response.

"Why are you still standing here?"

He didn't even think about the tour. His parting advice to me was to take as much time as I needed to make sure my mother was taken care of. He'd handle things out on the road.

When I got home, I learned that Chubby had suffered a stroke that left her unable to speak. Even worse, the diabetes had stopped the circulation in her legs. The doctors said amputation was the only way to save her. As horrifying as that was, there was no other choice. Chubby had to lose her legs so she wouldn't lose her life. And we weren't ready to lose her. The whole time I was home, Richard kept sending Chubby those flowers every day, like clockwork. While she couldn't speak, she was still alert, aware of the care we were giving and the kindness Richard was showing.

Even though I was reluctant to leave her, everyone told me the same thing: It was time for me to go back to work. I had made sure Chubby was as comfortable as possible, and there was nothing else I could do for her. Even Chubby told me to leave, in her own way.

When I rejoined the tour, I found that Richard had the biggest surprise of all still up his sleeve. It started one day when he saw me in the hotel lobby and asked for my help.

"Patti, I need to pick out a gift for my aunt."

The next thing I knew, we were driving up to a Cadillac dealership and Richard asked me to pick one out.

"You know my aunt and you know what kind of car would look nice for her to drive to church on Sunday."

"This one is nice," I said, pointing to an aqua 1979 Fleetwood. "It will go with her gray hair."

"Let me see how you look sitting behind the wheel."

"Do I look like I have gray hair?"

"Patti, just humor me," he insisted.

The whole time I sat there, I thought about the last time I had ever been behind the wheel of a car. The day I crashed Armstead's yellow Thunderbird into that tree.

"Here," he said, handing me the key. "Turn it on."

"I can't. I don't even know where the key goes."

"Right there," he said. "Now turn it on."

When the motor turned over, Richard was beaming. "You have just started your brand new Cadillac."

Was this a joke? I told Richard, as thoughtful as it was, I couldn't accept such an expensive gift. He had already given us the sauna and, besides, I didn't even drive. We had two cars at home, and Armstead drove both of those. Nothing I said could change Richard's mind. He was bound and determined to give me that car, and he even hired somebody to drive it to my house in Philadelphia. I knew I had to reach Armstead before that Cadillac did. So, after the show, when we all went out to dinner, I called home. I had to have a Courvoisier first to get up my nerve. And when Armstead answered, I started talking ninety miles an hour — at least fast enough to beat that Fleetwood on the highway, headed to Philly.

"Look, before you read this in *Jet*, Richard Pryor just gave me a Cadillac."

Silence.

"Now don't get the wrong idea. He's not even looking at me like that, and he's not expecting anything in return. He's just like my brother, and he won't take the damn thing back."

We went around and around for awhile, but Armstead finally saw my point. Richard was a kind and generous soul who wanted to pass along his happiness. Armstead may have accepted my point and we accepted the car. But I couldn't drive it and he never did. My sister Jackie, however, had a ball wheeling around Philly in a brand-new Caddy. Richard's generosity made everybody happy.

Chapter Thirty-four

God sent me an angel to tell me my mother died. I guess He knew that was the only way I could take it.

It was early on a Saturday morning when it came to me. I was back out on tour with Richard Pryor, and I had really turned the show out the night before so I was still deep down into a serious sleep — drapes taped shut, towels blocking the light under the door, sleep mask covering my eyes — when it came. Now, believe me, I know all about dreams that are so vivid that they seem real. I've had my share. And I know about having premonitions in dreams. But that's not what happened to me. The day my mother died, I didn't have a dream or a premonition. I had a visit. A rendezvous with an angel.

I felt it first. Before it spoke to me, I felt it. It started shaking the bottom of my bed, just real slow and easy at first, but I guess I didn't wake up fast enough because the bed started shaking harder and faster until the whole thing was rocking and swaying. I remember sitting straight up in bed thinking "What in Hell is going on?" I should have been thinking "What in *Heaven* is going on?" because it's clear to me now that's where my answer came from. The instant I sat up and pulled off my sleep mask, everything stopped. I don't just mean the bed stopped shaking. I mean there was this hush, this absolute stillness, that fell over the room. I probably *would* have thought the whole thing was a dream if it weren't for what happened next. In that absolute quiet, I heard a voice. It was soft, but it was crystal clear.

"Your mother's gone," it said into the silence.

My stomach turned over. I didn't move. Nothing moved. It was as if everything in the room had been frozen in time, as if time itself had stopped. All I could think was "I'm having a nightmare. This isn't real. I have to make myself wake up." And then I heard it again. It was the same voice, only this time it spoke right into my ear.

"Your mother's gone," it repeated in the darkness.

Right then and there, I knew it was no dream. I heard the words clearly. And suddenly I was filled with dread. I reached over to turn on the light. As my eyes slowly focused, I looked around the room and saw that there was nobody there. That's when I reached for the phone. It was on the table right next to my bed, but it might as well have been a million miles away. I felt paralyzed, numb — like I was trying to move with weights tied around my arms and legs. I knew I had to call the hospital, but I couldn't make my hands pick up the phone. My arms felt so heavy, like they belonged to somebody else. I was pushing against myself. Part of me was moving toward an answer that most of me didn't want to hear. My whole soul was stuck in the balance.

To this day, I can't tell you how I finally managed to dial the hospital and get a nurse from my mother's floor on the line. But I can somehow remember exactly what happened when I got her.

"Hello, this is Patricia Edwards, Bertha Holte's daughter. My mother just died, didn't she?" I asked calmly, coolly, as if I were asking her about the weather.

Silence.

"Answer me," I demanded. "I know she's dead, so you might as well tell me."

"I'm sorry, Mrs. Edwards. We can't give that information out on the telephone. You need to come in right away."

"And you need to put somebody on this phone who can answer me right now," I shrieked in my best diva-bitch voice. Within seconds, a somber-sounding doctor came on the line.

"Please, Mrs. Edwards," he said gently. "You need to come in right away."

"You don't know a damned thing about what I need," I hissed, slamming the phone down in his ear.

How could he have known what I needed? What I needed was for him to tell me that my mother wasn't dead. What I needed was one last chance to see her alive, the way she looked *before* — before the stroke stole her strength and her spirit. Before the diabetes ate away her body. Before they amputated both her legs. But what I needed more than anything else was a chance to say good-bye; just one last chance to look into her face and tell her how much I loved her, how all those years when all I saw in my mirror was an ugly little black girl, her love of my voice made me find something to love in myself. And if the time had come to say good-bye, everything I did, everything I was, would be her legacy. Until we met again.

If this were a movie, I would have made it home in time. But this is real life and I never got to tell Chubby any of those things I needed to tell her. I sent a message to Richard and was on the next flight to Philly. When I got off the plane, Armstead was waiting for me. He had been the first to make it to the hospital. The look on his face was indisputable confirmation of what the angel had come to tell me. What the hospital wouldn't. What I didn't really want to know. Without saying a word, I fell into Armstead's arms and cried like a baby.

I don't remember much about the five days my sisters and I spent planning Chubby's funeral. I know I didn't eat or sleep, and most of the time I wandered around in a daze. All I kept thinking was that it seemed like I had just buried my oldest sister and now here I was about to put my mother in the ground.

I do remember Barbara, Jackie, and I went shopping to buy her the prettiest dress we could find. It was pale blue, the soft color of the sky, and the minute we saw it we knew she would have loved it. Chubby always liked to look good, and my sisters and I weren't going to send her home any other way. We would wear the same color.

The morning of the funeral, the house was full of people, but you never would have known it. It was so quiet you could have heard an ant peeing on a cotton ball. By this time, the whole family knew I was going to do it. The way they were tiptoeing around, whispering back and forth to each other, you would have thought I had told them I was going to jump off the Brooklyn Bridge.

My sisters were appointed to talk me out of it.

"Please, Patsy," they pleaded. "This is crazy. You can't do this."

Armstead was a lot cooler, but I could tell by the way he kept watching me he didn't think I could either. The truth is, I wasn't sure I could do it myself. But I was sure of one thing. I had to try. If I didn't, I'd never be able to forgive myself. After all, from the time I was a little girl standing in front of the mirror singing into a broomstick, Chubby always was my biggest fan. I could sing her the phone book, and she'd say the same thing.

"Child you got the sweetest voice on this earth."

That was the voice I wanted her to hear as she was leaving it. I just had to sing one last song for her.

The Beulah Baptist Church was packed when

we arrived. I later learned that Jim "Mudcat" Grant had been the very first person to get there, to say good-bye to his dear old baseball buddy. The only person I saw there was Chubby. As we had done at Vivian's funeral, my sisters and I had Chubby's casket open, and throughout the sermon my eyes never left her face. That's how I made it up to the front when the time came for me to sing. Guided by Chubby. Eventually, that's how I made it through the song.

I could hear the stunned gasps, the shocked whispers, as I made my way to the front of the church. That's when it hit everybody — what only my family and close friends had known before. That the "Patricia Edwards" listed in the program, the soloist, was me: Patti LaBelle.

The first time I started the song, I thought I wouldn't even make it through the first four words. I will never forget them. How could I? They were everything I felt about my mother. They were the title of the song, Armstead's and Zuri's song. Chubby's favorite: "You Are My Friend." As my voice broke, and I fought back the tears, my sisters' warning echoed in my head: "Before you get out five notes, Patsy, you're going to lose it." Thank God, my musical director and friend, Budd Ellison, was at the piano and kept right on playing. That gave me a chance to look into my mother's face and listen for her voice. To steady me. To calm me. To comfort me. And somewhere in my heart her words came back to me.

"Child, you got the sweetest voice on this earth."

At that moment, I believed it. At that moment, I felt Chubby's love. At that moment, I began to sing.

You are my friend,
I never knew 'til then;
My friend, my friend.
I feel your love when you're not near;
It helps me make it knowing you care.
The thought of you helps me carry on;
When I feel all hope is gone . . .

The words flowed from my mouth, but I knew they were coming from someplace else. Someplace my mother had been the first to see in me. Someplace where she would live forever, strong and whole and beautiful again. That day, I sang as I've never sung before. This was a command performance.

When I finished, I walked over to my mother's casket, gently kissed her on the forehead, and pulled the blanket over her face. It was over. It was done. It was gospel.

I was thirty-four years old, and for the first time I saw one of life's great truths with crystal clarity: A girl never really becomes a woman until she loses her mother.

Chapter Thirty-five

The day after I buried my mother, I went back on the road with Richard. Armstead thought I should take some time off, but I told him I needed to work. I needed to keep busy. I needed to sing. I release everything I'm feeling through my songs. There was so much to let out. So much sorrow to let go. And it would continue. Not long after we lost Chubby, my best friend, Claudette, told me the shocking news. She had breast cancer. I couldn't believe it. Claudette was only thirty-four years old, and the whole time she lived with Armstead and me she wasn't sick so much as a single day. I was terrified, and I struggled to keep the fear out of my voice as I reassured her everything was going to be okay. The doctors said if she had a mastectomy, she could beat the cancer and, in 1979, Claudette went into the hospital twice — to have her breast removed, and later to have reconstructive surgery. Like Vivian, she was so brave. One afternoon, she came to our house for dinner. I thought I was going to have to cheer Claudette up, and she wound up cheering up everybody in the house. Armstead, Jackie, and I were sitting in the kitchen when she said she wanted to show us something. Her new breast. Armstead tried to excuse himself so she wouldn't feel uncomfortable, but Claudette insisted he stay. Then, as casually as she would have taken off her coat, she lifted her blouse and pointed to her new breast.

"See?" she asked. "Didn't they do a good job?"

I nodded.

"Touch it, you guys," she instructed us. "You, too, Armstead. Doesn't it feel natural?"

It did. But what was more important to me was that Claudette seemed so natural. She was okay, both physically and emotionally. She had lost her breast but none of her self-confidence and appeal.

It seemed we had barely gotten past Claudette's scare when Barbara started feeling weak and sickly. She told me she had some kind of bug but if she didn't feel any better soon, she was going to see a doctor. I didn't think any more about it, and life went on as usual. It was during this period that I recorded my last two albums for Epic, "It's Alright With Me" and the Allen Toussaint–produced LP, "Released." As the seventies were coming to a close, I had gone back to his New Orleans studio hoping he could re-create the magic he had worked for Labelle. While I had eight chart singles between 1977 and 1980, none of them made the Top 20. (My biggest single during those three years, the Toussaint-produced "I Don't Go Shopping," peaked at number 26.) I can summarize a big part of the problem in two words: disco fever. In 1977, The Bee Gees had five disco songs on Billboard's Top Ten list. At the *same* time. The following year, they walked off with five Grammys for their work on the "Saturday Night Fever" double sound-track album, which eventually sold millions of copies world-wide and remains the best-selling sound track ever.

While people tried to talk me into jumping on the disco bandwagon, I just couldn't do it. Like those boots and knickers Vicki wanted me to wear, I just didn't feel it. Part of finding out who you are is finding out who you're not. I had spent the last six years of my life learning that lesson the hard way. Now that I had finally found the strength to reclaim my music, myself, my life, I wasn't about to give it up for *any* price. That decision cost me a lot in both record sales and popularity, but I didn't care. As far as I was concerned, the price of doing it any way but my way was a whole lot higher. It just wouldn't be real. When it came to disco, I agreed with author and music critic Nelson George who said, "It was music with a metronome-like beat — perfect for folks with no sense of rhythm."

I stuck to my guns and pulled through it somehow. With the exception of the "star/rats" period, I have always been blessed to be able to get concert work even when I don't have a hit record. That held true even during disco fever. While Donna Summer, Gloria Gaynor, and Grace Jones became the diva darlings of disco, I went to England where I did some test runs of my new show before unveiling it in the U.S. One of my most memorable engagements was the week I spent with Jerry Butler at Broadway's Winter Garden Theater in 1980. I was happy to be reunited with "The Iceman," who I hadn't shared the stage with since The Bluebelles used to open his show and then sing backup for him.

This wound up being a busy period for me. I hadn't seen much of my sisters while I was out on the road and one day when I was home, I decided to visit them at the house on Washington Avenue. When Barbara came down the stairs, it was clear something was wrong with her. And it wasn't the flu as she had tried to make believe before. She was so thin and so frail, she looked like one of those starving children you see on the TV commercial fund-raisers. I was shocked. I was stunned. But most of all, I was scared.

"Tell me the truth," I demanded. "What's really wrong with you?"

That's when she told me. She had colon cancer. She thought she was going to be all right and hadn't wanted me to worry. She had sworn everyone to secrecy — no one was supposed to tell me. She knew how hard I had taken the deaths of Vivian and Chubby. I couldn't believe what I was hearing. What was happening to my family? Was this some kind of curse? Was Barbara really going to be okay, or was she lying to me again to spare my feelings?

"Just let me know what you need," I said. "Anything you want, I'll do it."

That's when she told me the one and only thing she wanted. A wedding. For years, she had been deeply in love with Donald Puriefoy, or "Shot" as everybody calls him. Like Armstead and me, they had practically grown up together. But their

302

lives had taken them in different directions and they were only now reconnecting. Shot knew Barbara had cancer, but he proposed to her anyway. Of course I would host her wedding, I told her. And she could have whatever she wanted. Ever since Barbara was a little girl, this had been her one big dream: to marry the man she loved in a fairy-tale wedding. And I was going to do whatever I could to make that dream come true.

It was a gorgeous day in September 1980 when we held the wedding ceremony at Chubby's house. It was a small and intimate affair with only a few close friends and family in attendance. But I went all out for the reception. The best food, the best champagne, the best spot in downtown Philly. We had a band, we had balloons, we had a blast. But best of all we had a beaming, beautiful bride. The Lord smiled on my sister on this day, the day she had always dreamed of, the day she wore her long white lace wedding gown. As I watched her dancing with Shot, I couldn't hold back my tears. They were tears of joy and sorrow. I marveled at the faith she and Shot must have had promising to share a new life together when life was the one thing Barbara was not promised. But my sister knew something then that it would take me many more years to understand: We must live in the moment. It is all we really have. The past is gone and the future may never come. If we spend all our time dwelling on yesterday or worrying about tomorrow, we lose all the joy and sweetness of today. We block all the blessings.

The following year, when my contract with Epic ran out, I signed with Philadelphia International Records. The label was owned and run by my old friend, singer-lyricist Kenny Gamble, and his partner, pianist-arranger Leon Huff, who I hadn't worked with since we recorded the Laura Nyro album. I don't know who was more excited, Kenny or me. For one thing, we were old friends going back to the days when we used to drink beer together in the alley behind my house. For another, Kenny said he was sure he could get a number-one hit with me and he was so talented, I believed him. He did it, but it didn't happen right away. The first album I recorded with him, "The Spirit's In It," didn't even crack the Top 100. Still, it brought me some magical moments. When I was previewing it at a four-night engagement at the Savoy in New York, both Nona and Sarah paid surprise visits to the show on separate nights. This wasn't the first time we had reconnected after the breakup of Labelle. I had called Nona on her birthday about nine months after the split. I talked with Sarah shortly after that. We also ran into each other at an Aretha Franklin concert at Carnegie Hall in May 1978. But there was something even more special about their coming to see me at the Savoy. When Sarah came on closing night, the audience was thrilled when she joined me onstage to sing "You Are My Friend." I was thrilled, too. It was already such a special song for me. But it took on even more meaning that night. Whatever our differences had been, I hoped Sarah could feel that I meant every word that wonderful night. I think she did. Years later, she asked me to duet with her on the cut "You're All I Need to Get By" on her solo album for EMI.

Since my solo albums were not selling big, Armstead had been talking to me for months about broadening my appeal. Slowly but surely, he had been taking over the management of my career and when Barry and Fran Weissler, the producers of the gospel musical *Your Arms Too Short to Box with God*, contacted me about starring in the show for a 1981-82 run, Armstead had very simple advice:

"Go for it."

My response was even more simple than that: "No way." And I meant it.

I didn't want to do the musical for a lot of reasons. I'm too spontaneous to stick to a script, and I knew I'd be throwing everybody else off their mark and their lines. And what about those costumes? They didn't have any Cinderella pumps in the Bible, and that's what the play was all about — the Gospel according to St. Matthew. And last, but not least, this was the third time around for this musical. I saw it the first time it ran in New York in the mid-seventies when Delores Hall played the lead. And just the year before, it was on Broadway starring Jennifer Holliday before she was a Dreamgirl. Why in the world were people going to come see the same play they had just seen with Delores and Jennifer? When Vinnette Carroll, the show's creator and director, offered to revamp the leading role for me, Armstead told me this was the perfect vehicle to expand my audience. I already had a number of loyal fans among the R&B and club set. A gospel musical would attract a whole new audience, people who had never heard of Patti LaBelle.

To make a long story short, Armstead talked me into it. While it was a great show, I had problems right from the start. When Vinnette revamped my role, she gave me about a dozen songs to sing. I tried it, but it was too much even for me. After our opening in Washington, D.C., in November of 1981, I strained my vocal cords and we had to cancel the L.A. shows. Even after Vinnette cut my numbers in half, I drove the stage manager crazy. Certain songs were supposed to run for a certain length but when the Holy Spirit filled me, they went on for a whole lot longer. The stage manager would be standing in the wings waving his arms and mouthing the words "Get off, get off." As I told him many times, I *was* getting off and so was the audience, which is why I couldn't stop singing. I hadn't felt this good onstage since I was singing in the Beulah Baptist Young Adults Choir with Armstead and Barbara. I could tell the music was touching people the way it was touching me, and there was a message in the lyrics that had so much meaning to me at this point in my life. It was a message of faith and forgiveness, despair and deliverance, renewal and redemption. It was a message that I thought about at the close of every show. And I knew what I had always heard was true: God gave us music so we might pray without words.

Chapter Thirty-six

After nine months touring the country, *Your Arms Too Short* made history on September 2, 1982, when this incarnation made its Broadway debut at the Alvin Theater. It was the third Broadway opening for the show since 1976. No other musical had opened on the Great White Way so many times in such a short period. The born-again, award-winning singing star, Al Green, ordained pastor of the Full Gospel Tabernacle of Memphis, joined the cast for what was supposed to be a four-week run. We wound up being extended three times to a total of ten weeks due to rave reviews and popular demand. Opening night was a star-studded affair. In the house were Cicely Tyson and her husband Miles Davis, Nick Ashford and Valerie Simpson, Patti Austin, Mary Wilson, Stephanie Mills, Millie Jackson, Rev. Ike — and Sarah Dash and Nona Hendryx. After the show, a motorcade of limos headed for the post-performance party at the Palace.

It was when the reviews came out that I really felt like celebrating. Most critics loved the show and some, like Joel Siegel of ABC-TV, were especially kind to me. "As for Patti LaBelle, it's hold your breath, chills up your spine time," he said. "She does things with notes that the notes didn't even know they could do." Another critic wrote, "When Patti lets loose, a chill tears down your spine and even your sinuses clear up."

It was during the show's Broadway run that Nona and I got together again. After she came to see me on opening night, I went to see her at the Ritz where she was performing. I ended up doing more than watching the show. I performed in it. After Nona asked me to come onstage and sing with her, we did two numbers, "What Can I Do For You?" and "Do What You Wanna Do." After our duets, I stayed to sing backup for the rest of the show. I can't tell you how good it felt singing with Nona again. It was such a spiritual experience for me, I would have sung Mickey Mouse — M-I-C-K-E-Y M-O-U-S-E — if she had asked me to. After all the years and all the tears, I realized something that night. I still loved Nona like a sister. Once again, we were in harmony. Once again, we had our groove back. That same year I sang background on Nona's self-titled RCA album on the tune "Design for Living."

While things couldn't have been any better for the show, they couldn't have been much worse for Barbara. By this time, it was clear just how sick she was. The cancer had spread and, like Vivian, Barbara was in so much pain, some days even the morphine didn't help. The only thing that seemed to soothe her was a phone call from me. Long distance. Every day. Barbara told me how much she loved one of the songs I sang in the second act, "I Love You So Much, Jesus." Each time we got to that number, a production assistant placed a call to Barbara so that she could hear me sing to her. Some days, my teenage niece, Stayce, would answer the phone and hold the receiver when Barbara was too weak to manage it. Stayce is Jackie's second child, born three years after Billy, and she loved her Aunt Barbara like a second mother. While I was working on this book, Stayce reminded me how much those calls meant to Barbara. I couldn't believe how bad things had gotten. Just that summer, Barbara had felt well enough to attend the annual reunion of all our childhood friends and neighbors from Elmwood. Had I known what would happen there, I never would have gone. Not many people knew how sick Barbara was. In fact, there were so many new faces, not many people knew who Barbara was. But, all the teenagers in the neighborhood knew me. And they kept flocking to our table, leaning over and bumping into Barbara and Shot, to get my autograph. When I saw how uncomfortable this was making Barbara, I asked my friend George Peters to try keep the autograph seekers away. While he and Shot did their best, some people managed to duck them and make it to the table anyway.

"Please, Miss LaBelle. Would you just sign this napkin?"

How could I say no? Looking back, I see what I should have done was just leave and let my sister enjoy what would turn out to be the last reunion she would ever attend. To this day, I wonder if I ruined it for her.

I was on Broadway when Barbara had to be hospitalized. When I talked to Armstead, I could tell by what he *didn't* say that she was fading. I knew I had to go home right away. I called a meeting of the cast and staff in the basement of the theater to tell them I was going to miss the Sunday matinee because I had to go and see about my sister. Everyone understood. Everyone except the one person I expected to be the most understanding: the Reverend Al Green. He was annoyed because he would have to sing some of my numbers and, if he had to sing my numbers, he wanted top billing — his name in front of mine on the marquee. I didn't give a damn about whose name came first. All I cared about was getting home to Barbara. And that's what I told Al. They could put his *picture* up in lights for all I cared. But that didn't satisfy him. He wouldn't let it go. As I sat there sipping my glass of Courvoisier, he demanded to know what was so critical about my sister that I had to go home when we had a show to do and leave him to carry the burden.

"She is very sick," I told him.

"Well, we can't help it if your sister is sick. The show must go on."

I couldn't believe my ears. My sister was lying in a hospital bed fighting for her life and this ordained minister, a man who had pledged his life to God, only seemed to care about how many new songs he had to sing for a single matinee. I stepped aside and let Priscilla deal with the good minister. Within seconds, I had broken my glass of Courvoisier and I was moving on Al with blood in my eye and a jagged edge in my hand. As I was going for the jugular, I heard Chubby's words coming out of my mouth.

"I will cut your throat," I said.

That's when I felt Norma Harris, my friend and hairdresser, pulling me back. She was screaming frantically.

"No, Pat, no. You need to get home to Barbara."

Hearing my sister's name is the only thing that brought me back to my senses. I made it to Philly to Barbara's side and I made it back to New York for the evening show. Al earned a Tony nomination for his work in *Your Arms Too Short* and, whatever our differences, I still felt good for him because he gave that show his all. But the only way I could ever make sense of what happened between us in the basement of the Alvin Theater was to realize that, if you aren't very careful, if you don't keep all the acclaim and recognition in perspective, anyone — even a man of the cloth — can go to Hollywood.

Not long after that Sunday, my niece, Stayce, came to my room at the Essex House in New York. I was putting on my makeup and I could see Stayce's reflection in the mirror. She had this pained look on her face, and I knew it wasn't good.

"Turn around, Aunt Patsy. I have something to tell you."

Her next words left me numb.

"Aunt Barbara died."

I wasn't ready to hear that. All I could do was sit there and cry. At the age of forty, Barbara had left this world. And just like Vivian, she left it without hearing from me how much I loved her. Worse, I never even told her how sorry I was for the way I had mistreated her over the years — for not spending enough time with her and wasting what precious time we did have fussing and fighting over the stupidest things. Like the day I embarrassed her at the Carmen Skating Rink for singing off-key, and the day I took my frustrations out on her at Chubby's house, the day I gave her a black eye over something so petty I can't even remember what it was. On October 21, 1982, I buried my second sister. In her wedding dress. The day she married Shot had been Barbara's happiest, and that's how Jackie and I wanted everyone to remember her.

Chapter Thirty-seven

I didn't say a word to anyone but, after Barbara's funeral, I was scared to death. More accurately, I was scared of death. It had struck my immediate family three times in seven years. Now, there seemed to be a pattern. Every three or four years, I was putting somebody else I loved in the ground. More frighteningly, my two sisters had died of cancer in their early forties, in the prime of their lives. Now, at thirty-eight, I was the next in line. I don't know if Jackie, my youngest sister, the baby, was scared, too. I never asked her. I never talked to her about anything personal, important, intimate. Not love and sex, not life and death. After Barbara died, it seemed we didn't talk much at all. All we did was argue. Mostly over Armstead. There was a lot of tension between the two of them. It started shortly after I got married. I think Jackie was scared Armstead was going to take me away from our family, especially from her. Armstead has one of those close-knit families like the Waltons on TV, and I'm sure Jackie thought once I was married I would become part of *his* family and she would lose me forever. I tried to reassure her that that wouldn't happen, and I reminded her of the old saying about what happens when a couple gets married: "A son is a son until he takes a wife, but a daughter is a daughter for the rest of her life."

"The same thing goes for a sister," I told her.

But that wasn't enough to quiet Jackie's fears, especially when I packed my bags to move out of Chubby's house and in with Armstead after we married. She was scared he would come between us and take priority. Because of that, they never really did get along. And once Armstead left his teaching job in 1983 to manage my career full-time, things got worse between them. Jackie had worked for a while in the promotion offices of a number of record companies, and she felt she knew more about the music business in general and my career in particular than Armstead. He wasn't exposing me to the right people or opportunities, she insisted. Jackie thought my talent was so awesome that had Armstead been managing me right, I would be bigger than Barbra Streisand. There was always some kind of tug-of-war between them, and I was in the middle. I finally knew how Sarah had felt between Nona and me. Awful. And awfully tired. It's hard being a buffer and a peacemaker. It will wear you out. Even though Jackie was wrong about Armstead, I wasn't angry with her because I understood her motivations: deep love and deep fear. Of all Chubby's daughters, we were the closest in age — just one year apart — and now that Vivian and Barbara were gone, I was the only sister she had left.

Two months after we buried Barbara, I was a mess. Emotionally raw and physically exhausted. As much as I loved doing *Your Arms Too Short*, it was draining doing daily shows and two on

315

Sunday. I was desperately in need of a lift. Only time would dull the pain of losing my sister, but I had to do something to raise my spirits, *anything* to distract myself from the sadness. One evening, Stephanie Mills, the award-winning singer who starred as Dorothy in the Broadway production of *The Wiz*, came to visit me in Philly. From the moment Stephanie walked through the door, I couldn't stop staring at her. She looked so radiant, so rested, so refined. I started firing questions at her.

"Girl, who is doing your hair? Are you wearing new makeup? Do you have a new stylist? Give me the name of whatever spa you've been going to."

That's when Stephanie gave me the 4-1-1 on her new look. It wasn't the hair, the makeup, or the clothes. It was her nose. She'd had it done. The way she described the procedure didn't sound like a cakewalk, but it didn't sound like something I couldn't handle, either. Besides, I figured if I could handle nine hours of labor, I could handle a one-hour nose job. Since I was a little girl, I had always hated my nose and now I saw a way to do something about it. When Armstead got home, I asked him to find a plastic surgeon who was not only skillful enough but sensitive enough to give me what I wanted: a more attractive nose that fit *my* face, not a white-girl nose that looked like it should be on *Barbie's* face. He found a surgeon in Philly and for Christmas, I treated myself to a brand-new me. While no one tried to talk me out of having the operation, they told me I should check into the hospital under an assumed name. I said, "Why? I'm not trying to hide anything." I registered as Patti La-Belle. I was awake during the surgery and, while I didn't have a lot of pain, I did get the chills when I heard the doctor break my nose. Of course, I never lost my sense of humor about the whole thing. As we left the hospital, I told Armstead people were going to look at my bruised face and swear he had beat me up.

My new nose healed in the New Year exactly as I had hoped. I was thrilled with the way it looked, but there would be even bigger thrills for me in the coming years. My first Grammy nomination, for starters. It would come for Best R&B Vocal Performance/Female for "The Best Is Yet to Come," the single I cut with sax man extraordinaire, Grover Washington, Jr. Boyfriend plays every kind of sax on the planet — alto, soprano, tenor, and baritone — as well as clarinet, bass, and piano. And while he had already snagged a few Grammys, this was my first nomination, and it was a big deal to me. I dreamed of that baby sitting on my mantel. Unfortunately, that's where the Grammy stayed — in my dreams. It never made it to my house. Chaka Khan would take it home when the winners were finally announced. And she deserved it, too. It's true what they say: It really is an honor just to be nominated. But, Patti won't lie to you. It's no fun losing.

What *was* fun was the steady rise in my popularity. Under Armstead's management, every-

317

thing seemed to be falling in place for my career. He had told me I would broaden my audience by joining the cast of *Your Arms Too Short*, but I don't think either of us expected all the rewards that would come. Needless to say, I was more than happy to finish the last leg of the musical's national tour after we left Broadway. We wrapped it at Baltimore's Lyric Theater two days before my birthday. I had spent almost two years with this talented cast and crew, and it wasn't easy to say good-bye. The only thing that made it bearable was all the wonderful memories I was taking with me. None was sweeter than the night we performed in New Orleans and Daddy came to hear me sing. Later, I took him on a try-and-buy, point-and-purchase Bourbon Street shopping spree. We had a wonderful time. Just Daddy and I.

The day the tour ended, the cast and crew threw me a surprise birthday party. I was turning thirty-nine, and while I tried my best to enjoy the festivities, something in the back of my mind kept pushing forward — a thought I had to keep pushing back. The thought of dying young. The next year, when I would hit forty, I'd enter the decade neither of my older sisters made it through. I couldn't help but wonder if I would be able to accomplish what they hadn't: living to see fifty. With all that I had achieved, all that I knew I could look forward to, that one goal filled me with so much doubt. It would become my obsession.

Chapter Thirty-eight

After my birthday, I found myself wanting to do something different to take my mind off of my fears. Fortunately, I didn't have to look long or far. The answer came to me in the form of one of those "coincidences" I believe are really Divine Guidance. It happened at the Walnut Theater on July 26, 1983, the night Armstead and I went to the Philadelphia opening of Charles Fuller's Pulitzer Prize–winning drama, *A Soldier's Play.* Charles is a friend from Philly and, after the show, he introduced us to Norman Jewison, who was about to direct a film version of the play called *A Soldier's Story.*

"That play is so moving," I told Norman, "I would love to be in your movie."

"Sorry, Patti. There aren't any roles for women," he explained.

"Honey, to be in this movie, I'd play a soldier in drag," I told him.

Charles and Norman cracked up. And then Norman said something I could hardly believe. "Patti, I love you so much, I'm going to write a part in this movie just for you."

And he did. In my first major film role, I played a singer/saloon owner named Big Mary. And since Norman had created that character just for me, I wrote a song, "Pourin' Whiskey Blues," just for her. The film, about the murder of a black Army sergeant in charge of an all-black platoon in the Deep South during World War II, starred some real heavy-hitting actors — Denzel Washington, Howard Rollins, and Adolph Caesar, to name a few. Just being in that kind of company made me a nervous wreck. What in the world had made me think I could hang with this kind of acting talent? My only other nontheatrical acting experience had been a couple of years earlier when I played a domestic named Maggie Holmes in the PBS television production of "Working," a musical based on the book by Studs Terkel and my more recent performance in the PBS production of Duke Ellington's "Queenie Pie," which had aired in the spring of 1983.

We shot *A Soldier's Story* on location in Fort Chaffe, Arkansas, and Norman's patience and guidance got me through the shoot. He helped me enormously with my technique. When the film was released the following year, the critics were full of praise for my work. One California newspaper even said I might "nab an Oscar nomination for Best Original Song," while Rex Reed wrote, "The feisty and iron-lunged singer makes a juicy debut as an entertainer who dispenses soul food and soul songs to the black recruits on the steamy side of town." Kind reviews like those made it a lot easier when I didn't get the parts I auditioned for in two big movies. In *The Color Purple* I lost out to Margaret Avery, and in *Ghost* I lost out to Whoopi Goldberg. To this day, I tease Whoopi that she owes me a part — a big part — in one of her movies.

In the fall of 1983, Armstead and I launched our first business venture — LaBelle Amie, a clothing boutique in Philadelphia. I had been thinking about starting some kind of business since the seventies. Once, Laura Nyro and I talked about opening a restaurant together. But we knew, as much as we loved food, we wouldn't have anything left to serve to the customers. Unfortunately, I wound up "eating up" all the profits from LaBelle Amie, snatching up all that beautiful drag before my customers could ever get a chance to buy it. Now you know why I didn't stay in the retail business very long.

Looking back, I can see that 1984 was the year my career really started gaining momentum. In January, I got my first number-one record as a solo artist. "If Only You Knew" hit the top of the R&B charts, where it held the number-one spot for several weeks. The morning I found out, I was so excited I remember running through the house to the guest room to wake up my friend Rudy Calvo, who was visiting from California for the holidays.

"Get up, get up!" I screamed, jumping up and down on the bed. "I'm number one!"

What few people know is that song's parent album, "I'm in Love Again," had been sitting in the can for almost two years before Kenny Gamble felt the time was right to release it. Kenny had always told me he could get a number-one record with me, and Boyfriend proved his point. I owe Kenny a big thank you for releasing me from my contract with Philadelphia International so I could pursue offers from larger labels. It was another "lucky coincidence" that I would be looking for a new record deal on the heels of that number-one single and a Top 10 duet. I had recorded the song "Love Has Finally Come at Last" with Bobby Womack for his album "The Poet II," and it went to the number-three spot on the R&B charts. With that kind of juice, one of the biggest and most respected record labels in the business, MCA, said they wanted me to join the label. The deal was struck and, in November of 1984, I signed with them and I have been there ever since.

The year had started off with another special event. In January, I went to Washington, D.C., to perform in an all-star tribute to Dr. Martin Luther King, Jr., on the occasion of the first federal holiday in his honor. I was moved by the program and its significance and I wanted Mrs. King to know how much her husband's life's work meant to me. We taped at the Kennedy Center for the Performing Arts and I sang "Over the Rainbow" with such passion and intensity I even surprised myself! When I received a rousing standing ovation, I remember telling Rudy that it felt like I had carried *myself* over the rainbow. (Luckily, I didn't burst a blood vessel that gives me a nosebleed as I do sometimes when I hit a certain note in that song.)

"Over the Rainbow" represented so much to me — the power of dreams and the magic of faith. It was a song and a message and a feeling that would give my career wings. I decided to name my upcoming fifty-six-city national tour in its honor. On May 2, 1984, I kicked off the Look to the Rainbow tour in Los Angeles at the Beverly Theater. It was my first concert tour in three years, and opening night was truly a *supreme* experience. When I looked out through the spotlights to see the crowd, I focused on two familiar faces. Two-thirds of The Supremes — Mary Wilson and my old friend Cindy Birdsong. I hadn't seen Cindy in at least a decade and when I spotted her sitting there smiling, it really choked me up. To see her applauding me after all the mean and nasty things I had said about her touched me so deeply. After all those years, I realized I still loved her. At that moment, I wanted Cindy, and everybody in the audience, to know it, too. I asked Mary and Cindy to join me onstage and as I saw Cindy approaching, I couldn't wait. I came down off the stage and we met halfway — at the staircase leading up to the stage. The three of us sang, "You Are My Friend," which was becoming my very special song of reunion.

Within two weeks of my L.A. opening of Look to the Rainbow, I performed on the *Tonight* show thanks to another long-time friend, Roberta Flack. When she wasn't able to make her scheduled appearance, she talked Johnny Carson's producers into letting me go on in her place. They were skeptical, but Roberta assured them they wouldn't be sorry. They weren't. As a matter of fact, after I sang "Over the Rainbow," Johnny Carson did something he had never done in the history of the show. He invited me back to sing the *same* week.

At the end of May, I had a badly needed week off and, while I was back East, Armstead threw me a surprise birthday party at the hot New York club the Red Parrot. So many special people came out to help me celebrate turning forty — Bette Midler, Ashford and Simpson, Teddy Pendergrass, and so many others. But my two older sisters weren't there and, in the back of my mind, I saw no reason why I should be spared, either. We all shared the same genes. We all had had the same things to live for. Throughout the night, I couldn't help wondering when it would come for me. This year, my fortieth, when it came for Barbara? Or would I get the three extra years given to Vivian? Either way, the countdown had begun.

Though I couldn't know it that night, in the coming months, death would continue to haunt me. Not just because of my fear of it, but because my best friend, Claudette, had begun to suffer again. Despite the mastectomy, the cancer spread and the chemotherapy was making her violently sick. To ease the pain, the doctors suggested that Claudette smoke marijuana, but she refused. Claudette hated the feeling of being high more than she hated the pain. Many days, she dug deep into her soul for the strength to cope with her suffering. I dealt with mine the way I always have.

Music. During the summer months, I was performing in a different city almost every night and I let everything I was feeling — all the fear, all the anger, all the pain, all the rage — I let all of that out onstage.

As we headed into fall, the Look to the Rainbow tour headed to Broadway. When I opened at the Gershwin on September eleventh, the nearly 1,200-seat theater was filled to capacity. Sarah and Nona came to see the show. They had a very special reason. Through the magic of technology, they were in it. Before I took the tour on the road, Vicki, Sarah, and Nona helped Armstead and me create a special-effects segment that never failed to drive the audiences wild. As we had done in Labelle, Sarah, Nona, and I performed "Can I Speak to You Before You Go to Hollywood?" only now, Sarah and Nona were singing onscreen instead of onstage. Labelle was back on Broadway! Opening night was a smashing success.

The next day I got the call from my sister, Jackie. Claudette was in the hospital and she had taken a turn for the worse. I should come right away. Armstead and I left immediately to make the ninety-minute drive from New York to Philly. When we got to the hospital, the closest people from the old days, from the old neighborhood, had gathered to say good-bye. Claudette's husband, Grant, broke the news. I was a little too late. She had died just fifteen minutes before we arrived. My heart shattered in a thousand tiny pieces, but I told Grant I still wanted to see her. He understood and he escorted me into her room so that I could be with my friend one last time. Four days later, two months before her thirty-ninth birthday, Claudette was laid to rest. The funeral was on a Sunday and, after paying my respects and leaving Armstead at the service, I was an hour late for my matinee performance. I tried to do the show, but my heart just wasn't in it. All I could think about was Claudette: how close we had been and how I would never see her smiling face again. Throughout the performance, I apologized, I wept, I shouted, I shrieked. When it was over, I offered everyone their money back.

"I couldn't give you one hundred percent today," I told the audience. "I can't go back to my dressing room today and say I gave you my all." I didn't know how many people asked for their money back and I didn't care.

The following week, when I performed back home in Philly at the Shubert, Grant brought his eleven-year-old daughter, Kelly, and I dedicated the entire show to her mother. I hoped Claudette could hear me when I sang "The Wind Beneath My Wings" to her and see her little girl when I brought Kelly onstage to dance with me. Afterwards, I brought a gospel choir onstage to sing "You Are My Friend" with me, and together we segued into the old gospel tune "What a Friend We Have in Jesus." I wanted Kelly to know that, as much as we all would miss her mother, Claudette was in a better place.

Even though Claudette and I weren't blood sisters, we were sisters in every other way — in mind, heart, and spirit. After I lost her to cancer like Vivian and Barbara, what had been a growing fear in me became an unshakable certainty. The cancerous chain of death was continuing unbroken. My immediate family, my extended family, everyone close to me was being attacked.

I was living on borrowed time.

Chapter Thirty-nine

In the months following Claudette's death, music was the only thing that kept me from going mad. For me, that mystical, spiritual connection between audience and performer, the way my voice could uplift people I knew were suffering as I was, held the key to my sanity. In October, I left Philadelphia and took the Look to the Rainbow tour to thirteen more cities before beginning the New Year back on Broadway in a second sold-out run at the Gershwin Theater. Just four months earlier, I had stood on the very same stage and offered everyone their money back when I thought I hadn't given my all. I'm grateful my fans thought otherwise. When this return engagement was announced, I learned lines were formed outside the box office before tickets went on sale.

In between live performances, I went in the studio and recorded two singles, "New Attitude" and "Stir It Up," for the sound track to the blockbuster Eddie Murphy movie *Beverly Hills Cop*. Both would become big hits for me with "New Attitude" making the Top 20 and earning me a second Grammy nomination. If this sounds like a crazy, frantic, mile-a-minute pace, it was. But, I wanted to keep busy. I *needed* to. It was the only thing that took my mind off death. To protect and preserve my voice from all the strain I was putting on it, I have a two-step routine that has always worked for me. After most performances, I stand in a hot shower for almost an hour, then drink a special brew — tea, honey, and spirit of peppermint — or, when I really need to open up my throat, warm water and cayenne pepper.

Fortunately, this combination continued to work its magic. It was during this period that I gave what many people thought was the performance of my career. I was one of more than sixty performers on The NBC TV special "Motown Returns to the Apollo." The show, which was taped live on May 4, 1985, before a black-tie audience, was celebrating the reopening of the newly renovated theater. The stars were out in force that night. The lineup included some of the biggest and the best: Stevie Wonder, Smokey Robinson, The Temptations, Sammy Davis, Jr., Gregory Hines, The Four Tops, Little Richard, Wilson Pickett, Sarah Vaughan, Mavis Staples, Rod Stewart, Boy George, Joe Cocker, George Michael, Billy Eckstine, Billy Preston, and Diana Ross. With that kind of talent in the house, you can see why I was so surprised, stunned really, that I received so many of the standing ovations the audience gave that night. I performed several numbers, including a gospel medley with Mavis Staples, Little Richard, Al Green, and the New Jersey Mass Choir and a duet, "You Are So Beautiful," with Joe Cocker. But the moment that stands out in my memory is when I sang the song that had meant so much to me from the first time I ever sang it for an audience at the Bartram High talent show: a song that had given so much encouragement to me each and every time I sang it and to thousands of others who heard me sing it over the years. When I saw Coretta Scott King in the audience, something came over me. Who more than this woman knew the pain of losing someone you love with all your heart? Someone so young and wonderful and brave? Someone gone too soon. Though it can't be seen in the edited version of the show broadcast a few months later, I pointed right to her. I wanted Mrs. King and everyone in the audience to know I was singing to her. What only I knew was that I was singing to Vivian and Chubby and Barbara and Claudette as well. "You'll Never Walk Alone."

Unfortunately, that wasn't the moment that everyone was buzzing about after the taping. It was the finale that got everybody talking. There were some people who said I stole the show from Diana Ross. Literally. Intentionally. Backed by the New Jersey Mass Choir, Diana had just finished singing the first verse of Foreigner's hit, "I Want to Know What Love Is," when she started inviting others to sing with her.

"Somebody help me," she said.

She didn't have to ask twice. I helped her. When I sang the first line, the audience went wild and gave me a roaring standing ovation. I didn't notice it, but the press reports later said Diana looked as if I had slapped her. "Ross looked as though she'd have given anything to take the moment, and that microphone, back," wrote the

Philadelphia Inquirer. It hurt me deeply when I heard people thought that I was trying to steal Diana's thunder. Nothing could be further from the truth. The truth is it had been such an emotional night for me that everything had been building to that stirring curtain call. I was being propelled by the magical musical moment.

Two months later, after I performed in Philadelphia at the "Live Aid" extravaganza, I heard the same criticism about my performance. This time people even went so far as to say that during the finale, "We Are the World," I had the only live mike on the stage. Not so. If I was louder than everyone else, I was just being Patti. I was singing my heart out. Like the song I sang to Mrs. King at the Motown special, this was another inspired song at the end of another emotional night. What's more, the promoters had gone all out to make sure I could be there. That very day, they sent a private jet to Reno where I was performing to fly me to Philly's Veteran Stadium for the show that would be broadcast live around the world. The least I could do was go all out for them. And I still hadn't come down from my experience earlier in the evening. When I sang John Lennon's "Imagine," I felt so much love from the audience. It was the same way I felt that day I performed on Aunt Hattie Mae's porch. It was that same life-giving, love-getting, spirit-lifting cycle. One writer said my voice "was like a hand that hovered over the stadium, comforting the masses." It sure felt like the audience was comforting me. When I left the stage I was shaking. I don't remember it, but people tell me my performance was so moving that, when I passed the many stars and crew on the way back to my trailer, no one said a word. They just stared as if seeing me for the first time. Just like the Young Adults Choir the day I sang "God Specializes."

Those experiences have left me wary of doing group finales. For a while, I even asked Armstead to make sure I didn't have to perform in them. Some people have tried to prevent my no-holds-barred performances before they're even scheduled. For instance, the same year I did "Live Aid," I was invited to perform in Washington, D.C., at "The Kraft All-Star Salute to Ford's Theater." It was suggested, however, that I tone down everything — my hair, my costumes, even my voice. At first I was hurt. But then I got mad. I said why? Why should I give less? If I can't come as me, then I shouldn't be invited. If I'm too outrageous for the pinstripe Powertown crowd, just tell me and I'll stay home. I accept people the way they are and I think everyone else should do the same. I sang three songs at Ford's Theater, and I'm happy to say the audience didn't think I was too much at all. I can't swear to it, but I think I even saw President Ronald Reagan tapping his foot.

It was one thing for strangers to ask me to change myself, but when the request came from a sister-friend, it was a real blow. When it happened in April of 1986, I couldn't believe what I was hearing. I was taping the HBO special that won a Cable Ace Award, "Sisters in the Name of Love," at the Aquarius Theater in Hollywood. I was thrilled to be starring in the show with two women I had played the chitlin' circuit with, and love dearly — Gladys Knight and Dionne Warwick. After the first time we ran through the show, Dionne called me into a side room.

"Patti," she said, "we're going to do it one more time. Do you think you can tone it down some this time around?"

You could have knocked me over with a feather. Here I was singing my heart out to make this show a smashing success. It was not only because I was singing with two sisters in the name of love, but because this was Gladys's debut as an executive producer. As hurtful as it was to listen to Dionne's request, I didn't feel that I had any choice. Dionne was a friend and I was crushed. I said "no problem," and then I excused myself and went into an empty room and cried like a baby. Later, it happened again when Dionne and I were together rehearsing a song for another special. This time Dionne didn't call me aside for a private conversation. Many of the band members looked as shocked as I was when she told me the way I was singing was interfering with her part. Why did Dionne want to go there? For the second time. And this time in front of people. This time Patti didn't run into a room and cry. This time Priscilla would run interference. "I've had it," I screamed. "Don't tell me another time what I can and cannot sing. I'm only trying to do my best and if my best is too much for you, that is not my problem."

I felt good that I had spoken up for myself but I felt bad that Dionne and I had argued in front of other people. We've put the whole incident behind us and, as far as I'm concerned, it hasn't affected our friendship. In fact, not only did the three of us get together to record the single "Superwoman," for Gladys's "Good Woman" album, we even went on *Oprah* together to perform it. That song snagged Grammy nominations for all three of us.

There was one television production on which I didn't have to worry about anybody closing the curtain on me or asking me to be anything other than who I am. Although I would earn an Emmy nomination for my performance on the Motown special, that wasn't the biggest surprise to come my way as a result of that show. Two days after the taping, Hollywood producer Marty Krofft was in Philly taking Armstead and me out for lobster dinner at Bookbinders and offering me my own prime-time television special. NBC Top Gun Brandon Tartikoff had seen my performance that night, and he quickly gave the project the green light.

I couldn't wait to get started. I wanted this show to be truly *special* and so I went all out. I asked four fabulous artists to guest-star and, to my delight, they all said yes. Bill Cosby, Luther Vandross, Amy Grant, and Cyndi Lauper were all there, although Cos' came on through a taped hookup in a beauty shop in Las Vegas. I wore a twelve-thousand-dollar gown that took twelve people two weeks to make. (It took only two *minutes* to tape my boobs down with gaffer's tape to make sure nothing that wasn't supposed to popped out of that gown.) Norma gave me a serious *Star Wars*/Art Deco hairstyle — half moon crescents studded with glittering rhinestones that Norma created by spraying pieces of hair with tons of hair spray and then putting them in the freezer overnight.

We started taping on a Tuesday and, even though we shot for ten to twelve hours a day, we didn't finish until close to midnight on Friday. By that time, I was so emotional I just stood in my dressing room and cried. In between tears, I was asking everyone how the last night of taping had gone, if I had done okay. Armstead just walked up to me, wiped the tears from my face, and handed me a beautiful velvet box. Inside was the most gorgeous antique diamond necklace I have ever seen.

"I think," he said quietly, "you are awesome."

I had an inkling that we were doing something right when, during *rehearsals,* the stage crew would give us standing ovations. But when Armstead said "awesome," that's when I knew this special was *really* special. The show aired on Thanksgiving Day 1985, just days after I had appeared on Sylvia Fine Kaye's musical for PBS-TV, a performance that would earn me my second Emmy nomination. When the reviews came in for my Thanksgiving Day special, the critics were particularly kind. " 'The Patti LaBelle Show' is the most exciting television pop-music event since 'Motown 25: Yesterday, Today, Forever,' the show that exposed the mass audience to Michael Jackson's moonwalk," wrote one. But the comment that meant the most to me came from the critic who described the way I sang "Over the Rainbow" as "a nervy assertion of will and personality. 'This is me,' LaBelle is saying between the lines. 'If Patti is too strong for you, change the channel.' "

Chapter Forty

In the years after Barbara died, when I started working like a madwoman, I was doing it to hold myself together. But, all that effort and energy had an unexpected benefit. By the end of 1985, it had taken my career to a whole different level. Late in 1984, when I started recording "Winner in You," my first album for MCA Records, I had no idea how successful it would become. Not only would the album go platinum, it would also earn me two more Grammy nominations — one for Best R&B Vocal Performance/Female and one for the number-one pop and R&B single, "On My Own," a duet I did with ex-Doobie Brother, Michael McDonald. I had already recorded the Burt Bacharach/Carole Bayer Sager ballad by myself when we decided it would sound better as a duet. Michael was brought in later to blend his voice with my recording. We even shot the video on separate coasts. We would not meet until we performed the song together on Johnny Carson's *Tonight* show.

There were other memorable events connected to the "Winner" production. Because she is close to Carole, Liz Taylor came to the studio when I was recording her friend's song. It was really good to see her again. She and I first connected back in May of 1983 when she and Richard Burton were starring on Broadway in *Private Lives*. After the opening-night performance, Liz invited Armstead and me to a private dinner. That's when she asked me to serve with her on a committee to salute an upcoming anniversary of the world-famous Alvin Ailey Dance Theater. I was only too happy to lend my support. Not only was Alvin Ailey a gifted artist, but I was honored to know he had been a huge Labelle fan. (I heard that months after Liz and I saw each other again in the recording session, she called a few radio stations and requested "On My Own." I can just imagine what happened when she said "Hi, this is Liz Taylor." Either they played the song that second or laughed as they were hanging up the phone in her ear.)

It was during those recording sessions for "Winner" in L.A. when I had a little mishap that led to a very special performance. I was preparing to head out to Malibu to meet Burt and Carole to record the song "Sleep with Me Tonight." I was rushing around my hotel room because Budd Ellison and our driver were on their way to pick me up for the session and I wasn't even close to being ready. In my haste to get dressed, I stepped on a needle in the carpet. One of my producers, Sami McKinney, was there when it happened and he told me under no circumstances should I put on my heels.

"Patti doesn't go anywhere without her fever pumps," I reminded him.

Ten minutes later, I was wishing I had listened to Sami. Budd and I hadn't even gotten out of

L.A. when my foot started aching and I told our driver to take a little detour — to the emergency room at Cedars Sinai. The X-ray revealed that half the needle was still in my foot. While the doctors were performing emergency surgery, I gave a mini-concert on the operating table. When I hobbled out of there, everyone in the room was still applauding and I was all warmed up for my recording session.

I unveiled the album's title song, "Winner in You," for a nonmedical audience in February when I returned to Broadway for a four-week engagement at the Minskoff Theater. The song's composers, Nick Ashford and Valerie Simpson, were in the audience opening night, and it was an affair to remember. When I invited some people in the audience to come onstage and sing with me, I met Louise. She was wearing one of the baddest gowns I have ever seen — a long, black, slinky number — and when I handed her the mike to sing her line, Miss Thing brought the house down with a voice as silky smooth as Barry White's. And just as deep! That's right. "Louise" was really a man. "Girlfriend," I said, "I'm scared of you." Later in the evening, my backup trio, The Sweeties, accompanied me on an a cappella version of "How Great Thou Art." People tell me the theater became a church that night. That engagement sure was a blessing for me. We broke a thirteen-year house record.

That May, three months after I was breaking records in New York, I was setting off alarms in

Las Vegas. I was performing at Caesars Palace, and Arsenio Hall was opening for me. This was Arsenio's debut in the Circus Maximus Showroom, years before Boyfriend made all his millions, and he was genuinely impressed with the huge, plush suite they had put me in. It *was* grand but, more important to me, it was set up just the way I like. I have been known to switch my hotel room in a heartbeat if the furniture arrangement doesn't feel right to me. For years, I thought I was just being compulsive. Then I found out about feng-shui (pronounced "fung shway"). People who practice this ancient Chinese philosophy believe the way we place our objects and arrange our furniture will create a setting that is either good or bad for the soul. I don't know how or why it works. All I know is that it does. When the room isn't right, *I'm* not right. My balance is off, I don't feel comfortable, and my creative juices don't flow. Not only was the feng-shui right that night in Caesars Palace, that suite had plenty of space for me to spread out my electric pans and groceries. Arsenio looked at me like I was about to commit a felony when I pulled out my hot sauce and garlic powder and onions.

"Patti," he said, "you're not going to cook in here, are you? Not in Caesars Palace."

"You don't think I'm ordering room service, do you?"

It had nothing to do with the food at Caesars Palace. It could have been great, for all I know. I've never had it. But, by 1986, I had been traveling with my electric pans for years. Ever since the day I ordered two twenty-five-dollar eggs at some chi-chi hotel that tasted like wet cardboard, I've packed those pans right alongside my designer gowns. That night at Caesars Palace, I had a craving for some liver and onions and cabbage and I told Arsenio to just kick off his shoes, relax, and dinner would be ready in a few. I was burning that night. Literally. I didn't know I had set off the hotel's fire alarms until a security guard was knocking on my door.

"Miss LaBelle," he said looking at my smoking pans, "you can't cook in here. Not at Caesars Palace. Besides, it's against the fire code."

"I'm sorry, baby," I said. "Can we open a window? I'll fix you a big plate."

Arsenio, the security guard, and I ate good that night.

Arsenio was with me another night I caused a fuss. He had taken me to an AIDS benefit in L.A., and I spotted Madonna at the table across the room.

"Take me over and introduce me to the Material Girl," I told him. That was an introduction Arsenio didn't want to make. All the way over to her table, Arsenio was telling me to keep my cool. He knew what happened the last time I had run into Madonna. Or, I should say when Madonna ran into me. It was at an American Music Awards Show, and she practically knocked me over trying to get to Earth, Wind and Fire star Philip Bailey. When I fell back, she didn't even apologize. She didn't even notice me. Now that I had a number-one hit, she noticed me. Of course, this time I made sure she did. I told her *everyone* deserves to be treated with dignity and respect whether they have a number-one record or not. To Madonna's credit, when I told her what she had done at the American Music Awards, she apologized and I really felt that she meant it.

Arsenio and I had so many adventures together, but two really stand out in my memory. Both involve the threat of death and opening your eyes to a new life. Arsenio would receive a letter that gave me the chills when he told me about it. It was from a woman who had decided to kill herself. For some reason, on the night she was going to do it, she came to see our show. As she wrote in her letter, Arsenio made her laugh at life and the message in my music gave her the courage to live it. When she left our show, she decided she had a reason to go on living. Hearing that woman's story had a lasting effect on me. I think that's when I really started to see that my suffering had meaning for other people. Whatever time I had left, I had to use to spread the message: *Love never dies.*

It takes some people a little longer to get the point, as I discovered after a concert Arsenio and I did together at the Paramount Theater in Oakland. As we were leaving the show and I was signing autographs, my friend Rudy Calvo, who was my makeup artist at the time, headed for the limos outside. When he opened the back door, he was met with a threat.

"Get your hands off my damn car."

Rudy turned around and saw the gun, and that's when he realized he was about to get into the wrong limo. As we pulled off a few minutes later, Rudy told me the story and pointed to the identical white stretch limo trailing ours.

"That's the guy?" I asked.

Rudy nodded.

"Stop this car right here, right now," I told the driver.

Everybody in the car went crazy.

"No, Pat," Norma said. "Let it go," our road manager chimed in. "Mom, no. The guy has a gun," Zuri pleaded.

I told them all to just chill. "I got this covered," I said, as I headed to the gunman's limo.

Arsenio and Budd were a few cars behind us, and the two of them jumped out to see what was going on. Zuri and Norma got out of our limo and followed me. As I approached the "gangster-mobile," the tinted-glass window slowly lowered to reveal one angry, mean-looking brother.

"Did you pull a gun on my friend?" I asked him calmly.

"Yeah," he answered. "He touched my motherfucking car."

"First of all, you should never talk to a lady like that."

That's when his girlfriend recognized me. "That's Patti LaBelle! That's Patti LaBelle!" she started screaming.

343

He backhanded her. "Keep your damn mouth shut, bitch."

Why did he want to do that in front of me? "Don't you ever disrespect a woman like that," I said.

Then I turned to her. "You deserve better than this. If this man can't treat you any better than this, then you need to get to stepping."

"And you," I said, turning back to him. "Don't you ever even *think* about pulling a gun on any of my people ever again."

To my surprise, instead of shooting me to death, Big, Bad Boyfriend shocked me to death. "I'm sorry, Miss LaBelle," he finally muttered. "I was wrong."

Zuri was furious that I had confronted someone with a gun. He had a right to be. It was a dangerous and stupid stunt, and I promised him I would never do something like that again. I could only hope it was worth the risk; that both of those people learned a lesson about respecting themselves and others.

Chapter Forty-one

With my career at an all-time high, my sister Jackie started traveling with me to handle the marketing and sale of all the Patti paraphernalia — the concert programs, the T-shirts, the posters. It was more than needing somebody to deal with the merchandise. After I lost Vivian and Barbara, I wanted to be with Jackie as much as possible. If there was one thing I had learned from losing my two older sisters, it was to take time together whenever you could. Sales were smooth, but our relationship was rocky. Jackie was always giving me career advice on things that didn't have anything to do with merchandising — my hair, my clothes, my songs, even how big my name was on the marquee. You name it, Jackie had something to say about it. She wanted me to be a superstar even more than I wanted it for myself.

"Patsy, with your voice, you should be bigger than Barbra Streisand," she always used to say.

Jackie was determined to do all she could to put me at the top — right where she thought I deserved to be. Unfortunately, we never agreed on anything. If I said "red," Jackie said "blue." If I said "up," Jackie said "down." If I said "yes," Jackie said "hell, no." The tension between us kept building and building. One night things came to a head. I was performing in Atlantic City, and Jackie was having problems with the hotel management about the placement of the merchandise.

"Patsy," she said, as I was getting dressed for the show, "you need to come out here and straighten these people out."

I looked at her like she had lost her mind. "Jackie, don't you see me trying to get myself ready to do a show? I don't have any time to straighten out anybody. I don't even have time to get myself together. And anyway, what would I look like going out into the lobby half dressed to make a fuss about some damned T-shirts. This is your department. You handle it."

Jackie went off. "Oh, so you think you're Miss Patti Hot Shit LaBelle. Too good to deal with the help?"

The next thing I knew, Jackie had ripped my bra off, tied it around my neck, and was trying to strangle me with it. You have to understand, at her heaviest, Jackie was a size six and weighed ninety-five pounds with a roll of quarters in each pocket. But for some reason, my baby sister thought she could fight. She was a fiery, feisty little thing. But I couldn't let her get away with this. Trying to strangle me with my own bra? Oh, no. I started swinging and cussing. I called her all kinds of witches with a capital B. My niece, Stayce, was screaming for us to stop. Norma was trying to pull us apart. And Jackie and I kept right on fighting. Before it was all over, they had to call security to pull us off each other.

I didn't understand what made Jackie act that

way. What made her so angry, so hostile. I didn't know it at the time, but Jackie was sick. Very sick. Once again, I was the last to find out. When Jackie started having problems with her eye, the doctors found a tumor behind it. I don't know how many people she told, but I know she didn't tell me. I learned later that when she told Budd, who was rooming with her at the time, she told him she didn't want me to know. She wanted to keep it from Stayce and Billy, too. Just like Barbara, Jackie was trying to protect me. She knew how upset I got when she was hurting. At another time, when some guy she was dating beat her up, she had Budd keep that from me, too. But when I was on the phone with him one night, he let it slip.

"Come over here right now and get me," I told him.

I knew where the guy lived, and I waited in Budd's car until he came home. Budd wound up having to pull me off the guy, but before he did, I gave him a warning: "Don't you *ever* touch my sister again or you will have to deal with me. And, believe me, you don't want to do that."

So, Jackie had kept the diagnosis from me as long as she could. She told Budd she didn't want it on my mind while I was trying to move my career into high gear. That's how much she loved me and yearned for my success. I found out the truth on Saturday, June 11, 1988. I was being honored for my charitable work at Philly's Franklin Plaza Hotel and it was one of the most emotional evenings of my life. So many people who have meant so much to me came out to make special tributes: Eileen Moran Brown, the teacher who had sponsored the talent show I had won at Bartram High; Bartram's principal, Louis D'Antonio; even the Beulah Baptist Choir came out to sing for me. And all three of my sons — Zuri, Dodd, and Stanley — made me so proud when they introduced their mom to the guests. But it was a particularly intense evening because of what Jackie had told me before we arrived. She had brain cancer. Jackie knew that I had specifically requested that the American Cancer Society be the primary beneficiary of the evening's proceeds, and I guess she thought there was never going to be a better time to tell me. After I made the presentation to Dr. Carl Mansfield, president of the organization's Philadelphia division, I choked up. Jackie and I both did. I called her to the podium with me and, together, we told the audience about the cancer. Between tears, we vowed to fight — and beat — this thing together.

As hard as Jackie fought, this was one battle she wouldn't win. She continued to travel with me, even as she was getting sicker and weaker. With every passing day, she seemed to become more and more consumed by her wish for my name to become a household word, for me to become a living legend. I kept telling her she needed to worry more about herself, and less about me. She needed to get off the road and just concentrate on getting better. She wouldn't even

348

hear it. And that's why the fighting continued. Once, for example, when I was performing in Washington, D.C., she and I had yet another argument about it. She didn't look good to me that night, so I told her she needed to go home and get some rest. That set her off. When I tried to ignore her ranting and raving, she found a way to get my full attention. Jackie almost bit my finger off. Under normal circumstances, it would have been war. But I knew the medicine was affecting her, so I just walked away. That was the night she got so sick we had to call an ambulance and put her in the hospital — we had her transferred back home to Philly the same night.

I wasn't handling Jackie's sickness well at all. I was in denial. I couldn't accept that my third and last sister had cancer, too. That what had happened to Vivian and Barbara was happening to her. I'm not proud of it, but the way I dealt with it was by not dealing with it. When Jackie would call me and ask me to come over, I would find some reason why I couldn't. One night when we were out on the road, she asked to use the sauna in my suite. I told her I was about to go to bed for the night. Another time, she wanted me to come over and visit, and I told her I wasn't feeling well. Looking at her forced me to see what I couldn't bear to see, to think the unthinkable. I could be losing my baby sister, too. I'd give anything to do things differently, to take those times back and spend them with Jackie. And, of course, there was that time she called and asked me to make her that egg sandwich.

As you know, after that phone call Jackie got worse. She was on a respirator and in and out of consciousness. She was so bad that the hospital called her daughter, Stayce, in New York and told her she needed to come quickly. Jackie's son, Billy, came, too. The week before, Armstead had called Aunt Hattie Mae and Aunt Joshia Mae in Georgia and asked them to come to Philly. Even though I was going to the hospital regularly, we needed someone with Jackie all the time. We needed the whole family to be there. On one of their visits, Billy and Stayce gave Jackie the Mother's Day ring they had specially designed for her with all three of their birthstones. Since it hadn't been ready in May, they decided to give it to her on her birthday — July 12 — but she had gotten so sick, we weren't sure she would make it. So, a week before her birthday, Stayce slipped it on her mother's finger. It was such a moving moment. Jackie hadn't been conscious, but at that moment she opened her eyes and Stayce and Billy wished their mother a happy birthday. She looked at the ring, she looked at them, she looked at me. She didn't have much strength left, but somehow she managed a smile as she pointed to the ring. Then she pointed at me. It was clear what she meant. Jackie wanted me to watch over her babies, to be their mother when she was gone.

Later, when I was alone with her and she was sleeping, I told her I would watch over Stayce and Billy like they were my own. She didn't have to worry. If the pain was too much, she could let go. I didn't know it at the time, but Stayce and Billy would tell her the same thing that same night. The next day, I got the call from Aunt Hattie Mae. She and Aunt Joshia Mae were sitting with Jackie at Lankenau Hospital when it happened. I didn't let her say more than my name before I cut her off.

"No. Don't tell me, Aunt Hattie Mae."

"It's true, baby. Jackie's gone. But she didn't suffer. She just slept away."

Five days before her forty-fourth birthday, my baby sister died. I don't know what I would have done without Aunt Hattie Mae and Aunt Joshia Mae. They helped us handle all the arrangements and, on the day before Jackie's birthday, we held her funeral at Liberty Baptist Church. We flew my father up from Georgia for the service, but we didn't tell him why. We instructed the nursing home personnel not to tell him, either. We wanted Daddy to hear it from a family member but we didn't want to tell him on the phone. Daddy was furious. He went nuts. He cussed us all out for waiting so long to tell him that his daughter had died. I think he was just letting out all the hurt and pain. I know he was. He couldn't even make it through the entire funeral. After I took him up to Jackie's casket to say his last good-bye, Daddy was so distraught Aunt Hattie Mae had to take him home. Maybe it would have eased his grief just a little if he had seen what some of us saw during the funeral service. A little butterfly fluttering around the church. Daddy knew how much Jackie had always loved butterflies — ever since she was a little girl, when she spent hours chasing and trying to catch them behind our house.

The story I'm about to tell you is so incredible I wouldn't believe it myself if it hadn't happened to me. But it did. It's real. Before Jackie went home, she came to me to say good-bye. To tell me she was all right and everything was all right between us. It wasn't until I was writing this book that I realized what it all meant, and that realization has helped me to begin to make peace with myself for the way I treated my sister.

So much of Jackie's funeral is a blur to me. But Stayce remembered what I had forgotten. That butterfly. And what it did. As the minister finished the eulogy, it came to me. It just landed on my shoulder and sat there for a few seconds. And then it was gone. I honestly believe it was a sign from Jackie. The one thing we shared as little girls was a love of butterflies. Jackie loved them even more than I did. She must have known I would get the message. She was in a better place. All was well. All was forgiven. All was fine between us. She had only been fighting me to get me to open my eyes. To get me to love myself as much as she loved me. She wanted me to take my glory while I'm here. And she died fighting to make sure I would.

When it was all over, Stayce handed me the

Mother's Day ring she and Billy had given Jackie in the hospital. It had been my sister's last request that I have it. She wanted me to carry on.

Chapter Forty-two

As you know, just as I had done after Chubby died, the day after Jackie's funeral, I went back to work. Somehow, I shot the "If You Ask Me To" video. But, as I said earlier, the whole time I was singing, I was thinking about Jackie. About all the things she had asked me to do. About all the things I never did.

The following month, in August, I played the "Acid Queen" in an all-star performance of The Who's rock opera, *Tommy*, at the Universal Amphitheater in California. It was a lavish production filled with fantasy. But, as much as I tried to lose myself in my work, something kept tugging at me. My inner voice was talking to me. It kept telling me there was something I needed to check on. It was Daddy. He had taken Jackie's death so hard and it had been awhile since I had visited him in the nursing home. But I just couldn't bring myself to do it. I hated seeing him so sick that he needed twenty-four hour care. His sisters and I hated putting him in a home. But we didn't really have a choice. The Alzheimer's was taking its toll, and Daddy had been getting progressively worse. One morning, for instance, he drove away and he didn't come back. Aunt Hattie Mae and Aunt Joshia Mae were frantic until somebody found him sitting in his car on the side of the road. Daddy had spent the night there when he couldn't remember how to get back home. It was so hard to have to see my father like that, and so I promised myself I'd go see him later, when I was feeling stronger. I never got the chance. On September sixteenth, two months after we buried Jackie, my father died. I was at home asleep when Aunt Hattie Mae called to say he was gone. Stayce was at the house, but she didn't want to wake me up and tell me. Armstead was out of town, so she called my cousin, Hazel, and asked her to come over and break the news. As I sat on the edge of my bed, half asleep, half dazed, wondering if I was just having a bad dream, pictures of the two of us — Daddy and me — flooded my memory like scenes from a movie. The days back in Elmwood when we sat on the front steps singing the songs he had written just for me. The night he and Chubby got together again to come to Atlantic City to see me perform with the original Ordettes. Our shopping spree down Bourbon Street. And the Father's Day in 1985 when I called him up onstage and sang to him. I sang the song that describes the way I will always remember him, "Forever Young." After he and Chubby broke up, he had three more children, my siblings, Monica, Henry, and Joshiala. Even though we didn't grow up together in the same household, over the years I have grown to love them as much as if we had. As I reflected on his life, I thought about a few lines from a poem I had once heard: lines I know my daddy would want me to take to heart:

Do not stand at my grave and cry.
I am not there.
I did not die.

On September 23, we buried my father back home in Georgia. After the funeral, my Aunt Hattie Mae reminded me that her brother had lived his life to the fullest. And that, when he got sick, I had done all I could, providing for him the way he once had provided for them.

"Patsy," she said, "your daddy didn't suffer from nothing but the sickness because you gave him everything."

Not nearly as much as he gave me.

Chapter Forty-three

With the fall release of my second MCA album, "Be Yourself," I hit the road again for an extensive four-month national tour beginning in November. It felt strange to be traveling without Jackie, and many many nights I cried myself to sleep. During the whole tour, there wasn't a day that passed when I didn't expect the phone to ring and hear my sister telling me off about something I had done wrong. I even missed her nagging. My anxiety was almost as strong as my grief. I was convinced more than ever that death was just toying with me. At forty-five, I was older than any of my sisters had been when they passed on.

Now, it was just a waiting game. But I was going to make good use of whatever time I had. Not only by filling it up with my work, but by making my work meaningful to other people. At my concerts, I started talking about my mistakes, hoping to save somebody else from making the same ones. I was on a mission. Everybody who came to hear me sing heard the same message: "If you love somebody, go home and tell them tonight because tomorrow is not promised." In the last few years, in addition to my sisters, I had also lost so many of my fans to AIDS and I knew a lot of other people were going through the same hell I was — losing someone you love before their time, before you say good-bye.

But as much as I thought about death, my own as well as my sisters', I wasn't feeling sorry for myself. I knew whatever time I had left was a blessing. And I wasn't going to block it by crying and complaining and moping around. I had already wasted way too much time doing that. What did I have to complain about? I wasn't sick. I didn't have to worry about where my next meal was coming from. I had a beautiful family that hung together in good times and bad. I thought about all the people who were barely scraping by but who still treated every new day like a blessing.

"What's wrong with me? I don't have anything to complain about," I said, as I was explaining my new attitude to one of my producers, Sami McKinney, on the phone one day.

The more we talked about it, the more we knew. There was a song somewhere in this realization. And what a song it turned out to be. After that phone conversation, Sami wrote, "I Can't Complain," and the minute I heard it I knew it had to go on the new album. What neither of us knew before it was released is that it would earn me another Grammy nomination. But, as moving as the song is, it still wasn't enough to move me into the winner's circle. When I lost for the fifth time, I started to feel like I was never going to win that trophy, and I had to ask myself why I even bothered to keep going to the ceremony. On Grammy night, I was always a bridesmaid, never a bride. A few months before the 1992 ceremony, when a reporter for USA Today asked me about losing *five* times, I couldn't resist.

"If I don't get one soon," I told him, "I'm going to snatch somebody else's."

I was half kidding, half serious. My career was going well, and I hoped Jackie was proud. In addition to the song "I Can't Complain," the "Be Yourself" album produced a number of popular songs for me including "If You Asked Me To" and "We're Not Making Love Anymore," a duet I did with Michael Bolton. Powerful and well-respected people in the film business had also noticed me. A few years earlier, producer Craig Zadan and screenwriter Dean Pitchford, who won an Academy Award for *Fame*, had created a starring role in a major motion picture just for me. They even waited until I found the time to shoot it. In the 1989 film *Sing*, I played the role of a Brooklyn high-school teacher trying to shake her class out of apathy. It was a fitting role for me at that time in my life. I also was a lot more confident about my acting ability in this film than I had been when I did *Soldier's Story*. Two years before we shot *Sing*, I had appeared in the NBC made-for-TV movie about Agent Orange, *Unnatural Cause*s, costarring Alfre Woodard and John Ritter. I also appeared in the movie *Fire and Rain*, made for the USA Network about the crash of a Delta Airlines plane.

There would be other acting opportunities in the coming years. In February of 1991, I co-starred in Truman Capote's musical, *House of Flowers*, at the Valley Forge Music Fair in Philadelphia. In this show about rival West Indian brothels, I played Madame Fleur opposite Carmen De Lavallade's Madame Tango. During this period, I also was making regular appearances on prime-time TV. First as the impossible-to-please Adele Wayne in the NBC hit show *A Different World*, and then, in the fall of 1992, the network gave me my own series, *Out All Night*. When that show was offered to me, I told Armstead I didn't want to do it. First of all, I didn't want to "go to Hollywood"; that is, move to L.A. where I would have to shoot the series. But more important, I thought a weekly show would be way too time-consuming to allow me to continue my concert performances. Giving those up would be out of the question, since singing is my blood supply. If I didn't sing, I'd be a crazy woman. Onstage is the one place where I can open up, vent my frustrations, cry out my pain. And that has freed me to be a better wife and mother. At first, Armstead tried to convince me with the same argument he'd used with *Your Arms Too Short*. Broader exposure. But that one fell flat. Then he made me an offer I couldn't refuse.

"I'll buy you a condo in L.A. and a Rolls-Royce to put in the driveway."

"Throw in a driver," I said, "and you have a deal."

After only one season, the show was canceled but it can still be seen on Black Entertainment Television's cable channel. And I still have that car and that condo.

There were even bigger rewards during this period. Sarah, Nona, and I recorded together for the first time since the breakup of Labelle. We reunited on my 1991 album, "Burnin'." Nona cowrote the song "Release Yourself," and it had the perfect message for our reunion. It talks about looking to each day as a new beginning and listening to your inner voice and your heart.

We sang that very song on our old stomping grounds, the Apollo stage, when I shot a live concert video there in September 1991. It was the first time the three of us had performed together in fifteen years.

Following the release of "Burnin'," I made yet another trip to the Grammys, this time with two nominations — one for that album and one with Gladys and Dionne for the single "Superwoman." When I lost that nomination, at least I felt that I was in good company. But something totally unexpected happened that night. When they announced the winner of the Grammy for Best R&B Vocal Performance/Female, there was a surprise. I heard "Patti Labelle." And "Lisa Fischer." It was a tie. I was happy to share the honor with Lisa, who had also sung on "Burnin'." As I told Armstead, I would have taken that award if I had been nominated in the category of Best Male Vocal Performance. I just *wanted* a Grammy. It's sitting right next to the American Music Award I won the following year for Favorite Female Artist in the Rhythm & Blues Category.

It was fitting that "Burnin' " would be the album that would capture the Grammy. Two of my favorite songs are on it, and each of them contains a message I hoped my fans were taking home from my concerts: "When You've Been Blessed (Feels Like Heaven)" and "Love Never Dies." In the first song, I sing about how important it is to share, to give, and to appreciate one another while we can — and to pass the blessings on. In the second, I deal with the everlasting power of love. While this song's message has special meaning to me personally, it's also giving a larger benefit to others. Some of the proceeds earned from the record sales are donated to three charitable causes dear to my heart: the Minority AIDS Project, L.A., Gentleman Concerned, L.A., and T. J. Martell Cancer and AIDS Research for Children.

But I didn't want to just contribute money. I had given my sisters plenty of things and stuff but not enough of the one thing they wanted — me. Now I was giving of myself to causes that would honor their lives and their memory. In 1991, I became the spokesperson for the National Cancer Institute, traveling the country and taping videos and public-service announcements to urge women to educate themselves and get regular medical checkups. Later, when Flori Roberts introduced my signature line of lipstick and nail polish, I asked that the net proceeds from the "My Boy Z" shade go to the Patti LaBelle Breast Cancer Research and Scholarship Fund, which is administered by the National Medical Association.

I continue to serve as the national spokesperson for the National Minority AIDS Council's multimedia Live Long, Sugar campaign, which encourages people living with AIDS to seek the health care they need. We kicked off the campaign at Philadelphia's Four Seasons Hotel on May 17, 1994 — exactly one week before my fiftieth birthday. God had given me His greatest blessing — the blessing of life. As I approached a date I thought I would never live to see, I was doing everything I could to pass that blessing on.

Chapter Forty-four

It was a long and rocky road to fifty. A real trip. But I made it. The journey, and the revelations it brought me, have changed me forever. I'm no longer that scared, shy, insecure little girl who didn't see her worth or her blessings. It took me a long time to understand that so much of my pain was about me. Me not listening to my heart. Me needing others to love me because I didn't love myself. Me holding on in fear instead of letting go in faith. Me not living for today because I was worrying about tomorrow. Me blocking the blessings.

All that is past. As I write these last pages, there's a brand new me. Unafraid. Unbroken. Unleashed. Unblocked. But I didn't make this journey of self-discovery all by myself. Not hardly. I have learned something from everyone who has touched my life, from everything that has shaped it. Those who have left this world have left me with something precious. My reason to carry on. My blueprint for living. I've learned to assert myself — to speak up, to throw down, to walk out when I need to. Thank you, Chubby. I've learned to squeeze two hours of life out of every single hour I'm given. Thank you, Daddy. I've learned to face the worst tragedy with the best attitude — with grace and style and courage. Thank you, Vivian. Thank you, Claudette. I've learned to say it now. "I love you."

"I miss you." "I'm sorry." Thank you, Barbara. I've learned to accept my good, to love, honor, and cherish myself, to appreciate all the wonderful gifts I have to share with the world. Thank you, Jackie. Thank you so very much.

From the loved ones who are still here with me — Armstead, Zuri, Billy, Stayce, Dodd, and Stanley — I've learned the joy of sharing. Not just stuff you pick out and pay for, but stuff that really matters. Years ago, when Zuri was just a little boy, Armstead started a tradition in our house that came to mean so much to all of us. On Christmas, we couldn't just exchange store-bought gifts. We had to give something of ourselves. A letter from the heart to the family member whose name we would pick out of a hat. In it, we would tell how we felt about each other, how that person had touched us during the course of the year. That tradition created so many special moments in our household, all because we took the time to say "I love you."

From my fans, friends, even strangers who come up to greet me on the street as if we really *are* friends (never "Hi, Miss LaBelle"; always, "Hey, Patti, girl"), I have learned so much about the power of giving. Not money and things. But time and effort. Every time I take the stage, it's like being on Aunt Hattie Mae's porch down in Georgia. I feel that same cycle. I'm sending out all my love and energy, but I'm getting it all back. And then some. We all have a special gift to share with others. When I sing to an audience, I'm sharing mine. When I hear their roaring applause, I feel them giving something back to me. And that's such a critical thing to understand. The power of that cycle of love. As I was writing this book, something hit me. Even though I've been knocking myself out with recording sessions and live performances and film, TV, and charitable work, I never get tired. I feel more and more energy all the time. When you share love, it's like a boomerang. Every time you throw it out there, it comes right back to you. Stronger and stronger. When you pass on the blessings, you become a magnet for more and more to flow to you. It can be little things, big things, in-between things. It really doesn't matter. All that really matters is that you keep the cycle going. A few years ago, for example, I gave Armstead a special gift for his fifty-second birthday. The gift of "yes." It would be his "trump card." If we reached a point where we disagreed on something really important and we came to a standoff, a stalemate, a deadlock, he could use his "yes" to have his way. To this day, he never has. Boyfriend must be saving that gift for something really serious. Maybe I should have put an expiration date on it.

At my concerts, fans always bring me flowers. Bushels of bouquets. I want you all to know I don't throw one single stem away. Before I head for the next stop, the next city, the next show, I make sure those flowers are delivered to a local hospital and placed in the rooms of AIDS and cancer patients. I want to share with others the joy others have shared with me. It keeps the cycle going. As often as I can, I try to share this life lesson. For example, when I was shooting my first video, "New Attitude," in L.A., a buffet for cast and crew was set up on the street. Some homeless people went over to the table to help themselves. Every time they tried to fix a plate, some assistant would shoo them away. When I was told what was going on, I came out of my trailer in my robe and told those hungry people to help themselves. "And if you have any friends," I said, "go get them and bring them back, too."

What does it cost you to show a little kindness, a little love, a little compassion? Not much. Unless, of course, you are Oseola McCarty, who worked her fingers to the bone washing other people's clothes to earn a living. And what did she do with most of her life savings? She gave it away — $150,000 to the University of Southern Mississippi to, as she put it, "give some child the opportunity I didn't have." When *Essence* magazine recognized Ms. McCarty's unbelievable generosity with a special award, they asked me to make the presentation. I wanted everybody to know just how special this woman is. And so I sang to her. But not from the stage. From the floor. Down on my knees at her feet. In front of everybody in the audience and everybody watching on national TV.

If there's one thing this life has taught me, it's what Ms. McCarty knows, what President Bill Clinton gave her the Presidential Citizens Medal for. There is so much to gain by giving. In 1992, my fans nominated me for one of my most cherished honors: a star on the Hollywood Walk of Fame. Record companies usually recommend their artists and pay the required $5,000 fee. I am proud to say I am the first and only recording artist who was not only nominated but whose star was paid for entirely by fans. In March of 1993, the Patti LaBelle star was dedicated. Thank you, Rachel Cobb, Kellie Boyce, and Alan Fox for spearheading that effort. It was one of the greatest surprises of my life.

Once I stopped dwelling on what I *didn't* have, on what I thought I was going to lose, and began to give freely, everything opened up for me. Everything began to flow into my life. My eighth Grammy nomination, this one for the appropriately titled song "All Right Now." My own three hundred-seat cabaret theater in Philly, Chez LaBelle. A halftime performance before millions at Super Bowl XXIX. And a truly unexpected honor. On Mother's Day 1996, I was awarded an honorary doctorate of music from Boston's Berklee College of Music. Not bad for a kid who once dropped out of high school.

Yes, I have learned a lot from people who love me, but I have also learned a great deal from people who didn't necessarily have my best interests at heart. They taught me there are no mistakes, only lessons. There are no problems, only opportunities to learn and grow. Everything is just the way it should be at the moment. We must never struggle against it. No matter how bad it might seem, there is a lesson in the experience to make us stronger. You must learn it, and then use the lesson to move your life forward. People come into our lives for reasons — important ones. To teach us something about ourselves, something we need to know. I know now that when I was fighting other people, I really was fighting myself. I don't do that anymore. There is an old African proverb: "I am not what you call me; I am what I respond to." And that is so true. Nobody can make you feel inferior without your consent. Well, baby, I've taken back my consent. And I've taken back *myself* in the process. Nona had it exactly right in the song she wrote for Labelle's first reunion: "Release Yourself." I have found that the more "Patti" I release, the more people I reach. When I performed for President Clinton at his forty-eighth birthday bash, even Armstead was surprised when I gave him *double* Patti. As I do in many of my concerts, I got down on the stage floor and rolled across it while I sang to him. I sang so hard that, even though I didn't pop that blood vessel that always gives me a nosebleed, I did burst the seams in the back of my dress. Armstead was backstage having a baby. "Tell me she's not rolling on the floor in front of the president," he kept saying to people. He needn't have worried. Even the First Lady got a kick out of it. After the show, Hillary Clinton said to me, "Patti, you're the funniest lady." I said, "I'm funnier than that, honey. Feel the back of my dress." The First Couple liked me just fine, thank you. Seven months later, the president and Mrs. Clinton surprised me by coming to my show at Washington's Warner Theater. They even brought along a few of their friends — lawyer Vernon Jordan and Deputy Secretary of State Strobe Talbott. Once again, they saw the real me. The me it took me so long to see. The Patti I traveled around the world and over the rainbow to find. And all along she was right here. Inside me. Just where I would find everything I ever thought I needed. Just where we all can find everything we need to get by. Right there inside.

When Cindy Birdsong and I reconnected as I was writing this book, she said something that really touched me. Cindy, who has dedicated her life to the Lord, said that God was using me to spread a message. I hope she's right. I know what I do is blessed or God wouldn't have left me here to carry on. He wouldn't have given me a voice that people want to hear. People from all walks of life. From the president in Washington to the homeless of L.A. People have told me they leave my concerts different than when they came. Stronger. Better. More in touch with what's really important. I think it's why God put me here. I *know* it is. That's the only way I can explain why the older I get the stronger my voice becomes. I can hold a note longer. I can take a song higher. I can carry a message farther. And I can't hold back. This is what I'm living for. To share my gift. And now that I know it, death has lost its power over me. It took me fifty years to *really* get the message given a long time ago by two wise people: James Baldwin who, before his death, was a big Labelle fan, and Sojourner Truth, who I have a feeling would have been a fan if she hadn't been born before her time and ours. As Brother James said: "If you're afraid to die, you will not be able to live." And Sister Sojourner sure spoke the truth and nothing but the truth for me when she said: "I'm not going to die; I'm going home like a shooting star."

Discography

TITLE	LABEL	NO.	DATE
The Blue-Belles Singles			
I Sold My Heart to the Junkman/Itty Bitty Twist	Newtown	5000	1962
Pitter Patter/ I Found a New Love	Newtown	5006	1962
Patti LaBelle and the Bluebelles Singles			
I Found a New Love/ Go On (This Is Goodbye)	Newtown	5006	1962
Tear After Tear/ Go On (This Is Goodbye)	Newtown	5007	1962

Title	Label	Number	Year
Cool Water/When Johnny Comes Marching Home (Issued as the Blue-Belles)	Newtown	5009	1963
Love Me Just a Little/Pitter Patter	Newtown	5010	1963
Decatur Street/Academy Award	Newtown	5019	1963
Down the Aisle/C'est La Vie	Newtown	5777	1963
Down the Aisle/C'est La Vie	King	5777	1963
You'll Never Walk Alone/Decatur Street	Parkway	896	1964
Danny Boy/I Believe	Parkway	935	1964
One Phone Call/You Will Fill My Eyes No More	Parkway	913	1964
Where Are You/You'll Never Walk Alone	Nicetown	5020	1964
You'll Never Walk Alone/Decatur Street	Nicetown	5020	1964
Love Me Just a Little/The Joke's on You (issued as Patti LaBelle)	Newtime	510	Unknown

Title	Label	Number	Year
All or Nothing/			
You Forgot How to Love	Atlantic	2311	1965
Over the Rainbow/			
Groovy Kind of Love	Atlantic	2318	1966
Ebb Tide/Patti's Prayer	Atlantic	2333	1966
I'm Still Waiting/Family Man	Atlantic	2347	1966
Take Me for a Little While/			
I Don't Want to Go On			
Without You	Atlantic	2373	1967
Always Something There to			
Remind Me/Tender Words	Atlantic	2390	1967
Dreamer/Unchained Melody	Atlantic	2408	1967
Oh My Love/I Need Your Love	Atlantic	2446	1967
He's My Man/Wonderful	Atlantic	2548	1968
Dance to the Rhythm			
of Love/He's Gone	Atlantic	2610	1969
Pride's No Match for Love/			
Loving Rules	Atlantic	2629	1969
Trustin' in You/Suffer	Atlantic	2712	1969

Labelle Singles

Morning Much Better/Shades of Difference	Warner	7512	1971
Moonshadow/If I Can't Have You	Warner	7579	1972
Ain't It Sad It's All Over/ Touch Me All Over	Warner	7624	1972
Sunshine/Mr. Music Man	RCA	0157	1973
Going on a Holiday/ Open Up Your Heart	RCA	0965	1973
Lady Marmalade/Space Children	Epic	50048	1974
What Can I Do for You/ Nightbirds	Epic	50097	1974
Messin' with My Mind/ Take the Night Off	Epic	50140	1975
Far As We Felt Like Goin'/ Slow Burn	Epic	50168	1975
Get You Somebody New/ Who's Watching the Watcher	Epic	50262	1976

Title	Label	Catalog	Year
Isn't It a Shame/Gypsy Moths	Epic	50315	1976
Miss Otis Regrets/ Too Many Days (UK only)	Track	2094	1976
Lady Marmalade/ Messing with My Mind (12")	Epic	69180	1989
Turn It Out (12")	MCA	55113	1995

Patti LaBelle Singles

Title	Label	Catalog	Year
Joy to Have Your Love/ Do I Stand a Chance	Epic	50445	1977
You Are My Friend/ I Think About You	Epic	50487	1977
Little Girls/You Make It So Hard (to Say No)	Epic	50583	1978
Teach Me Tonight/Quiet Time	Epic	50550	1978
It's Alright with Me/ My Best Was Good Enough	Epic	50659	1979
It's Alright with Me/ Music Is My Way of Life	Epic	50659	1979

Title	Label	Number	Year
Love and Learn/ Love Is Just a Touch Away	Epic	50763	1979
Release/ Come and Dance with Me	Epic	50852	1980
I Don't Go Shopping/ Come and Dance with Me	Epic	50872	1980
Don't Make Your Angel Cry/Ain't That Enough	Epic	50910	1980
Over the Rainbow/ Rocking Pneumonia	PIR	02309	1981
The Spirit's in It/Family	PIR	02655	1981
If Only You Knew/ I'll Never, Never Give Up	PIR	04248	1983
I'm in Love Again/ Love, Need and Want You	PIR	04399	1983
Pourin' Whiskey Blues/ Low Down Dirty Shame (France only)	Milan	259	1984
Shy/Love Symphony	PIR	05658	1985

Living Double/I Can't Forget You	PIR	05436	1985
If You Don't Know Me by Now (parts 1 & 2)	PIR	05755	1985
New Attitude/Shoot Out	MCA	52517	1984
On My Own (with Michael McDonald)/Stir It Up	MCA	52610	1984
Stir It Up/Discovery	MCA	52610	1984
Oh, People/Love Attack	MCA	52877	1986
Kiss Away the Pain/Instrumental	MCA	52945	1986
If You Asked Me To/Instrumental	MCA	53358	1989
The Last Unbroken Heart (with Bill Champlin)/Miami Vice: New York Scene Instrumental (by Jan Hammer)	MCA	53064	1986
Just the Facts/Instrumental	MCA	53100	1987
Yo Mister/I Can Fly	MCA	53728	1989
I Can't Complain/I Can Fly	MCA	53774	1989
When You Love Somebody/Temptation	MCA	54481	1991

Title	Label	Number	Year
When You've Been Blessed	MCA	54376	1991
We Haven't Finished Yet	Virgin	98824	1991
All Right Now	MCA	54513	1992
The Right Kinda Lover	MCA	54673	1994
Eyes in the Back of My Head/			
Save the Last Dance for Me (12")	Epic	50573	1978
Music Is My Way of Life/			
Instrumental (12")	Epic	50664	1979
If Only You Knew/I'll Never,			
Never Give Up (12")	PIR	04176	1983
New Attitude (12")	MCA	23534	1984
Stir It Up (12")	MCA	23567	1985
If You Don't Know Me by Now			
(parts 1 & 2; 12")	PIR	2245	1985
Shy (12")	PIR	05296	1985
Oh, People (12")	MCA	23651	1986
On My Own/Stir It Up (12")	MCA	23607	1986
Kiss Away the Pain (12")	MCA	23679	1986
Something Special (12")	MCA	23649	1986

Just the Facts (12")	MCA	23773	1987
Yo Mister (12")	MCA	23984	1989
Feels Like Another One (12")	MCA	54238	1991
All Right Now (12")	MCA	54541	1992
The Right Kinda Lover (12")	MCA	54851	1994
All This Love/Our World (12")	MCA	54933	1994

Labelle CD Singles

Lady Marmalade (4-Track EP, Holland only)	Epic	611	1988
Lady Marmalade/What Can I Do for You (Holland only)	Epic	655153	1989
Turn It Out	MCA	55113	1995

Patti LaBelle CD Singles

If You Asked Me To (UK only)	MCA	1357	1989
If You Asked Me To (Japan only)	Warner	6067	1989
Yo Mister (Germany only)	MCA	2573672	1989

Title	Label	Catalog No.	Year
Feels Like Another One (Japan only)	MCA	MVDM-10	1991
All Right Now	MCA	17847	1991
When You've Been Blessed	MCA	54421	1992
The Right Kinda Lover (UK only)	MCA	1995	1994
The Right Kinda Lover (UK only)	MCA	32222	1994
My Love, Sweet Love	Arista	12930	1995

Patti LaBelle and the Bluebelles Albums

Title	Label	Catalog No.	Year
The Apollo Presents the Bluebelles	Newtown	631	1962
Sleigh Bells, Jingle Bells and Bluebelles	Newtown	632	1963
On Stage	Parkway	7043	1964
Over the Rainbow (mono & stereo)	Atlantic	8119	1966
Dreamer (mono & stereo)	Atlantic	8147	1967
At the Apollo	Upfront	129	Unknown

Merry Christmas from LaBelle & the Bluebelles	Trip	8016	Unknown
LaBelle & the Bluebelles Early Hits	Trip	9525	Unknown
Greatest Hits Labelle & the Bluebelles Superpak	Trip	3508	Unknown
Merry Christmas from LaBelle & the Bluebelles	Mistletoe	1204	Unknown
The Very Best of Patti LaBelle and the Bluebelles	United Artists	LA504E	1975

Patti LaBelle and the Bluebelles CD's

Christmas with Patti LaBelle & the Bluebelles (Germany only)	Pilz	5452	1991
Sleigh Bells, Jingle Bells & Bluebelles	Relic	7043	1992
Down the Aisle	Relic	7044	1992
The Early Years (UK only)	Ace	441	1993

Title	Label	Number	Year
Island of Broken Hearts (Germany only)	Legend	90048	1993
Golden Classics	Collectables	5090	1993
The Early Hits (Canada only)	ISBA	102	1993
Our Christmas Songbook	Collectables	5091	1994
The Early Hits (UK only)	Classic Soul	1171	1994
Sleigh Bells, Jingle Bells & Bluebelles (Japan only)	P-Vine	1983	1994
Over the Rainbow/The Atlantic Years	Ichiban	2501	1994
Sweethearts of the Apollo	Collectables	5092	1995

Labelle Albums

Title	Label	Number	Year
Labelle	Warner	1943	1971
Moonshadow	Warner	2618	1972
Pressure Cookin'	RCA	10205	1973
Nightbirds	Epic	33075	1974
Nightbirds (quadraphonic)	Epic	33075	1974

Title	Label	Number	Year
Phoenix	Epic	33579	1975
Phoenix (quadraphonic)	Epic	33579	1975
Chameleon	Epic	34189	1976
Pressure Cookin' (Reissue with cover variation)	RCA	4176	1981

Labelle CD's

Title	Label	Number	Year
Nightbirds	Epic	33075	1988
Chameleon	Epic	34189	1989

Patti LaBelle Albums

Title	Label	Number	Year
Patti LaBelle	Epic	34847	1977
Tasty	Epic	35335	1978
It's Alright with Me	Epic	35772	1979
Released	Epic	36381	1980
The Spirit's in It	PIR	37380	1981
Best of Patti LaBelle	Epic	36997	1982
I'm in Love Again	PIR	38539	1983
Miss Soul (cassette only)	Sony	19933	1983

Title	Label	Number	Year
Patti	PIR	40020	1985
Winner in You	MCA	5737	1986
Be Yourself	MCA	6292	1989
This Christmas	MCA	10113	1990
Burnin'	MCA	10439	1991
Live!	MCA	10691	1992
Gems	MCA	10870	1994

Patti LaBelle CD's

Title	Label	Number	Year
I'm in Love Again	PIR	38539	1986
Patti	PIR	40020	1986
Winner in You	MCA	5737	1986
Best of Patti LaBelle	Epic	36997	1987
Patti LaBelle	Epic	34847	1989
The Spirit's in It	PIR	37380	1989
It's Alright with Me (Germany only)	Epic	35772	Unknown
Be Yourself	MCA	6292	1989

Title	Label	Number	Year
This Christmas	MCA	10113	1990
Burnin'	MCA	10439	1991
Live!	MCA	10691	1992
LaBelle	Sony	20313	1993
I'm in Love Again	The Right Stuff	66690	1993
The Spirit's in It	The Right Stuff	27629	1993
Gems	MCA	10870	1994
Lady Marmalade: The Best of Patti & Labelle	Epic	66339	1995

Patti LaBelle and the Bluebelles Guest Appearance Albums & CD's

Title	Label	Number	Year
Exciting Wilson Pickett (with Wilson Pickett) (album track 634-5789; also issued as Atlantic single no. 2320)	Atlantic	8129	1966
Processes (with Tony Kosinec) (album track "Simple Emotion")	Columbia	9832	1969

Labelle Guest Appearance Albums & CD's

Truth Is on Its Way (with Nikki Giovanni) (album track "Peace Be Still")	Right-On	5001	Unknown
Gonna Take a Miracle (with Laura Nyro) (album tracks "I Met Him on a Sunday," "The Bells," "Monkey Time"/ "Dancing in the Street," "You Really Got a Hold on Me," "Jimmy Mack," "Nowhere to Run," "It's Gonna Take a Miracle.")	Columbia	30987	1971
Rock of the Westies (with Elton John) (album track medley: "Yell Help," "Wednesday Night," "Ugly")	MCA	464	1975

Patti LaBelle Guest Appearance Albums & CD's

Title	Label	No.	Year
Walk in the Light (with Eric Robinson) (album track "In His Hands")	RCA	8033	1982
The Best Is Yet to Come (with Grover Washington, Jr.) (album track "The Best Is Yet to Come," also issued as Elektra single no. 69887)	Elektra	60215	1982
Nona (with Nona Hendryx) (album track "Design for Living")	RCA	4565	1983
Fred Schneider and the Shake Society (with Fred Schneider) (album track "It's Time to Kiss")	Warner Bros.	25158	1984
The Poet II (with Bobby Womack) (album tracks "Love Has Finally Come at Last," also issued as Beverly Glen single no. 2012;			

"Through the Eyes of a Child," also issued as Beverly Glen single no. 2014; "It Takes a Lot of Strength to Say Goodbye," also issued as Beverly Glen single no. 2018)	Beverly Glen	10003	1984
Harold F (with Harold Faltemeyer) (album track "Them Changes")	MCA	42165	1984
Where the Fast Lane Ends (with the Oak Ridge Boys) (album track "Rainbow at Midnight")	MCA	5945	1987
Desiree (with Desiree Coleman) (album tracks "Till We Put Our Heads Together" & "You Wouldn't Hurt Me (Would You)")	Motown	6262	1988

You're All I Need (with Sarah Dash) (album track "You're All I Need to Get By")	EMI	90036	1988
Forgotten Eyes — "For the Children" (with various artists)	Motown	4681	1989
Music Speaks Louder Than Words (various artists) (album track "There's Always Love")	Epic	45380	1990
The Sun Will Shine Again (with Wintley Phipps) (album track "The Sun Will Shine Again")	Coral	84822	1990
Garfield "Am I Cool or What?" (various artists) (album track "I Love It When I'm Naughty")	GRP	9641	1991
Back to the Grindstone (with Ronnie Milsap) (album track "Love Certified")	RCA	2375	1991

Title	Label	Catalog	Year
Fourplay (with Fourplay) (album track "After the Dance")	Warner Bros.	26656	1991
Good Woman (with Gladys Knight & Dionne Warwick) (album track "Superwoman")	MCA	10329	1991
Time, Love and Tenderness (with Michael Bolton) (album track "We're Not Making Love Anymore")	Columbia	46771	1991
Love's Alright (with Eddie Murphy) (album track "Yeah")	Motown	374636354	1992
For Our Children, The Concert (various artists) (album track "What a Wonderful World"/ "Sing a Rainbow")	Disney	60620	1992
Sing-Songs of Joe Raposo (various artists) (album track "Just a Little Bit (at the Beginning)")	Golden Music	5684	1992

Title	Label	Catalog	Year
A Little More Magic (with Teddy Pendergrass) (album track "Can't Help Nobody")	Elektra	64197	1993
A Touch of Music in the Night (with Michael Crawford) (album track "With Your Hand upon My Heart")	Atlantic	82531	1993
Rhythm Country and Blues (with Travis Tritt) (album track "When Something Is Wrong with My Baby")	MCA	10965	1994
Duets II (with Frank Sinatra) (album track "Bewitched")	Capitol	18232	1994
Joyful Christmas (various artists) (album track "Away in a Manger")	Columbia	66187	1994

I'll Be Home for Christmas: Voice of the Homeless II (various artists)(album track "Angel Man")	MCA	11383	1995
The Songs of West Side Story (various artists) (album track "America," with Natalie Cole & Sheila E)	RCA	62707	1996
Saxtress (with Pamela Williams) (album track "The Secret Garden," with Teena Marie)	Heads Up International	3034	1996

Patti LaBelle and the Bluebelles Sound Track Appearances

Stonewall (album track "Down the Aisle")	Columbia	76502	1996

Labelle Sound Track Appearances

Carlito's Way (album track "Lady Marmalade")	Epic	57620	1993

Title	Label	Catalog	Year
To Wong Foo, Thanks for Everything Julie Newmar (album track "Turn It Out")	MCA	11231	1995

Patti LaBelle Sound Track Appearances

Title	Label	Catalog	Year
Beverly Hills Cop (album tracks "New Attitude" & "Stir It Up")	MCA	5553	1984
Jazz and Country in the Movies (album tracks "Pourin' Whiskey Blues" & "Low Down Dirty Shame"; France only)	Milan	8126	1985
Into the Night (album track "Don't Make Me Sorry")	MCA	5561	1985
Miami Vice II (with Bill Champlin; album track "The Last Unbroken Heart")	MCA	6192	1986
Running Scared (album track "I Know What I Want")	MCA	6169	1986

Title	Label	Catalog	Year
Dragnet (album track "Just the Facts")	MCA	6210	1987
Licence to Kill (album track "If You Asked Me To")	MCA	6875	1989
Sing (album track "Total Concentration")	Columbia	45086	1989
The Five Heartbeats (album track "We Haven't Finished Yet")	Virgin	91609	1991
Fried Green Tomatoes (album track "Barbeque Bess")	MCA	10461	1991
Leap of Faith (album tracks "Ready for a Miracle" & "Rain Celebration Medley")	MCA	10671	1992
Beverly Hills Cop III (album track "Right Kinda Lover")	MCA	11021	1994
To Wong Foo, Thanks for Everything Julie Newmar (album track "Over the Rainbow")	MCA	11231	1995

Waiting to Exhale (album track "My Love, Sweet Love")	ARISTA	18796	1996

Patti LaBelle Videos

Look to the Rainbow Tour	I.V.E. Video	1985
Patti LaBelle Live in New York	MCA Music Video	1991

Patti LaBelle Laser Discs

Look to the Rainbow Tour	Pioneer Artists	1985
Live in New York	Pioneer Artists	1991

Note: The discography reflects only commercially available product and does not include all entries for compilations, imports, promotional material, reissues and remixes, as they are too numerous to list. (Compiled by Rudy Calvo and Michael Ecker.)

Laura B. Randolph is a Washington-based journalist and lawyer. Currently, she is Senior Editor at *Ebony* magazine, where she also writes the monthly column "Sisterspeak."